Transformation of the Welfare State

Transformation
of the Welfare State

The Silent Surrender of
Public Responsibility

Neil Gilbert

OXFORD

UNIVERSITY PRESS

2002

OXFORD
UNIVERSITY PRESS

Oxford   New York
Auckland   Bangkok   Buenos Aires   Cape Town   Chennai
Dar es Salaam   Delhi   Hong Kong   Istanbul   Karachi   Kolkata
Kuala Lumpur   Madrid   Melbourne   Mexico City   Mumbai   Nairobi
São Paulo   Shanghai   Singapore   Taipei   Tokyo   Toronto

and an associated company in Berlin

Published by Oxford University Press, Inc.
198 Madison Avenue, New York, New York 10016

www.oup.com

Oxford is a registered trademark of Oxford University Press

Library of Congress Cataloging-in-Publication Data
Gilbert, Neil, 1940–
Transformation of the welfare state: the silent surrender of
public responsibility / by Neil Gilbert.
    p.   cm.
ISBN 0-19-514074-5
1. Welfare state.   2. Social policy.   3. Capitalism.
4. Means tests.   5. Privatization.   I. Title.
JC479 .G55 2002
330.12'6—dc21   2002020040

9 8 7 6 5 4 3 2 1

Printed in the United States of America
on acid-free paper

For
Evan, Jesse, Nathaniel, and Nicole

Acknowledgments

This book is the outgrowth of a large-scale comparative project on the changing landscape of modern welfare states, which I initiated in 1997 with the assistance of a generous foundation grant. The project engaged a group of leading international scholars to analyze the course and implications of social policy trends in their countries. I am indebted to all the outstanding people who contributed reports at various stages of the project:[1] Jens Alber, Jean-Claude Barbier, Linda Bauld, Jill Duerr Berrick, Espen Dahl, Abraham Doron, Jon Anders Dropping, Valeria Fargion, Maurizio Ferrera, Sven Hort, Ken Judge, Piet Keizer, Ross Mackay, Francois X. Merrien, Neung-Hoo Park, Roland Sigg, Bruno Theret, and Rebecca Van Voorhis. Their findings and ideas did much to shape my thinking about how and why modern welfare states have been fundamentally altered.

In 2000, phase three of the project concluded with a five-day conference at the fabled Rockefeller Foundation Conference Center in Bellagio, Italy. This meeting was cosponsored by the International Social Security Association and the Center for Comparative Study of Family Welfare and Poverty at the University of California, Berkeley. In addition to members of the research team who were involved during this phase of the project, the conference participants included a number of outside experts whose wisdom deepened our understanding of the magnitude and implications of recent shifts in social policy. For their frank and thoughtful observations, I should like to thank the members of this expert group: Lucy apRoberts, Cathy Drummond, Keith Fontenot, Chris Foster, Richard Hauser, Dalmer Hoskins, Inger Marklund, Warren McGillivray, Stein Ringen, and Hans Svensson. In

2000, I also had the good fortune to serve as a visiting scholar amid a host of congenial colleagues at the International Social Security Association (ISSA) in Geneva, which gave me access to considerable expertise and a copious body of data on social welfare developments around the world. I am grateful to Warren McGillivray, Xenia Scheil-Adlung, Mike Gautrey, Donatella Fabbri-Lovatti, Roland Sigg, and Donate Dobbernack for their friendly support and assistance during my stay at ISSA, with special thanks to Dalmer Hoskins for making it all possible.

Although my work has drawn freely on the good counsel and views of numerous people from diverse countries and institutional arenas, none of them bear any responsibility for the interpretations made and conclusions reached in this book. Indeed, I imagine some of them would disagree with the conclusions or want to qualify various aspects of my analyses.

Initial formulations of several sections of this book were presented in papers delivered at meetings and conferences between 1998 and 2000. Early drafts of parts of chapters 1 and 2 were given in a colloquium at the Fafo Institute for Applied Social Research in Oslo (later published in Norwegian and English)[2] and in a plenary session at the Conference on the Future of the Danish Welfare State, sponsored by the House of Mondag Morgen in Copenhagen.[3] Sections of chapter 3 were delivered in a report for a consultation meeting, Social Policies for Middle Income Countries, organized by Peter Berger at the American Enterprise Institute in Washington, D.C., under the sponsorship of the Center for Development and Enterprise. A portion of chapter 4 was presented at the International Conference on Playing the Market Game in Social Services at the University of Bielefeld, Germany (later translated and published in German).[4] Part of chapter 6 was given in a plenary lecture at the International Social Security Association's Second Technical Conference on Social Security as an Instrument of Social Cohesion, in Naples. Sections of chapter 7 were presented in the International Symposium for Sharing Productive Welfare Experiences sponsored by the Korea Institute for Health and Social Affairs in Seoul. I thank the sponsors of these learned gatherings and the publishers for the chance to test out my initial observations in public fora, which provided constructive feedback on a number of issues.

Once again, I am indebted to the family members who established the Milton and Gertrude Chernin Chair in Social Services and Social Welfare at the University of California, Berkeley, which afforded me the time and resources to gather the evidence and pursue the lines of analysis developed in this study. Finally, I want to express my deepest appreciation to my family: Bekki Van Voorhis, our children Nathaniel and Nicole, and my sons Evan and Jesse. Bekki surveyed the ideas in this book with an intelligent eye and delivered critical judgments with a winning smile. Her warm support and gentle encouragement helped me to bring this work to fruition in more ways than she knows.

NOTES

1. Two edited volumes based on these reports have already come out of the initial phases of this project: Neil Gilbert, ed., *Targeting Social Benefits: International Perspectives and Trends* (New Brunswick, N.J.: Transaction Publishers, 2001); and Neil Gilbert and Rebecca Van Voorhis, eds., *Activating the Unemployed: A Comparative Appraisal of Work-Oriented Policies* (New Brunswick, N.J.: Transaction Publishers, 2001).

2. Neil Gilbert, *Selvhjelpsstaten et Nytt Paradigme for Sosial Trygghet* (*The Enabling State: An Emerging Paradigm for Social Protection*), Fafo, Norwegian Institute for Applied Social Science, 1999, Report 312 in the series from the Fafo project The Welfare Society in the 21st Century.

3. An initial version of part of chapter 1 was also published, in Neil Gilbert, "Remodeling Social Welfare," *Society*, July–August 1998.

4. Neil Gilbert, "Dienstleistungskontrakte: Strategien und Risiken" ("Contracting for Services: Methods and Pitfalls"), in Hans-Uwe Otto and Stefan Schnurr, eds., *Privatisierung und Wettbewerb in der Jugendhilfe* (Neuwied, Germany: Luchterhand, 2001).

Contents

Foreword

This profound book has a special quality to it, rarely achieved by any other: after it was written (albeit before it was published) its analysis was fully vindicated by the 2001 assault on America and the new sense of community and, above all, respect for the role of government that grew out of it. History rarely tests paradigms so quickly and in such a dramatic fashion—and leaves them confirmed. There are, however, two issues on which there is room for additional dialogue. One concerns the relationship between rights and responsibilities.

As communitarians see it, at least this one, a good society combines respect for individual rights with the expectation that members will live up to their own responsibilities to their families as well as to the community at large. One of the greatest achievements of the communitarian approach is the curbing of the language of rights, some of which had turned many wants and interests into legal entitlements and had fostered unnecessary litigiousness. "Rights talk," which fostered a disregard of social responsibility, was dominant in the 1980s, the days of rampant individualism. By now it has been largely replaced by a wide recognition that both individual rights and social responsibilities must be respected.

Basic individual rights are inalienable, just as one's social obligations cannot be denied. However, it is a grave moral error to argue that there are no rights without responsibilities or vice versa. Thus, a people who evade taxes, neglect their children, or fail to live up to their social responsibilities in some other way are still entitled to a fair trial, free speech, and other basic rights. There may be fewer rights than some claim, but our constitutionally protected rights are not conditional. We cannot and should not be required to do anything to "earn" them. Hence, policies that deny criminals the right to vote while jailed should be modified. And nobody should be denied the basic necessities of life, even if they have not lived up to their responsibilities, for example, finding work.

On the other hand, a person whose rights have been violated (say, one who has been denied the right to vote because of a registration foul-up or a jail sentence) is still not exempt from attending to his or her children, not littering, and other social responsibilities.

The core tenet of the good society, as this book so correctly assumes, is that people must assume responsibility for others. No one is exempt from this expectation, although individuals vary greatly in the contributions they can make. A mental experiment may help: consider a paraplegic who has lost the use of his limbs and is permanently institutionalized. He uses a small stick in his mouth to turn pages of a book. Should we provide him with a nurse's aide to turn the pages or expect him to take that much responsibility for his own well-being? In order to both respect the person's dignity and to remain in line with the expectation that everyone should do as much for the common good as they can, we would expect the paraplegic to turn the pages himself (assuming he can do so without undue effort). If assuming responsibility to the best of one's abilities applies under these circumstances, surely no one is exempt from contributing to the common good in line with their ability.

For the same reasons, high school students should be encouraged to do community service as part of their civic practice. Senior citizens should be expected to help each other, members of their families, and their community. Likewise, those who receive welfare and cannot find gainful work should hold community jobs. People with contagious diseases should be expected to do their best not to expose others, and so on. All this follows from the paradigm laid out in the book before us.

The reference here is not primarily to legal commitments, enforced by courts and by the police, but to moral expectations. Discharging one's responsibility should not be considered a sacrifice or a punishment but an ennobling activity, something good that people do. For instance, high school students can gain a deep satisfaction from working in soup kitchens, as senior citizens can by volunteering to run social centers for other seniors, and so on.

Responsibility from all is to be paralleled by responsibility for all. That is, communities in a good society assume a moral responsibility for ensuring that no one is treated inhumanely, which occurs when they are denied the basic necessities of life. Voluntary associations, extended families, friends, mutual saving associations, and religious charities can carry part of this burden. Given that communities may be overwhelmed by needs, especially following war or natural disasters, the final responsibility to ensure that all are attended to falls on the state.

Communities can play an especially important role in ensuring that everyone is included and treated with the full respect entitled to them by the mere fact of their humanity, as ends in themselves. An obvious example is to ensure that no one will be subject to discrimination based on race, ethnicity, gender, sexual preference, religious background, or disability. Discrimination, which generates humiliation, breeds hate, and sets people against people, not only violates our elementary sense of justice but is also incompatible with treating people as ends in themselves. Here, too, the state must be the ultimate guardian against mistreatment. Millions of Americans who believed otherwise changed their minds in this regard after September 11, 2001.

Policies that impinge on the balance between individual rights and social responsibilities should be reviewed and adjusted accordingly. The right to privacy, for example, is to be respected, but it should not take priority over protection of life and limb. Mandatory drug testing of school bus drivers, train engineers, and air traffic controllers is legitimate because in this case the violation of privacy is limited while the danger to those whose lives they are directly responsible for is considerable. After all, although the Fourth Amendment dictates that there be no *un*reasonable search and seizure, it does not ban searches altogether. And reasonable searches have long been considered acceptable when there is a strong public interest. It is hard to imagine a greater public interest than a bus full of children or a train full of civilians. Some other professions and occupations that meet the same criteria might well be included (for instance, pilots), but at the same time there is no compelling public interest in testing most people. In contrast, violations of the privacy of our medical records, which concern the most intimate parts of our lives and yield at best minimal social benefits, should be summarily banned.

One of the core implications of the paradigm advanced here is that one and all deserve a rich basic minimum standard of living. These are things that everyone is due simply by being human. People deserve at least shelter, clothing, food, and elementary health care. People who act in antisocial ways or do not discharge their social responsibilities—whether because of their genes, parents, "the system," poor upbringing, or character failings—are not to be denied the elementary life necessities we provide to inmates, prisoners of war, and pets.

Providing a basic minimum will not kill the motivation to work for most people, as long as work is available, and they are able.

Though some will abuse the system, a good society should consider this a small price to pay for affirming the basic humanity of everyone. Throwing mental patients, alcoholics, mothers with small children, or anyone else onto the streets and cutting off their benefits is not compatible with treating all people as ends in themselves. For example, mental patients who are homeless need either to be provided with the kind of safe and healing community centers and family support that were assumed to exist when they were deinstitutionalized, or they must be reinstitutionalized. Such a change in public policy is important both out of respect for their humanity and for the safe and orderly living of all other members of the community.

During the 1990s, welfare systems, which badly needed to be reformed, as Gilbert shows so well, were finally restructured. However, here we see a clear case of overcorrection. The reform entailed cutting off some people in toto—not lowering benefits but terminating them—and terminating not merely cash support but also housing allowances, food stamps, and Medicaid assistance for children. These reforms need to be re-reformed if we are to cease the violation of this basic tenet of a good society. There is much room for deliberation concerning what exactly society owes each person and at what level benefits will cut into motivation to work and to refrain from antisocial behavior. For instance, furnishing cash would not necessarily be a part of such a state (or even charity) provided package. To ensure that community jobs keep people above the poverty line of the kind already discussed, their income from wages publicly provided *and* from other kinds of benefits—whether in kind or in cash—should be high enough to meet the "minimum" test.

These deliberations merely help to illustrate how much thought this book evokes, how fruitful it is.

Amitai Etzioni

Transformation of the Welfare State

Introduction

As the century turns, state-sponsored care and social protection in all of the advanced industrialized countries have entered a new era, marked not just by a temporal rotation but also by material developments that have deep and lasting implications. In the United Kingdom, Tony Blair's New Labour policies show no hesitation in privatizing the delivery of public services; the Social Democrats in Sweden have initiated the partial privatization of old-age pensions; reforms in Germany have introduced significant incentives for citizens to open private pension accounts for their old age; and throughout Europe and the United States changes in unemployment, disability, and social assistance programs have demonstrably qualified historic rights to public aid by a persistent emphasis on the responsibility to work and to be independent. As the generous scope of and access to public benefits contract, change is in the air, as well as in the substance of social provisions—to which some will no doubt respond, "Yes, well, *la plus ça change. . . .*" But in regard to state-sponsored social protection, things have really not stayed the same.

In exploring the direction and essential quality of the changes underway, this book pursues three lines of analysis. The main line, as the title signifies, furnishes evidence that the welfare states of advanced industrial nations are undergoing a major transformation. To transform is not to dismantle or obliterate but to fundamentally alter the existing framework in such a way that a new design emerges. In this case, what is being altered involves the essential framework for social policies that heretofore molded the foundation on which the most progressive welfare states were established. Briefly put in the language of social architects, this change is from policies framed by a *universal* approach to *publicly delivered* benefits designed to *protect labor* against the vicissitudes of the market and firmly held as *social rights* to policies framed by a *selective* approach to *private delivery* of provisions designed to promote *labor force participation* and *individual responsibility*—summed up by the maxim "public support for private responsibility." Or to put it more bluntly, a change from the ideal-type Scandinavian model of social welfare to a market-oriented version, which is identified with the Anglo-American approach that I term the *enabling state*.[1]

The second line of analysis, signified by the subtitle, suggests that the true magnitude and significance of this change have been minimized by policymakers and many welfare state advocates on the Left, while they go about actively supporting the shift to an enabling state. Since reforms from the Left increasingly draw on social policies of the Right, the substantive shift in orientation is muted as new initiatives are rhetorically couched in terms that permit the Left to distinguish itself from the Right. The third line of analysis argues that although the conversion to the enabling state introduces a much needed corrective to the unbridled growth of social rights and public expenditures from the 1960s to the 1980s, from a broader perspective the overall consequences of this development have troubling implications, which are difficult to address in the currently vaporous climate of political discourse.

To claim a basic transformation in a long-standing, well-entrenched social institution is a large charge. This is a small book, and the evidence is not unequivocal. However, I think that the trends documented in the following chapters lend plausible weight to the conclusions drawn on that score. It is one thing to document that social policies are changing—they almost always change—and another to understand the reasons why, which requires studying the change in a larger context. Thus, part I of the book begins by examining the competing theories about how welfare states are shaped by social, fiscal, and political pressures, as well as the evidence of how these forces are driving the transformation of the welfare state in modern times. I do this to lodge the more detailed analyses of the dimensions of policy reform in a broad framework that allows them to be seen not as isolated events but as part of a systematic shift, which conforms to diverse theoretical expectations.

The fundamental characteristics of these policy reforms, their variations, and how they are played out in the advanced industrial nations are discussed in part II, which analyzes the substance of measures recently initiated and data on the directions of change over the last few decades. These chapters illustrate empirical patterns of convergence toward market-oriented social policies in the industrialized nations. In interpreting the political discourse of *empowerment, solidarity, social inclusion, activation, equity,* and *social responsibility* which has accompanied the redesign of social policy, these chapters also ponder the ramifications of change that run contrary to the inspirational rhetoric of reform.

It has been said that social researchers examine empirical data to discover relationships and trends, theoreticians tell why these findings occur, and philosophers speculate about what they mean for the human condition. In the last part of this book, I make a brief foray into the broader implications of the triumph of capitalism, which is palpably manifest in the increasingly market-oriented design of social welfare reforms. Policies inspired by concerns for competition, choice, productivity, and rational weighing of measurable costs and benefits drive the provision of social care and protection into the domain of commercial life; that is, private responsibility supplants the public quest for communal security. Branching off from analysis of policy reforms to reflection on the larger meaning of these developments, this chapter cautions that as a handmaiden to the economy the enabling state bows too low to the market, resulting in a social imbalance that elevates the values and purpose of commercial exchange above all else.

Taken separately, I would imagine that there is a fair amount of agreement among social policy scholars about the trends, documented in these chapters, toward work-oriented policies, privatization of social welfare, increased targeting of benefits, and the shift from an emphasis on the social rights of citizenship to the civic duties of community members. Movement in these directions is evident in almost all of the industrial nations, if not at the same speed or on exactly the same heading. There is no doubt less agreement about whether the joining of these lines of change represents a magnitude of convergence that justifies the title of this book, whether the decline of public responsibility is as large and muffled as the subtitle suggests, and whether the apprehensions expressed about what these developments augur for the future health of society are credible. I leave these matters for the reader to decide.

NOTES

1. In the late 1980s my initial conception of the enabling state was seen as a uniquely American phenomenon, characterized primarily by the increasing use of indirect social expenditures to finance the private delivery of social services. By the early 1990s, I could distinguish additional features of the enabling state that were taking shape in the United States at the same time that similar changes appeared

to be unfolding in other industrialized nations. See Neil Gilbert and Barbara Gilbert, *The Enabling State: Modern Welfare Capitalism in America* (New York: Oxford University Press, 1989); and Neil Gilbert, *Welfare Justice: Restoring Social Equity* (New Haven, Conn.: Yale University Press, 1995).

PART I

CURRENTS OF CHANGE

1

New Course or Marginal Adjustment?

Over the last decade, arrangements for social protection have undergone a series of policy changes that are redrawing the boundaries and transforming the character of welfare states in many, if not all, of the industrialized nations. The significance of these changes is subject to varying interpretations. Some see them as a marginal adjustment in the borders of the welfare state—a retreat to the core—or a "fine tuning" of existing policies.[1] Summarizing a study of the adaptations of welfare states in the mid-1990s, Gosta Esping-Anderson concludes that almost everywhere political forces have conspired "to maintain the existing principles of the welfare state. This means that cutting occurs at the margin, that trimming is largely limited to the 'fat.' "[2] Others perceive the changing landscape of industrialized welfare states as the embodiment of major revisions in the principles and philosophy of social protection—amounting to an emergent shift in the conventional welfare state paradigm.[3] Observing a worldwide consensus "that social security is at a critical juncture in its development," Dalmer Hoskins, secretary general of the International Social Security Association, expresses the need to resolve such basic issues of social welfare as what risks should be covered and where state responsibility for protection should end and individual responsibility begin. Moreover, he sees the process of redefining a new social contract with respect to income security as well underway.[4]

Whatever their disagreements about the depth and implications of the changes underway, most welfare state analysts acknowledge that these reforms are spurred, in part, by the need for greater labor force adaptability and productivity as national markets are absorbed into the competitive sphere of the global economy. In U.S. classrooms, students are told that "to reestablish the legitimacy of the welfare state it is necessary to demonstrate how social programs can contribute positively to the nation's productivity"[5]—a sentiment echoed by the Dutch minister of Social Affairs and Employment, who calls for "reshaping the welfare state into an economic performer."[6] In New Zealand, Anne de Bruin sees the subordination of social policy to the demands for labor flexibility and the constraints of international competition as a distinctive feature of the changing institutional framework for social protection.[7] Similar observations appear in Sweden, where Staffan Marklund finds social welfare reforms stimulated by "an effort to increase the productivity and competitiveness of the economy," and in Britain, where Anthony Giddens counsels movement toward the "social investment state," emphasizing public investments in human capital over the provision of customary social welfare benefits.[8]

Along with the growing need for labor force flexibility, concerns about the erosion of individual responsibility have fostered policy reforms that offer incentives for people to work in the market economy or to contribute actively to the community in other ways. This development has been variously characterized as moving from "Keynesian Welfare to the Schumpeterian Workfare State,"[9] "social rights to social obligations,"[10] "passive to active social policy,"[11] and—for those who favor more evocative metaphors—"safety nets to trampolines."[12] In the United Kingdom, this shift is referred to as the "third way."[13]

Institutional arrangements for social protection are also being redesigned with a heightened regard for the benefits of competitive markets. Thus, for example, Niels Ploug and Jon Kvist find that in Sweden the case for less state and more market in the field of social welfare is supported by several of the nonsocialist parties along with some members of the Social Democratic Party.[14] Market-oriented reforms are reflected in the movement toward privatization, which has inspired descriptions and analyses of the "Hollow State," the "Contracting State," and the "Mixed Economy of Welfare."[15] Commenting on this trend, Zsuzsa Ferge sees the formal rationality of the market being imposed not only on the "Post-Modern Welfare State" but also on all spheres of activity: "Works of art, the organisation of Oxford Colleges, the activity of social policy, or even the most insignificant acts of everyday life are all subjected to the profitability calculus."[16]

In a flourish of neologisms—the Schumpeterian workfare state, the hollow state, the contract state, the hidden welfare state, the social investment state, the active state, the mixed economy of welfare, the third way, the post-modern welfare state, and the enabling state—welfare theorists around the world have tried to capture the essential features of change. What do all these new classifications add up to? Do they signal a paradigm shift or the need to lend analytic discourse on social welfare a fashionable currency by cloaking old models in new conceptual garb? Before addressing this question, let us take a brief glance backward to reflect on some of the concerns about the welfare state that were being voiced prior to the 1990s; a broader context lends sharper focus to the meaning and significance of recent changes.

From the early 1970s to the mid-1980s, there was an ongoing debate in the literature about the "crisis" of the welfare state.[17] Ramesh Mishra detected serious doubts about the intellectual and moral legitimacy of the welfare state.[18] From a neo-Marxist perspective, the fiscal crisis of the state was seen, in part, as a problem of public expenditure brought about as the state sought to legitimize and advance the capitalist system through such provisions as education that socializes some of the costs of production and welfare benefits that mitigate the afflictions of surplus labor.[19] Michael Hill and Glen Bramley found some evidence and much public concern that in the mid-1970s the British government would not be able to finance social expenditures to which it was committed, but they remained skeptical that this constituted a real crisis.[20] Similarly Rudolf Klein and Michael O'Higgins concluded that there was no crisis in the British welfare state in the sense of an impending bankruptcy. However, they recognized that although the welfare state of the mid-1980s was a response to the problems and values of the first Industrial Revolution, future arrangements for social protection will "have to cope with the consequences of the second Industrial Revolution: this will, almost inevitably, mean responding to a new set of problems and perhaps a new set of values."[21]

In retrospect, the discourse of the 1990s can be seen as closely related to the earlier debates on the crisis of the welfare state. The term *crisis* connotes an emergency in which there is danger of serious harm and ruin; in the debates up through the mid-1980s, this connotation referred to what some saw as the impeding moral and fiscal depletion of the welfare state. But there is another meaning in which *crisis* signifies a turning point. The replacement of the analyses of crisis in the 1970s and 1980s with the 1990s discourse on reclassifications of arrangements for social protection suggests that the earlier crisis was not signaling an impending bankruptcy so much as a turning point—a change of course in response to new problems and values, emerging partly, as Klein and O'Higgins suggested, from the second Industrial Revolution.

Only a Matter of Degree?

But, to return to my earlier question, has this change of course moved recent social welfare policies only a few degrees to one side, or have developments veered so far over in a different direction that one might speak of a paradigm shift toward a new institutional framework for social protection? At some point a change in degree becomes palpably a change in kind: we withdraw our hands as the once cool water starts to boil and eventually evaporates. The transformation of the welfare state is more difficult to pin down. Reasonable people who are reading the same facts can disagree on how much change is taking place and what it all means. Consider the various meanings one might attribute to the numbers in table 1.1.

What would the reader take as the most striking feature of these numbers? One straightforward assessment is that they show that the welfare index was declining in three out of the four countries over a period of six years. Another account might note that whereas the welfare index remained fairly stable in one country, it declined an average of 11 percent in the other three countries, not a monumental fall but a serious drop, given the relatively brief period of six years during which it registered. Further interpretation of these data might even offer a generalization about where these Anglo-American, "liberal" welfare states seem to be headed—that is, away from generous, accessible, and high-quality welfare provisions.[22] These plausible interpretations of the hypothetical data in table 1.1 reinforce the conventional perception of "liberal" welfare states as less progressive than the social democratic regimes in the Nordic countries.

But what if the countries in table 1.1 were Denmark, Finland, Norway, and Sweden instead of the United States, England, Australia, and New Zealand? And what if the changes in mean welfare index between 1990–91 and 1996–97 represented changes in the mean of

Table 1.1 How Much Change?

Country	Changes in Mean Welfare Index of Accessability, Generosity, and Quality of Social Benefits for Children, the Elderly, and the Unemployed Between 1990–91 and 1996–97 (percent)
United States	− 4
England	− 25
Australia	+ 1
New Zealand	− 14

membership scores of these countries in the ideal-type, Nordic welfare model (based on measures of generosity, accessibility, and quality of benefits)? In fact, the differences shown in table 1.1 are the same as the percentage difference in mean scores for membership in the Nordic model of welfare reported in Jon Kvist's study of welfare reform in Denmark, Finland, Norway, and Sweden. Placing less emphasis on the magnitude and direction of the percentage change, his analysis considers mainly whether the absolute change in the membership scores is large enough to warrant a claim that a country's correspondence to the ideal-type model changed in kind or degree. He concludes that "perhaps the most striking feature of welfare reform in the Nordic countries in the 1990s is the extent of resilience and restructuring. None of the countries has left the club of countries belonging to the Nordic welfare model despite the adverse national economic performance in Finland and Sweden and the significant changes in the surrounding world."[23]

But Kvist's ideal-type model did not capture changes in all the essential characteristics of the Nordic welfare state—such as increasing levels of privatization, targeting, and obligations to work—or what was soon to come. For example, 1998 reforms to the Swedish pension system included a measure to reallocate 2.5 percent of the 18.5 percent pension contribution (or almost 14 percent of total contributions to the public system) from the public system to private investment in individual reserve accounts.[24] (In the United States, up through 2001, equivalent proposals to privatize from about 2 percent to 5 percent of social security contributions encountered firm resistance from mainstream Democrats as too radical a departure from government protection.[25]) The Swedish reform will shuttle billions of dollars from the public coffers to private insurance companies, a development that architects of the Swedish system would have found almost inconceivable a mere 30 years ago.[26]

In a later study that analyzed reforms in unemployment compensation schemes in the 1990s, Kvist arrives at a somewhat different conclusion. Although accessability to unemployment benefits and their generosity declined from 1990 to 1998, these changes were not deemed great enough to be a major deviation from the Nordic model. However, Kvist interprets the profound revisions in the rules that govern claimants' obligations to work in Denmark and Sweden "as resulting in a qualitative change" in their unemployment compensation policies, which marks the arrival of a "New Social Democratic model" that was also evident in Norway.[27]

Does the advent of a *new* social democratic model signal a fundamental change of course? A recalibration of individual and communal responsibility for welfare? Is it the beginning of what Anton Zijderveld construes as the "end of comprehensive state succor?"[28] Not according to Sven Hort, who reassuringly describes the reform of public pensions as a change under which "a minor part of contribution will be set aside for individual risk investment. Each insured will have the opportunity to save a certain amount according to one's own ideas. Failure will be an individual responsibility and winners take all." Operating alongside Kvist in the vein of "marginal adjustments," Hort's analysis of recent Swedish reforms maintains that "decisions taken during the last decade point towards a slimmed and somewhat more market-oriented version of the old model, and not a radically new one."[29] Similarly, although Nordlund acknowledges that the "Nordic welfare states have unquestionably been subject to a sequence of important changes during the 1980s and 1990s," he finds that these changes have not been far-reaching enough to constitute a "dismantling of the welfare state."[30] Even in the United States and United Kingdom under the Reagan and Thatcher administrations, there was no dismantling of the welfare state up through the early 1990s, according to Pierson's widely cited study.[31]

Short of dismantling modern arrangements for social protection, the point at which increasing degrees of change in these arrangements amount to a fundamental transformation of the welfare state is to some extent a subjective matter.[32] Of course, one need not wait for the boiling water to evaporate to draw the conclusion that putting one's hand in a simmering pot will evoke a qualitatively different experience than when it was cold. Since the welfare state is not being dismantled and the heat created by the friction of legislative changes rarely drives participants from the chambers of power, we must rely on our analytic faculties to measure the degrees of change and to judge their meaning.[33] These judgments are invariably complicated by the all too human tendency (to which social scientists are hardly immune) to mingle impartial analysis of what is happening to the welfare state and normative prescription of what the observer would like to see happening—a tendency that is heightened when matters relating to social values are concerned, and the welfare state is surely a value-laden subject.[34]

The impartial analytic task may be further swayed by the workings of national pride and political convictions. As for national pride, it is difficult to find homegrown (or any other) welfare scholars and experts who point to the United States as a model for social protection with much enthusiasm. The Nordic countries are another matter. Setting an international standard, Peter Baldwin suggested that until recently, "Sweden under the Social Democratic reign was the welfare Mecca that all other nations were striving towards or reacting against."[35] The faithful are naturally prone to interpret evidence of change more as a marginal adjustment in the boundaries of the "welfare Mecca" than a full-scale relocation (from, say, Stockholm to London, or even to Washington, D.C.). Politically speaking, it is fair to say that most welfare state scholars lean toward the Left, though over the last two decades one finds an increasing number on the Right, particularly in the United States, where conservative foundations have made concerted efforts to encourage thinking and research in this area.[36]

All of these factors—politics, nationalism, and social values—can shade one's reading of the evidence of change and what it means for the welfare state. As the title of this book suggests, I think the evidence indicates that a basic shift has occurred in the institutional framework for social protection (or to hedge the bet, at least is far enough along that one might speak of an emerging paradigm), most prominently in the United States and England, with the other advanced industrialized nations moving steadily in the same direction. This is a large claim, on which the reader will ultimately decide. In weighing the evidence on this issue, the reader is advised to judge how closely the facts fit the interpretation, how well the pronouncements about the need for change reflect the actual passage of legislative reforms, and the extent to which reforms that are on the books coincide with the implementation of these measures. Before examining the evidence based on a range of empirical indicators and social policy reforms, my line of analysis starts in this chapter by placing the tides of change in a broad theoretical context, which integrates competing ideas about the role of social forces and human initiative in the development of the welfare state. This is followed by an appraisal of the forces currently reshaping the central character of the welfare state and the essential features that typify the new institutional framework for social protection.

First, however, we must make a brief digression. If a new institutional framework for social protection is in the offering, it needs a name—a conceptual representation that differentiates it from the conventional welfare state model. Among the neologisms identified earlier, the distinction between the Keynesian welfare state and the Schumpeterian workfare state is the intellectually toniest conceptualization, contrasting John Maynard Keynes's ideas about the merits of state intervention in the market with Joseph Schumpeter's views on the fiscal limits of taxation beyond which the state would sabotage innovative activity and entrepreneurial drive.[37] Although the emphasis on workfare, which stimulates productive activities, describes an important facet of the recent developments in social protection, it captures only one dimension of a multifarious change. Similarly, the other models tend to accent unidimensional attributes: references to the contract state and the hollow state suggest that the spreading privatization of social welfare is the essential feature of change; the hidden state draws attention to the increasing use of tax expenditures and other indirect measures to effect social transfers, often to the middle classes;[38] and akin to the Schumpeterian workfare state, the social investment state and the active society refer to policy measures designed to enhance human capital and move people into the labor force.

In contrast to these one-dimensional characterizations, the mixed economy of welfare conveys a rather sketchy framework, which incorporates a broad range of designs for social protection based on a combination of efforts emanating from the state, market, voluntary, and informal sectors. The postmodern welfare state, outlined by Ferge, embodies a number of the basic attributes of the new institutional framework for social protection.[39] However, the *postmodern* emblem has been tagged to so many social phenomena—music, architecture, literature, and philosophy—with various meanings, that applying it to the changing character of the welfare state adds little clarity to this process. The postmodern sensibility is associated with questioning the positivistic formulations of objective reality—for example, emphasizing the fervently subjective interpretations of literary deconstruction—which forms a curious mix with the staunchly objective, what Weber termed "formal," rationality of market-oriented profit-loss calculations that is coming to dominate social welfare policy.[40] The "third way," another nebulous formulation, has been used by Prime Minister Tony Blair to describe New Labour's path of welfare reform, which treads between the right-wing calls for dismantling of welfare and the old Left's advocacy for continuation of collectivist welfare policies.

Finally, there is the *enabling state,* a term that has been used to illustrate the essential character of change in the United States and England, which is captured by the tenet of public support for private responsibility—where "private" responsibility includes individuals, the market, and voluntary organizations.[41] By building on this principle, social welfare arrangements are increasingly designed to enable people to work and to enable the market and the voluntary sector to assume an expanded role in providing social protection. This conception of the enabling state transmits a somewhat sharper picture of the role of government in the emerging framework for social protection than the unidimensional alternatives and imparts a clearer sense of the direction of change than the mixed economy model. Hence, among these options, I have selected the enabling state to represent the emerging paradigm for social protection. Whether or not this nomenclature sticks (there are ideological and sentimental reasons to cling to old labels, as well as political reasons to choose new ones that evoke, perhaps, a more dubious image), in practice the welfare state as we knew it is being replaced in many nations by new arrangements under which social provisions are transferred through work incentives, tax benefits, purchase of service contracts, and other measures designed to offer public support for private responsibility. Let us see how and why this has come about.

How Welfare States Evolve

The transformation of the welfare state is a story most clearly articulated by starting from a vantage point that places the currents of change in their theoretical context. Among the various accounts of the rise of the modern welfare state, much of the theory and research is concentrated along two apparently competing lines of analysis, which emphasize the influence of either impersonal structural forces or sociopolitical pressures that stem from human discord.[42] These approaches frame the major theoretical debates on the development of the welfare state. Analyses of structural forces, such as economic growth, industrialization, and demographic shifts, are associated with convergence theory. Simply put, convergence theory posits that in response to disruptions caused by structural changes, countries tend to increase public expenditure on a similar set of institutional arrangements—programs such as public assistance for the poor and social security for the elderly—that perform the functions of social protection previously rendered by the extended family, church, and feudal traditions. Coming from a different angle, we see that studies on the impact of sociopolitical pressures are associated with the theory of distinct welfare state regimes, which holds that different institutional arrangements for social protection evolve according to the strength and cultural dispositions of contending interest groups.

The argument that welfare states converge derives from theoretical works in the 1950s and 1960s that examined the relations between the rise of industrial society and the development of social welfare benefits and social rights.[43] Building on these theoretical foundations, a series of comparative studies followed, which empirically explored the links among levels of economic growth, demographic change, and social security spending. The results from many of these studies generally support the underlying thesis of convergence.[44] Analyzing patterns of social welfare policy development in Sweden, Norway, Germany, and the United Kingdom from 1960 to 1993, for example, Olli Kangas finds that countries that have often been described as representing different welfare state models at specific points in time show distinct signs of convergence when analyzed from a longitudinal perspective. He concludes that "much of what is happening is structural," although politics will eventually influence how countries respond to structural problems.[45] At the same time, a number of empirical studies have generated findings that challenge the soundness and utility of convergence theory. Some of these studies have found no relationship between levels of industrial development and the timing of the adoption of social insurance programs.[46] Other studies have detected evidence of divergence rather than convergence between levels of economic development and social security expenditures.[47]

Also, compelling questions have been raised about the methods used to measure social spending and the normative assumption underlying these studies—that countries that spent the highest proportion of their gross domestic products (GDPs) on social welfare were leaders and those that did not were laggards. Measuring welfare effort as a simple function of social expenditure divided by GDP ignores the interaction of spending and need; a country with low unemployment, a low proportion of elderly citizens, a small percentage of single-parent families, and relatively few people living in poverty would be likely to spend a smaller proportion of its GDP on social welfare programs than a country that ranked comparatively high on these indices. Does this difference in social spending reflect lower "welfare effort" or fewer social needs? Moreover, most measures of spending on social welfare do not take into account the degree of tax effort. If one country consumes 10 percent more of its GDP on social expenditure than another but collects taxes at a rate 40 percent higher, which one is making the greater welfare effort relative to taxation? When social expenditures are analyzed by controlling for levels of need and taxation, notable shifts appear in national rankings on welfare effort.[48] More generally, convergence theory has drawn criticism for a deterministic countenance that attributes the development of welfare states essentially to impersonal social forces, ignoring the role of human intervention.

In contrast to the impersonal forces of convergence theory, those who stress the importance of sociopolitical processes argue that what appear to be broadly similar institutional patterns for social protection at a high level of abstraction on closer inspection actually represent different types of welfare states, fashioned by human hands. Here the analytic perspective focuses less on the structural determinants and more on the clash of group interests and the processes of political mobilization that shape the development of distinct welfare state regimes. One strand of sociopolitical analysis models the welfare state as a continuous compromise in the ongoing class struggle between workers and capitalists in democratic societies. Based on the strength of numbers, organized labor mobilizes political power through the democratic process to offset the economic power exercised by capitalists—thereby extracting concessions on the distribution of resources in society.[49] As Rebecca Van Voorhis points out, Social Democrats tend to see these concessions as a victory for labor, whereas neo-Marxists perceive social spending as merely a capitalist safety valve, which controls labor by letting off steam when the pressure gets high enough.[50] A number of comparative studies show that countries with the most powerful unions and strongest or longest ruling social democratic parties have the highest rates of social expenditure.[51]

The corpus of empirical evidence for the distinct regime theory was substantially advanced by Gosta Esping-Andersen's influential work, which identified three types of welfare states—liberal, corporatist, and social democratic—based on quantitative measures of social policy in 18 advanced industrialized nations.[52] But like the empirical research on convergence theory, the methods and measures used to analyze distinct regimes are open to serious criticism on several counts. One of the key, and oft-cited, distinguishing features of the different welfare regimes in Esping-Andersen's model, for example, is the extent to which a country's social policies give workers a certain degree of immunity from market forces, protecting their labor from being treated purely as a commodity; thus, labor is "decommodified" by unemployment benefits that are easily accessible, last for years, and pay replacement rates of 80 percent to 90 percent of previous earnings—allowing workers to withhold their labor from the market until a suitable job is available. Esping-Andersen developed a decommodification index, which provides an empirical estimate of where the various countries rank on this attribute of social policy, showing a clustering of distinct regimes.

A close look at how this index was devised, however, reveals that despite the use of several indicators, the double weighting of replacement rates effectively makes this indicator the operational definition of the decommodification score for pensions.[53] At best, the use of pension replacement rates that fail to adjust for differential costs of living affords a crude measure for comparing the level of support actually sustained by these benefits. At the same time, the pension index takes no account of the legal age of retirement—a critical variable that affects the workers' ability to withhold their labor. Moreover, in the final calculation of overall decommodification scores, the additive approach to raw scores on sickness, unemployment, and pension policies ignores the large difference between the mean values on unemployment and pension policies, which inadvertently weights pension scores (which mainly reflect replacement rates) almost 50 percent more than unemployment.[54]

Shortly after it appeared, scholars found the three-regime model in need of refinement. Francis Castles and Deborah Mitchell proposed four types of regimes: conservative, social democratic, liberal, and radical welfare state.[55] Maurizio Ferrera and others argued that the Southern model, which includes Italy, Spain, Greece, and Portugal, constitutes a fourth regime.[56] Indeed, unlike works of convergence theory, which draw attention to broad resemblances among welfare states, efforts to distinguish distinct regimes tend to slice the conceptual patterns of welfare thinner and thinner, advancing toward the ultimate conclusion that each country's system evolves out of its unique heritage. Even the oft-cited Scandinavian model begins to unravel under close examination.[57] Thus, if convergence theory is sometimes charged with being too vague and abstract, affording unduly broad generalizations, in the course of refinement the distinct regime theory runs the risk of yielding results that are too country-specific to draw any general conclusions about the development of the welfare state.

A second strand of sociopolitical analysis focuses not so much on class struggle as on the processes through which government officials, public bureaucracies, and interest-group demands influence the development of the welfare state.[58] The public choice school of thought, a major line of discourse in this vein, suggests that public spending in the welfare states tends to spin out of control because the actors involved are motivated by narrow self-interests.[59] This thinking is informed by several propositions: (1) special-interest groups (organized around, for example, gender, ethnicity, disability, occupational associations, sexual orientation, age, veteran status, forms of victimization, animal rights, and religious convictions, as well as industrial lobbies) have a strong incentive to pressure the government to provide goods and services for their members since the benefits will be concentrated on the group and the costs are spread out over all taxpayers; (2) driven by self-interest, politicians have a strong incentive to cater to the demands of these organized groups, currying favor for the next election; (3) special-interest groups have little incentive to oppose the demands of other interest groups because with the cost of one group's benefits spread out over all taxpayers, for any given concession the net amount charged to other groups' members is too small to get excited about; and (4) operating outside the constraints of competition and profits, self-interested bureaucratic officials seek to expand their power bases by increasing public expenditures on the programs under their control. From this perspective, once they are established, social programs are easier to expand than to cut back. Their constituencies—service providers, public bureaucrats, consumers, and advocacy groups—quickly develop strong attachments to the social provision. Policy reforms are, in the current vernacular, "path-dependent," which means that where they go depends to a large extent on the strength and momentum already created by their core constituencies. Wherever it is headed, the path is usually difficult to reverse, although not impossible.[60] Giuliano Bonoli and Bruno Palier, for example, identify the British Social Security Act of 1986 and the 1995 French program for social security reform as innovative measures that, so to speak, jump the track and transfer programs to an alternative path.[61]

Social transfers derived from direct public expenditures are not the only source of benefits distributed to interest groups. Although the reduction of U.S. federal discretionary spending in the 1990s has constrained the politicians' scope to dispense benefits to interest groups funded with tax dollars or through deficit financing, Pietro Nivola suggests that the concessions have shifted to expand what he labels "social regulatory pork"—the use of government regulatory measures and special preferences to benefit some interest groups at the expense of other people, creating what amount to social transfers off the budget books.[62]

As with the other theories, there are studies that dispute or qualify the propositions advanced by the public choice school about the influence and utility-maximizing behavior of politicians, bureaucratic officials, and voters.[63] Summing up the counterevidence, Amitai Etzioni maintains that "Public Choice is but an extreme example of a neoclassical theory that finds little support in the facts, and is widely contradicted, precisely because it does not tolerate moral factors as a significant, distinct, explanatory, and predicting factor."[64]

Finally, in contrasting the two major lines of analysis, it should be noted that although many studies tend to emphasize trends toward either convergence or divergence, their authors often recognize that both structural forces and sociopolitical processes have shaped the development of welfare states.[65] And in some cases, efforts are made to integrate the structural and sociopolitical perspectives. Einar Overbye, for example, develops an inventive model that joins the utility-maximizing behavior of public choice with the structural influences of industrialization to illustrate convergence toward a dual public pension arrangement that provides contribution-based, earnings-related pensions to the working population and tax-financed, means-tested pension supplements to those only marginally connected to the labor force.[66]

Tides of Change: A Unifying Metaphor

After surveying the theories and weighing the relevant research, the question still remains, Do welfare states converge under the pressures of broad impersonal structural forces or diverge in response to human interventions shaped by sociopolitical factors in different countries? Viewed from a distance, these apparently competing lines of analysis can be united to form a coherent metaphor for the development of modern welfare states and the transformation currently underway. Imagine the advanced industrial nations as ships of the welfare state, afloat on a large bay at ebb tide. As the tide recedes, they are all pulled in the same direction—converging toward the mouth of the bay—by the powerful, impersonal forces of nature. However, these ships of state are not thoroughly adrift on tides of change; they are democratically manned by elected leaders who weigh the passengers' interests and preferences in deciding on the destination toward which to steer as they approach the widening mouth of the bay. Moving in roughly the same direction, away from shore, but not exactly toward the same final destination, some of the ships form small clusters that sail along on similar headings, whereas others chart independent courses. Thus, the modern welfare states expanded and branched off in various directions as they rode the ebb tide of economic development from the early 1960s to the late 1980s. But the tide has changed. When the 1990s came to a close, the ships of the welfare state were drawn back into the bay as a flood tide of new structural pressures and sociopolitical forces narrowed the channel of maneuverability and transformed the conventional arrangements for social welfare. Let us examine these shifting tides a bit more closely.

The initial convergence began to gain momentum in 1960 as welfare state expenditures were poised for a historic takeoff in almost every Western democracy. At about that time, Daniel Bell declared that capitalist societies had arrived at the "end of ideology," in part because of political compromises that included a rough consensus on the acceptance of the welfare state.[67] In the same vein, Gunnar Myrdal saw the internal political debates in advanced welfare states as "becoming increasingly technical in character, ever more concerned with detailed arrangements, and less involved with broad issues, since those are slowly disappearing."[68] Regarding the role of government, he thought that "all private enterprises in the advanced Welfare State are already in essential respects publicly controlled or are becoming so—without nationalization." And he also thought it possible that in "the Welfare State of the future, public ownership and public management will come to play a somewhat larger role, perhaps in the very long run, a much larger one." Myrdal was so convinced of the harmony created by welfare state programs that much of his analysis in *Beyond the Welfare State* was addressed to the need for building a "welfare world."

The optimism expressed by Myrdal and Bell at that time was not misplaced. Indeed, over the next two decades public spending on social welfare in Western democracies nearly doubled as a proportion of the gross domestic product, climbing from an average of 12.3 percent of the GDP in 1960 to 23.3 percent in 1980, among 21 member nations of the Organization for Economic Cooperation and Development (OECD).[69] (Although spending in the United States also multiplied from 9 percent to 18 percent of the GDP, it was nevertheless considered a laggard in welfare state development, ranking just above Greece, Spain, Portugal, and Australia.) It is fair to say that despite occasional criticism, the value of social welfare schemes financed and produced by the state during this period was largely taken for granted as a useful corrective for the vicissitudes of the market economy. Riding on a tide of public approval, these schemes expanded in political environments that rarely questioned the mounting costs and functions of the welfare state.

This golden era of welfare state expansion ended in the wake of the oil crises that hit the world economy in 1974 and 1979. Since the late 1970s the growth rate of public social expenditure slowed down and actually started to reverse after 1993. As illustrated in figure 1.1, data from Eurostat (Statistical Office of the European Communities) show that in the early 1990s the average social expenditure as a percent of GDP increased about 1 percent a year for the 15 countries of the European Union, topping out at 29 percent of the GDP in 1993, after which social spending relative to GDP began a slow decline. A similar trend is evident in the OECD data, which define social expenditure more narrowly than the Eurostat classification.[70] The trend in social expenditure is partly accounted for by the rising rate of unemployment in the European Union, which peaked in 1994 and then started to fall.

Not only has the rise of social expenditure halted, but also social welfare policies have come under increasing criticism. Rather than being seen as a remedy for the flaws and insecurities of capitalism, welfare programs have been repeatedly recast as part of the very problem they were designed to solve. Critics claim that the welfare state promises more than can be delivered without creating deleterious effects on the market economy by undermining incentive, hampering competitiveness, inhibiting savings, and increasing national debt.[71]

Although financial strains from the 1970s oil crises began to check the rise in social expenditure, the mounting challenge to the welfare state has been fueled by a more powerful combination of broader eco-

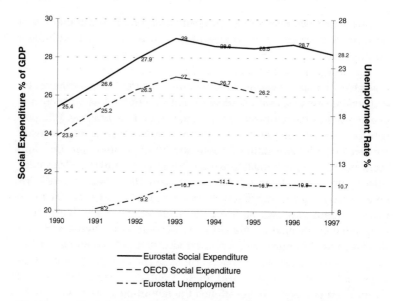

Figure 1.1 Social Expenditure and Unemployment Rate EU-15.
Sources: Eurostat, *Social Protection Expenditure and Receipts: Data
1980–1997* (Luxembourg: European Communities, 2000), p. 12;
OECD, Social Expenditure Database; 1980–1996 (including all the
EU-15 countries except Greece); Eurostat, *Eurostat Yearbook: A Statistical Eye on Europe 1987–1997* (Brussels: European Communities,
1999).

nomic and social forces. The economic forces that are reshaping the
welfare state are generated by demographic shifts and realignments of
production and distribution, spurred by the mobility of capital; these
structural changes have created conditions that pose fiscal constraints
on social spending. The social forces are the product of changing ideas
and values about the relations between welfare and work and the limits of government intervention, which transform the normative context for social welfare planning. These economic and social forces
converge along several lines of influence that have joined to mobilize
a drive beyond the welfare state toward a new paradigm of social
protection—in directions that Myrdal's earlier forecasts did not anticipate.

NOTES

1. Paul Pierson, "The New Politics of the Welfare State," *World
Politics*, 48:2 (1996), 143–79; Sven Olson Hort, "From a Generous to
a Stingy Welfare State? Sweden's Approach to Targeting," in Neil Gil-

bert, ed., *Targeting Social Benefits: International Perspectives on Issues and Trends* (Rutgers, N.J: Transaction Publishers, 2001), characterizes recent policy changes in the Swedish welfare state, including the unprecedented move toward the privatization of old-age pensions, as "fine tuning" (p. 198).

2. Gosta Esping-Anderson, ed., *Welfare States in Transition: National Adaptations in Global Economies* (London: Sage, 1996), p. 265; curiously, the claim that only fat was being cut is followed on the very next page with a description of successful welfare state cutback policies, for example, "the succession of increasingly severe cutbacks in the Swedish welfare state, including the most cherished programmes such as pensions, sickness absence and parental leave" (p. 266).

3. See, for example, Zsuzsa Ferge, "The Change of the Welfare Paradigm—The Individualisation of the Social," paper presented at the Annual Conference of the British Social Policy Association, Sheffield, July 16–18, 1996. For an analysis of the change in universalist principles and the institutional welfare model in Sweden, see Sune Sunesson, Staffan Blomberg, Per Gunnar Edebalk, Lars Harrysson, Jan Magnusson, Anne Meeuwisse, Jan Petersson, and Tapio Salonen, "The Flight from Universalism," *European Journal of Social Work*, 1:1 (1998), 19–29. See also Howard Glennerster, "Which Welfare States Are Most Likely to Survive," *International Journal of Social Welfare*, 8: 1 (January 1999), 1–13, for a view of the distinctive arrangements for social protection taking shape in the United Kingdom.

4. Dalmer Hoskins, "The Redesign of Social Security," *Developments and Trends in Social Security 1996–1998* (Geneva: International Social Security Association, 1998), pp. 1–9.

5. Howard Karger and David Stoesz, *American Social Welfare Policy: A Pluralist Approach* (New York: Longman, 1994).

6. A. P. W. Melkert, "Conclusion," in *Family, Market, and Community: Equity and Efficiency in Social Policy* (Paris: OECD, 1997).

7. Anne de Bruin, "Transformation of the Welfare State in New Zealand: From Welfare State to Schumpeterian Workfare State," paper presented at the 9th International Conference on Socio-Economics, Montreal, July 5–7, 1997.

8. S. Marklund, "The Decomposition of Social Policy in Sweden," *Scandinavian Journal of Social Welfare*, 1: 1 (1992), 10; Anthony Giddens is quoted in "Ideology: Beyond Left and Right," *The Economist*, May 22, 1998, p. 52. Over the last decade, recommendations in the international arena, for the redesign of social policy to support productivity were initially expressed in publications of the Organization for Economic Cooperation and Development and the International Social Security Association; see, for example, OECD, *The Future of Social Protection* (Paris: OECD, 1988); and ISSA, "Developments and Trends in Social Security: 1978–1989," *International Social Security Review*, 42: 3 (1989), 247–349.

9. B. Jessop, "From Keynesian Welfare to the Schumpeterian Workfare State," in R. Burrows and B. Loader, eds., *Towards a Post-Fordist Welfare State?* (London: Routledge, 1994).

10. Lawrence Mead, *Beyond Entitlement: The Social Obligations of Citizenship* (New York: Free Press, 1986).

11. OECD, "Editorial: The Path to Full Employment: Structural Adjustment for an Active Society," *Employment Outlook*, July 1989.

12. Jacob Torfing, "From the Keynesian Welfare State to a Schumpeterian Workfare Regime—The Offensive Neo-Statist Case of Denmark," paper presented at the 9th International Conference on Socio-Economics, Montreal, July 5–7, 1997.

13. Tony Blair, Foreword and Introduction, Green Paper on Welfare State Reform (1998). The British "third way" is reminiscent of the "middle way," Childs's popular account of Sweden's efforts to wend the path between individualism and collectivism in the 1930s. See Marquis Childs, *Sweden: The Middle Way* (New Haven, Conn.: Yale University Press, 1936).

14. Niels Ploug and Jon Kvist, *Social Security in Europe: Development of Dismantlement?* (The Hague: Kluwer Law International, 1996)

15. Tony Eardley, "New Relations of Welfare in the Contracting State: The Marketisation of Services for the Unemployed in Australia," Social Policy Research Center Discussion Paper 79, SPRC, University of New South Wales, 1997; Adalbert Evers and Ivan Svetlik, eds., *Balancing Pluralism: New Welfare Mixes for the Elderly* (Aldershot, Eng.: Avebury, 1993); Brinton Milward and Keith Provan, "The Hollow State: Private Provision of Public Service," in Helen Ingram and Steven Rathgeb Smith, *Public Policy for Democracy* (Washington, D.C.: Brookings Institution, 1993), pp. 222–37; Richard Weatherley, "From Entitlement to Contract: Reshaping the Welfare State in Australia," *Journal of Sociology and Social Welfare*, 3: 13 (1994), 153–73

16. Ferge, "Change of the Welfare Paradigm."

17. OECD, *The Welfare State in Crisis* (Paris: OECD, 1981).

18. Ramesh Mishra, *The Welfare State in Crisis* (Brighton, Eng.: Wheatsheaf Books, 1984).

19. James O'Connor, *The Fiscal Crisis of the State* (New York: St. Martin, 1983).

20. Michael Hill and Glen Bramely, *Analyzing Social Policy* (Oxford: Basil Blackwell, 1986).

21. Rudolf Klein and Michael O'Higgins, eds., *The Future of Welfare* (Oxford: Basil Blackwell, 1985), p. 230.

22. The "liberal" welfare state represents a popular distinction drawn by Esping-Andersen in his analysis of alternative welfare regimes; see Gosta Esping-Andersen, *The Three Worlds of Welfare Capitalism* (Princeton, N.J.: Princeton University Press, 1990).

23. Kvist employs fuzzy set theory to define categories of membership scores, a method of approximation that lends the weight of hard numbers to qualitative judgements. See Jon Kvist, "Welfare Reform in the Nordic Countries in the 1990s: Using Fuzzy Set Theory to Assess Conformity to Ideal Types," *Journal of European Social Policy*, 9:3 (August 1999), 231–52.

24. Ministry of Health and Social Affairs, "Pension Reform in Sweden, 1998," paper presented at the Stockholm Conference on the Future of Social Security, Stockholm, June 29–July 1, 1999.

25. For an analysis of these various proposals, see Rebecca A. Van Voorhis, "A Socio-Economic Analysis of Three Paths to Social Security Reform," *Journal of Sociology and Social Welfare*, 26:2 (June 1999), 127–49. In 2001, President George W. Bush appointed a bipar-

tisan commission to plan for the partial privatization of social security, which may well be underway as this book goes to press.

26. Myrdal, for example, saw the public sector role in advanced welfare states as continually expanding. See Gunnar Myrdal, *Beyond the Welfare State* (New Haven, Conn.: Yale University Press, 1960).

27. Jon Kvist, "Changing Rights and Obligations in Unemployment Compensation: Using Fuzzy Set Theory to Explore the Diversity of Northern European Policy Developments in the 1990s," p. 21, paper presented at the International Social Security Conference on Social Security in the Global Village, Helsinki, September 25–27, 2000.

28. Arguing that the days of the European comprehensive welfare state are over, Zijderveld concludes that "most post-welfare state countries in Europe will become more 'American' in their policies (p. 162)." Anton Zijderveld, *The Wanning of the Welfare State: The End of Comprehensive State Succor* (New Brunswick, N.J.: Transaction Publishers, 1999).

29. Sven Hort, "From a Generous to a Stingy Welfare State? Targeting in the Swedish Welfare System in the 1990s," in Neil Gilbert, ed., *Targeting Social Benefits: International Perspectives and Trends* (New Brunswick, N.J.: Transaction Publishers, 2001), p. 206.

30. A. Nordlund, "Social Policy in Harsh Times: Social Security Development in Denmark, Finland, Norway, and Sweden during the 1980s and 1990s," *International Journal of Social Welfare*, 9: 1 (January 2000), 40.

31. Paul Pierson, *Dismantling the Welfare State? Regan, Thatcher and the Politics of Retrenchment* (Cambridge: Cambridge University Press, 1994). It might be noted, however, that shortly after his study was completed, one on the most radical reforms in the history of income maintenance policy was implemented in the United States, and under the heading of a "New Deal" policy, a number of workfare initiatives were launched in the United Kingdom.

32. On this score Nordlund, "Social Policy in Harsh Times," observes that the frequent first-order changes have pushed Nordic social policy qualitatively in the direction of an achievement model, in the sense that "there are indications of an increased emphasis on labour market performance in the rules governing income protection" (p. 40). However, he suggests that if one goes back to the overarching goals of the Nordic welfare states established after World War II, what looks like a qualitative change in policy over the last two decades is really just a return to first principles.

33. Occasionally public officials do quit in protest to legislative changes that they judge as too radical or conservative. During the Clinton administration, for example, several top officials in the Department of Health and Human Services resigned in response to the 1996 welfare reform, which marked a serious departure from the historic federal guarantee of public assistance. But I would not base the case for a qualitative change in the welfare state on any single legislative reform.

34. All social welfare policies must address the questions of who gets what social benefits, how these benefits are delivered, and how they are financed. For a detailed discussion of how social values inform the responses to these questions, see Neil Gilbert and Paul Ter-

rell, *Dimensions of Social Welfare Policy*, 5th ed. (Boston: Allyn & Bacon, 2002).

35. Peter Baldwin, "Beveridige in the *Longue Duree,*" *International Social Security Review*, 45: (1992), 53–72.

36. Much of the work has come out of think tanks such as the Cato Institute, the American Enterprise Institute, the Pacific Institute, and Heritage Foundation. The American Enterprise Institute is probably the most centrist of this group. The Cato Institute is the most forceful advocate for the privatization of social security. See, for example, Martin Feldstein, "Privatizing Social Security: The $10 Trillion Opportunity," *The Cato Project on Social Security Privatization,* No. 17 (January 31, 1997); Michael Tanner, "Privatizing Social Security: A Big Boost for the Poor," *The Cato Project on Social Security Privatization*, No. 4 (July 26, 1996).

37. For a discussion of these views, see David Prychitko, "The Welfare State: What Is Left?" *Critical Review*, 4:4 (Fall 1990), 619–32 and Daniel Bell, *The Cultural Contradictions of Capitalism* (New York: Basic Books, 1976), pp. 227–39.

38. See, for example, Christopher Howard, *The Hidden Welfare State: Tax Expenditure and Social Policy in the U.S.* (Princeton, N.J.: Princeton University Press, 1997).

39. Ferge, "Change of the Welfare Paradigm."

40. Max Weber, *The Theory of Social and Economic Organization*, Talcott Parsons, ed., A. M. Henderson and Talcott Parsons, trans. (New York: Free Press [1947] 1964).

41. For a sample of this usage, see Maria Evandrou, Jane Falkingham, and Howard Glennerster, "The Personal Social Services: 'Everyone's Poor Relation but Nobody's Baby,' " in John Mills, ed., *The State of Welfare: The Welfare State in Britain Since 1974* (Oxford: Clarendon, 1990); Neil Gilbert and Barbara Gilbert, *The Enabling State: Modern Welfare Capitalism in America* (New York: Oxford University Press, 1989); Neil Gilbert, *Welfare Justice: Restoring Social Equity* (New Haven, Conn.: Yale University Press, 1995); Will Marshall and Martin Schram, eds., *Mandate for Change* (New York: Berkley Books, 1993); Ben Wattenberg, "Let Clinton Be Clinton," *Wall Street Journal* January 20, 1993, p. A12.

42. For a comprehensive study of these lines of analysis, see Rebecca A. Van Voorhis, "Three Generations of Comparative Welfare State Theory: From Convergence to Convergence," *Journal of European Social Work* 1:2, (1998), 189–202.

43. Classic statements in this line of analysis include T. H. Marshall, *Class, Citizenship and Social Development* (New York: Anchor Books, 1964); and Harold Wilensky and Charles Lebeaux, *Industrial Society and Social Welfare* (New York: Russell Sage, 1958).

44. Some of the major findings on convergence are reported in Henry Aaron, "Social Security: International Comparisons," in O. Eckstein, ed., *Studies in the Economics of Income Maintenance* (Washington, D.C.: Brookings Institution, 1967), pp. 13–48; R. M. Coughlin and P. K. Armour, "Sectoral Differentiation in Social Security Spending in OECD Countries," *Comparative Social Research*, 6 (1983), 175–99; P. Cutright, "Political Structure, Economic Development, and National Social Security Programs," *American Journal of Sociology* 70, (1965), 537–50; F. L. Pryor, *Public Expenditure in Communist and*

Capitalist Nations (Homewood, Ill.: Richard D. Irwin, 1968); J. Verner, "Socioeconomic Environment, Political System, and Educational Policy Outcomes: A Comparative Analysis of 102 Countries," *Comparative Politics*, 2 (1979), 165–67; Harold Wilensky, *The Welfare State and Equality* (Berkeley: University of California Press, 1975); J. Williamson and J. J. Fleming, "Convergence Theory and the Social Welfare Sector: A Cross-National Analysis," *International Journal of Comparative Sociology*, 8 (1979), 242–53.

45. Olli Kangas, "The Merging of Welfare State Models: Past and Present Trends in Finnish and Swedish Social Policy," *Journal of European Social Policy*, 4:2 (1994), 79–94.

46. See, for example, C. Collie and R. Messick, "Prerequisites Versus Diffusion: Testing Alternative Explanations of Social Security Adoption," *American Political Science Review* 69 (1975), 1299–131; and Peter Flora and Jens Alber, "Modernization, Democratization, and the Development of the Welfare State in Western Europe," in P. Flora and A. J. Heidenheimer, eds., *The Development of Welfare States in Europe and America* (New Brunswick, N.J.: Transaction Publications, 1981).

47. F. G. Castles, *The Impact of Parties* (Beverly Hills, Calif.: Sage, 1982); K. Taira and P. Kilby, "Differences in Social Security Development in Selected Countries," *International Social Security Review* 16:3 (1969), 1–28.

48. Neil Gilbert and Ailee Moon, "Analyzing Welfare Effort: An Appraisal of Comparative Methods," *Journal of Policy Analysis and Management* 7:2 (1988), 326–40.

49. The class struggle or power resources perspective informs analyses such as Walter Korpi, "Social Policy and Distributional Conflict in the Capitalist Democracies: A Preliminary Framework," *Western European Politics* 3 (1980), 296–315; Walter Korpi, *The Democratic Class Struggle* (London: Rutledge, Keegan, Paul, 1983); and J. D. Stephens, *The Transition from Capitalism to Socialism* (London: Macmillan, 1979).

50. Van Voorhis, "Socio-Economic Analysis."

51. Castles, *Impact of Parties*; Stephens, *Transition from Capitalism*; J. Myles, *Old Age in the Welfare State* (Boston: Little, Brown, 1989); and M. G. Schmidt, "The Welfare State and the Economy in Periods of Economic Crisis: A Comparative Study of Twenty-three OECD Nations," *European Journal of Political Research* 11 (1983), 1–26.

52. Gosta Esping-Andersen, *The Three Worlds of Welfare Capitalism* (Princeton, N.J.: Princeton University Press, 1990).

53. This is the result because double weights were given to replacement rates for both minimum pension benefits (allotted to production workers) and standard benefits (allotted to normal workers) as two of the four indicators used to calculate the decommodification score for pensions. For a methodological deconstruction of the decommodification index, see Rebecca A. Van Voorhis, "Different Types of Welfare States? A Methodological Deconstruction of Comparative Research" *Journal of Sociology and Social Welfare* (forthcoming).

54. The bias caused by overweighting pension scores could have been avoided by transforming the raw scores to standardized z scores on which to calculate the totals.

55. F. G. Castles and D. Mitchell, "Three Worlds of Welfare Capitalism or Four," The Australian National University Discussion Paper No. 21, Canberra, 1990.

56. Maurizio Ferrera, "The 'Southern Model' of Welfare in Social Europe," *Journal of European Social Policy*, 6:1 (1996) 17–37; as an alternative to Esping-Andersen's three worlds, Liebfried distinguishes among Germanic, Scandinavian, Anglo-Saxon, and Levantine regimes, the last including the "Latin Rim Countries"; see Stephan Leibfried, "Towards a European Welfare State? On Integrating Poverty Regimes into the European Community," in Zsuzsa Ferge and Jon Kolberg, eds., *Social Policy in a Changing Europe* (Boulder, Col.: Westview, 1992). In contrast to the case for a distinct Southern model, Katrougalos's reading of the data suggests that arrangements for social protection in Greece, Portugal, and Spain are "merely underdeveloped species of the Continental model." George Katrougalos, "The Southern European Welfare Model: The Greek Welfare State, in Search of an Identity," *Journal of European Social Policy*, 6:1 (1996), 43.

57. In a comparative analysis of social assistance schemes, for example, Bradshaw and Terum find substantial variations among the Nordic countries—a welter of differences that make it difficult to produce a classification of the Nordic model—as well as similarities with some countries outside of Scandinavia. See J. Bradshaw and L. I. Terum, "How Nordic Is the Nordic Model? Social Assistance in Comparative Perspective," *Scandinavian Journal of Social Welfare*. 6:4 (October, 1997), 247–256.

58. Representative works in this vein include A. De Swann, *In Care of the State: Health Care, Education, and Welfare in Europe and the United States in the Modern Era* (Cambridge, Eng.: Polity, 1988); E. Nordlinger, *On the Autonomy of the Democratic State* (Cambridge, Mass.: Harvard University Press, 1981); Theda Skocpol, *States and Social Revolutions* (New York: Cambridge University Press, 1979); Theda Skocpol, "Bringing the States Back In: Strategies and Analysis in Current Research," in Peter Evans, Dietrich Rueschemeyer, and Theda Skocpol, eds., *Bringing the State Back In* (New York: Cambridge University Press, 1985).

59. For a classic statement on this perspective, see James Buchanan, *The Limits of Liberty* (Chicago: University of Chicago Press, 1975); see also James Buchanan, "Why Does Government Grow?" in T. E. Borcherding, ed., *Budgets and Bureaucrats: The Sources of Government Growth* (Durham, N.C.: Duke University Press, 1977); and Denis Meuller, *Public Choice* (New York: Cambridge University Press, 1979).

60. See, for example, Pierson, "New Politics."

61. Giuliano Bonoli and Bruno Palier, "Changing the Politics of Social Programmes: Innovative Change in British and French Welfare Reform," *Journal of European Social Policy*, 8:4 (November 1998), 317–30.

62. Pietro Nivola, "The New Pork Barrel," *The Public Interest*, 131 (Spring 1998), 92–104.

63. For qualifying assessments of public choice, see J. P. Kalt and M. A. Zupan, "Capture and Ideology in the Economic Theory of Politics," *American Economic Review*, 74:3, (1984) 279–300; Walter Korpi, "Power, Politics, and State Autonomy in the Development of

Social Citizenship: Social Rights During Sickness in Eighteen OECD Countries Since 1930," *American Sociological Review* 54:3, (1989), 309–28; Gerald Marwell and Ruth E. Ames, "Economists Free Ride, Does Anyone Else?" *Journal of Public Economics*, 15 (1981) 295–310.

64. Amitai Etzioni, *The Moral Dimension* (New York: Free Press, 1981).

65. See, for example, G. Therborn, "Welfare State and Capitalist Markets," *Acta Sociologica*, 30:3/4 (1987), 237–54; Wilensky, *Welfare State and Equality*; and P. Wong and J. M. Daley, "Long Term Development Versus Crisis Management in Welfare States," *Social Policy and Administration*, 24:1 (1990), 2–12.

66. Einar Overbye, "Convergence in Policy Outcome: Social Security in Perspective," *Journal of Public Policy*, 14:2 (1994), 147–74.

67. Daniel Bell, *The End of Ideology* (New York: Free Press, 1960).

68. Myrdal, *Beyond the Welfare State.*

69. OECD, *Future of Social Protection.*

70. One of the differences is that under the Eurostat scheme, some privately paid benefits are classified as public spending if they are mandated by the government. For a detailed comparison of the two classifications, see *OECD Social Expenditure Database 1980–1996* (Paris: OECD, 1999), p. 20. This OECD database includes information on social expenditures in 1996 for only four of the European Union (EU) countries—Portugal, Netherlands, Ireland, and Denmark—which are not shown in table 1.1 (because of the small number). For this group, the average social expenditure as a percentage of the GDP continued to decline in 1996.

71. Some of the most trenchant critical analyses include Douglas Besharov, "Bottom-up Funding," in Peter Berger and Richard J. Neuhaus, eds., *To Empower the People: From State to Civil Society* (Washington, D.C.: AEI Press, 1996); Nathan Glazer, *The Limits of Social Policy* (Cambridge, Mass.: Harvard University Press, 1988); Lawrence Mead, *Beyond Entitlement: The Social Obligations of Citizenship* (New York: Free Press, 1986); Charles Murray, *Losing Ground: American Social Policy 1950–1980* (New York: Basic Books, 1984); Dennis Shower, "Challenges to Social Cohesion and Approaches to Policy Reform," in *Societal Cohesion and the Globalization of the Economy: What Does the Future Hold?* (Paris: OECD, 1997); and World Bank, *Averting the Old Age Crisis* (Oxford: Oxford University Press, 1994)

2

Toward the Enabling State

Just as tides go in and tides go out, social and economic forces change over time. Although those forces that are currently pressing toward convergence may shift in time, for the foreseeable future four lines of influence flow in the same direction. Two of these lines of influence stem from large-scale structural changes that involve demographic trends and the globalization of the economy; these changes generate the kind of impersonal forces that drive the development of welfare states, according to convergence theory. The other two lines of influence stem from changing ideas and normative views about the consequences of social policies and the appropriate role of the state; these changes animate socio-political processes that give rise to different types of welfare states, according to the theory of distinct regimes.

First, in the realm of structural change, immense fiscal pressures are projected in response to the interaction of mature social security systems with sociodemographic trends. When Otto von Bismark introduced the first state-sponsored social security scheme in 1889, life expectancy was only 45 years and retirement was at age 65. Since then life expectancy has climbed to 76 years in the OECD countries. Along with people living longer, these societies are getting older. In most OECD countries, for example, between 1960 and 2040 the proportion of people over age 65 is expected to more than double, from an average of 9.7 percent to 22.2 percent of their populations, with about half of those elderly over age 75.[1] At the same time, the average age of retirement has declined. In the United States, for example, men and women retired in the 1990s at the average age of 63.5, about five years earlier than the average retirement age in 1940, and workers in the United States retire at a later age than those in most, if not all, of Europe.[2]

With Social Security entitlements widely available, the rising number of elderly will exact an increasing level of public spending for retirement, health services, and social care throughout the industrialized nations. In the United States, estimates of the Social Security Board of Trustees indicate that the cost of Old Age, Survivors, and Disability Insurance (OASDI) will begin to exceed revenues from OASDI contributions shortly after 2015, with the accumulated reserves and interest within the OASDI Trust Funds exhausted by the year 2037.[3] The Health Insurance Trust Fund for the Medicare program is in even worse shape. In 1995, health insurance income was less than expenditures; to meet the shortfall it was necessary to draw on the funds' assets. To ensure the fiscal integrity of these programs, eventually the tax rate must be raised, benefits must be cut, or some combination of both must be tried.[4] European old-age pension systems face similar burdens. In France there are currently 3 workers contributing for every person who is drawing a pension; recent projections indicate that by 2030 this support ratio will drop almost 50 percent to 1.6 contributors for each retiree.[5] And France is by no means the exception, as seen in figure 2.1, which shows that by 2010 the ratio of persons over the age of 65 to the number of people employed is expected to start climbing steeply among the advanced industrialized countries (shrinking the available support from about 3 to 1.6 workers for each retired person).[6]

The trend illustrated in figure 2.1 poses a daunting challenge to the financing of social transfers, particularly old-age pensions. There are only so many avenues through which governments might address this precipitous rise in the ratio of the number of people over the age of 65 to the number of people employed. The most obvious adjustments are to raise taxes or lower benefits—neither of which is politically attractive. Efforts can also be made to increase the number of people who are employed by raising the age of retirement, particularly for women (which is already being done or is under consideration in many countries).[7] Training the hard-to-employ or boosting the productivity level of those currently employed would also be beneficial. But short of a baby boom, the broadest and most immediate avenues to lowering the dependency ratio is by opening the highways of immigration to an enormous flow of foreigners. Just to maintain the European population at its maximum level, reached in 1995, requires an average of almost 2 million immigrants a year, or a total of almost 96 million immigrants for the next 50 years. At that rate, in 2050, close to 18 percent of the European population would be post-1995 immi-

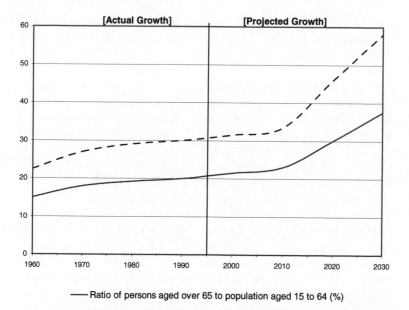

Ratio of persons aged over 65 to population aged 15 to 64 (%)

Ratio of persons aged over 65 to total employment (%)

Figure 2.1 Ratios of Persons Aged Over 65 to the Working Age Population and Number in Employment. *Source:* OECD, *Maintaining Prosperity in an Aging Society* (Paris: OECD, 1998), figure 1.2.

grants or their descendants. Moreover, an incredible number of immigrants would be needed to hold the support ratio constant at its 1995 level. To keep a constant relationship between the number of people aged 15 to 64 and people 65 years of age and over requires an influx of more than 1.3 billion people over the next 50 years. Then almost three-quarters of the European population would be post-1995 immigrants or their descendants.[8] The numbers involved in these scenarios are not trivial, nor are the cultural implications, particularly for small, relatively homogeneous countries, which may feel threatened by cultural annihilation.

Rising costs from the aging of the population are compounded by other demographic trends. Extramarital births and divorce rates are at almost record heights. Over the decade between the early 1980s and the early 1990s, the number of single-parent families increased an average of 25 percent (and as a percentage of all families, rose proportionately by an average of 17 percent) in 21 of the OECD countries for which these data are available.[9] The proliferation of two-income households, as well as single-parent families, has reduced the modern family's capacity to provide in-person care for children, the elderly, and other infirm relatives—what Valeria Fargion terms "defamiliza-tion" of traditional family responsibilities.[10] This situation creates additional demands on the state to supply child care, financial assistance, and other supportive services. The changes in the age of populations and family structures (including the appearance of "din-kies," dual-income-no-kids) that have emerged since the 1960s are so large scale as to constitute what some label a "second demographic transition."[11] Overall, the forecasts of the near future illuminate a period of sociodemographic change that will generate new demands and eliminate virtually no existing needs.[12]

The new claims for increased public spending create severe pressures because they seem to have hit a ceiling on how much governments can tax, as well as their propensities for deficit spending. As shown in figure 2.2, although the gross debt in 10 major OECD countries rose from 1980 to 1995, between 1995 and 1999 the debt declined in 7 of the 10 countries. Overall, the average gross debt among these countries climbed from 47.3 percent to 83.4 percent of their GDPs, after which it leveled off and declined slightly to 80.3 percent in 1999. As the mean deficit rates increased and leveled off, the dispersion of countries around these rates has narrowed (as indicated by the decline from 29.2 to 27.9 in the coefficient of variation), which signifies a slight convergence toward the mean.[13]

Despite the fact that public spending outstripped taxes in all the OECD countries, the average tax rates still climbed by more than a quarter, from 25.8 percent to 32.8 percent of the GDP, over the 15 years between 1965 and 1980. From 1980 to 1997, however, the rate of increase slowed down considerably (and was even reversed in a few countries), creeping up from 32.8 percent to 36.9 percent of the GDP over 17 years.[14] With tax rates at an average of 36.9 percent of the GDP in 1997, there may still be wiggle room for governments to maneuver, but the plateauing of taxes after 1980 lends weight to the observation that many governments are approaching a tax ceiling that will be difficult to raise for political and economic reasons.[15]

Where the tax ceiling rests is a matter of speculation. In 1918, Joseph Schumpeter had already asserted that levels of taxation were pushing the fiscal limits of the state.[16] Today, the ceiling is increasingly influenced by one's neighbors. Although the plural of *anecdote* is not *data*, a good story can still drive home the point. Under the glaring headlines FRENCH TAX EXILES FLOCK TO BRITAIN, the *Sunday Times reported* that there were now about 250,000 French people living in Britain, with one in seven new homes in London being bought

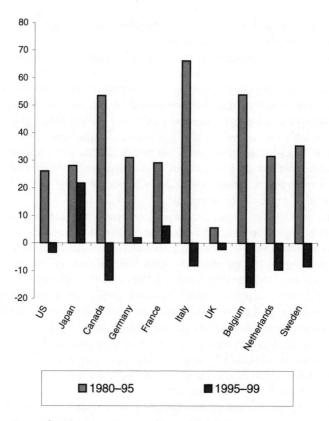

General government gross financial liabilities: 1980,
1995, and 1999

	1980	1995	1999
Mean	47.3	83.4	80.3
S.D.	13.8	26.2	22.4
Coefficient of variation	29.2	31.4	27.9

Figure 2.2 Change in General Government Gross Financial Liabilities as a Percentage of Nominal GDP, 1980–95 and 1995–99. *Source:*
OECD, *Maintaining Prosperity in an Aging Society* (Paris: OECD,
1998), table 11.1.

by Europeans, predominantly the French. "There is a massive flow of wealthy individuals leaving France. Traditionally they headed for Switzerland. Today London is the No. 1 destination. Your top rate of income tax in Britain is 40%; in France it is 60%." It is not only individuals who are crossing the channel. According to the *Times*, "more than 150 French companies have relocated their headquarters and staff to Britain," where an employer's outlay in tax and social security amounts to 32 percent of labor costs, compared to 48% in France. The story ends with a French entrepreneur, who moved his business from Paris to Britain in 1997 and is totaling his account: "Yes, here it is. I am paid 79,000 pounds a year, which with a pension is net 55,000 pounds. If I lived in France, working in the same job, my net pay would be 32,000 pounds. Vive le difference."[17] Politically, there is a practical limit on how much citizens are willing to pay; economically, restraining taxes is one way to keep production costs down in an increasingly competitive international market—an apt segue to the next point.

The second structural change involves the globalization of the economy. The central features of globalization include accelerated mobility of capital, which reflects the integration of capital markets; the growth of transnational corporations that organize production on a global scale; and rapid technological change, particularly in the realm of information and communications—all of which have magnified economic interdependencies and shrunk time and space. Although everyone agrees that it is happening, there are differences of opinion about what the process of globalization represents and its implications for the future of state-sponsored social protection. Some people characterize globalization as the logical progression to an advanced stage in the development of world capitalism, whereas others see it as more of a break with past forms of capitalism.[18] Splitting the difference, one observer suggests that it is "almost as if a threshold was reached in which long-term trends became sufficiently strong as to induce a profound change in perceptions of policy options."[19] These views about the meaning of globalization are related to the transformation of the welfare state. If the welfare state serves as an arrangement to protect citizens from the vicissitudes of life in a capitalist economy, a fundamental change in the nature of capitalism—whether to an advanced stage or to a new form—is likely to be accompanied by a substantive change in the character of social protection.

The full effect of globalization on the future of state-sponsored social protection is currently unclear. Although the policies of industrialized nation-states have always been somewhat attentive to the demands of international markets, the strength of local and national markets allowed for the pursuit of independent national economic

policies. With the emergence of a well-integrated global market, however, national policymakers are increasingly being disciplined, and
spending on redistributive social benefits is squeezed by the mobility
of capital to go where production costs are low.[20] Most analysts would
agree with Guy Standing's assessment that globalization has intensified pressures to scale back labor rights and welfare benefits, which
are seen as hindering a country's capacity to compete on the world
market and to attract foreign investment.[21] With all welfare state operations under tighter fiscal constraints, Fritz Scharp sees difficult and
painful policy adjustments looming, which endanger the political legitimacy of the postwar commitments to social security.[22]

Yet globalization manifests contradictory tendencies. On the one
hand, to maintain a competitive edge there is a push toward the state's
retrenchment of workers' rights and social spending, which would
heighten workers' vulnerability to the increasing social risks that accompany the vagaries of rapid technological change and escalating
global competition. On the other hand, to ensure that workers' inse-
curity does not reach an intolerable level, there is a pull toward expanding the state's efforts to cushion the growing social risks, which
would help avoid a backlash against globalization. Werner Sengenberger, former director of the International Labour Organization, counsels that the principal remedy to this dilemma "has to come from a
shift in the policy paradigm with a view to spreading the benign effects of globalization, especially to those who are losing their employment and/or their income entitlements."[23] But exhortations for
governments to play a greater role in regulating the global marketplace
and recasting their social safety nets do not resolve the inherent tensions of globalization. The welfare state can be both a necessary institutional prerequisite for absorbing the risks of globalization and a
hindrance to national competition in the global market. At the moment, one is tempted to side with Elmar Rieger and Stephan Leibfried's conclusion that the extent to which governments will be able
to reconcile the conflicting pressures of globalization in the long run
remains an open question.[24]

Globalization is not entirely about the hypermobility of capital.
Whereas the competitive discipline of the global market builds pressure to suppress local public spending on social benefits, a counterforce of increasing demand is being exerted by the rising tide of
immigration—another aspect of globalization. Technological advance-
ments and political alignments have not only expedited the mobility
of capital but also provided new highways for the movement of labor.
Just as capital can go to where standards of living, social benefits, and
labor costs are low, labor is more and more able to move to where
standards of living, wages, and social benefits are high. In the early

1990s, for example, 10.6 million inhabitants of the European Union were nationals of non-EU states, and an additional 5 million nationals of the EU were living in other than their member states.[25] And as previously noted, millions of immigrants will be needed to bolster the declining population of Europe in the coming decades. Driven by both the advent of the EU and the dissolution of the Soviet Union, the accelerating mobility of labor has heightened demands and competition not only for jobs but also for social provisions as new immigrant families arrive, seeking their fortunes in the lands of opportunity (with relatively generous social welfare benefits). This is not occurring only in Europe. Immigrants to the United States often bring their elderly parents. Between 1982 and 1994, the number of noncitizen immigrants who were receiving aid from the Supplemental Security Income (SSI) program soared from 127,900 to 738,000—a 580 percent increase in 12 years.[26] Welfare reform legislation in 1996 imposed stringent limits on legal immigrants' eligibility for assistance under federal programs such as SSI and food stamps.[27]

The third line of influence is in the realm of changing ideas and normative views. Public perceptions of the consequences of generous welfare policies are being remolded by the weight of accumulated experience gained during the decades of welfare state growth. These experiences lend credible support to the charge that social welfare provisions have inadvertently created disincentives to work. It is a conclusion frequently drawn not only in the United States but also throughout Europe. Thus, for example, an OECD report on the Netherlands finds "clear indications that the generosity of social benefits and high effective marginal tax rates implicit in income-dependent subsidies create strong disincentives to work and underlie the exceptionally high dependency ratio in the Netherlands, where one employed person supports almost one person on social benefits."[28] To combat what they had labeled as the "Dutch Disease," the government initiated corrective measures, tightening eligibility requirements for disability, reducing benefits, and requiring single mothers to become active in the labor market when their children reach the age of 5.[29]

The Dutch experience is not unique. From the Revenu Minimum d'Insertion in France to the Newstart program in Australia, sociopolitical deliberations in the industrialized welfare states over the last decade have produced numerous legislative reforms to "activate" the beneficiaries of disability insurance, unemployment insurance, and social assistance.[30] These reforms have injected into programs that offered "passive" income supports an array of sanctions and incentives designed to promote labor force participation and other active contributions to the community. This approach to social policy comes largely in response to an increasing acceptance of the idea that social welfare provisions produce "poverty traps" or "enforced dependency," phrases prudently crafted not to blame the victims.[31] One report goes so far as to say that "dependency traps are an unintended outcome of most social security systems."[32] And even in Sweden, the paragon of the modern welfare state, Prime Minister Carl Bildt declared in the early 1990s that benefit levels had become so high as to reduce the incentives to work.[33] Indeed, one might well conclude that Charles Murray's rendition of the disincentive to work bred by public welfare, which was viewed as heresy by welfare state advocates in the mid-1980s, became the received wisdom of the late 1990s.[34]

Finally, normative views about the proper relationship between the state and the market have undergone a significant conversion as the collapse of command economies in Russia and eastern Europe has raised to record levels the stock of capitalism's public approval in the marketplace of ideas. Writing in 1942, Joseph Schumpeter found that the public had grown so entirely antagonistic toward capitalism that its condemnation was almost a requirement of polite conversation.[35] Today, the tides have turned to such an extent that Francis Fukuyama finds the overwhelming intellectual triumph of free-market economic theory accompanied by a considerable degree of arrogance.[36] Of course, not everyone believes that the revival of economic liberalism has gone quite as far as Fukuyama contends or that it will continue to carry the day.[37] And as Fukuyama points out, although markets are efficient allocators of resources, there is more to the creation of prosperity than such factors, as competition and self-interest, which are featured in the neoclassical model. In particular, his analysis draws attention to the significance of social factors, such as trust and the ability to cooperate.

Another explanation for the rising faith in the private sector can be found in Albert Hirschman's provocative thesis of a cyclical movement in the pursuit of happiness through public and private involvements. His basic proposition is that acts of consumption and participation in the public or private sector eventually yield disappointment and dissatisfactions because human nature is such that people are never entirely satisfied: "Don't we all know, instinctively and intuitively, as well as from the writing of poets and philosophers, that disappointment and discontent are eternally the human lot, regardless of achievements, be they distinction, wealth or power?"[38] When disappointment with public consumption and involvement in public affairs loses its attraction, people turn to the private sphere in the alternating quest for satisfaction. Applying this thesis, one might say that by the 1980s, after decades of welfare state expansion, romance with the public sector began to cool. Even in Sweden, the delivery of public services came under fire during the 1980s as "consumers increasingly expressed dissatisfaction with the delivery of welfare state services in general. Specifically, citizens in their roles as clients, patients, and parents felt that they had no choices as to type of services or where to obtain them."[39]

Whether driven by outside events like the fall of communism, by citizens' critical appraisals of their own experiences, or by a reinforcing combination of both, ascendency of the neoclassical model and renewed public faith in the virtues of the private sector have impelled social welfare transactions to adopt the values and methods of the market economy. Today the results are conspicuous in the myriad arrangements for the privatization of social welfare functions.[40] Privatization almost swept the field in Texas when corporate giants such as Andersen Consulting and Lockheed Martin lined up for competitive bidding on a contract to manage the state's entire welfare operation, budgeted at over half a billion dollars annually. Although the all-encompassing plan was denied approval (because of reluctance to have the determination of eligibility for benefits conducted by private employees), the state was authorized to contract with private firms to perform all the other operations that do not involve enrollment into the system. After more than a decade of privatization under Margaret Thatcher, a defining moment for the Left arrived in England with Tony Blair's pronouncement that the New Labour Party is no longer entirely opposed to the privatization of government activities.

Without much fanfare, old-age pensions in a number of countries are marching on a steady course of incremental privatization. In the United States, retirement benefits from employee pensions increased between 1976 and 1992 from 25 percent to 33 percent of the total received by the elderly from employee plans and federal social security payments.[41] The U.S. experience follows that of private pensions in some of the more generous Nordic countries. In Denmark, for example, private pension expenditure between 1980 and 1992 jumped from 20 percent to 30 percent of the total share of public and private pensions. After 1985, the share of private pensions also increased in Norway, although at a slower pace. A comparative analysis of these country's experiences suggests that the introduction of a second tier of income-related public pensions in Norway helps to account for the relative containment of private schemes, whereas in Denmark a second public tier did not develop.[42]

Although by the late 1990s, left-of-center parties had come to power across the European Union, in comparison to the old Left these new governments appear to be charting a middle course, which is remarkably market friendly and determined to control deficit budgets and public spending.[43] Under their watchful eyes, the movements toward privatization and welfare reform continue apace. Sweden, as previously noted, in one fell swoop privatized 14 percent of the total public pension contributions. Overall, the normative shift in favor of the private sector is accompanied by an infusion of the capitalist ethos into the realm of social protection, as seen in contemporary social policies devised to create market and quasi-market conditions that stimulate competition and promote the work ethic.

Thus, complex and multiple forces lend impetus to the transformation of the welfare state. It is not demographic factors or tax ceilings, globalization, or the normative changes shaped by knowledge and experience with social policies or the rising faith in the market economy that by themselves account for the fundamental change in the character of social protection; rather, it is the combination of these forces. Also, what gives these pressures for change particular weight is that they all push in the same direction, that is, away from the conventional welfare state model based on government delivery of an expanding range of social benefits under a system of broad-based entitlements. The United States is probably furthest along the course that has veered away from social rights to welfare and toward social responsibilities to work, cost containment, and privatization. Here the movement for change is sustained by a remarkable convergence of liberal and conservative opinion that work incentives are necessary, that some degree of privatization is desirable, and that the projected levels of welfare costs cannot be upheld.

Most of the European welfare states are moving in this direction at varying paces, often covering their tracks in a haze of denial. For instance, an OECD report suggests that "within a framework that respects individual rights some form of training could be made a mandatory part of any income support package."[44] The report does not indicate how "mandatory" training can be squared with an individual's "right" to income support if the individual is unable or refuses to attend the training program. Another OECD report advises that "without calling into question its central tenets, the welfare system should be refocused and made less generous in terms of eligibility and benefits."[45] But if designs for eligibility and benefits—who gets what—are not among the central tenets of the welfare system, what is left? More bluntly, on the European front Henri Lepage asserts, that "the welfare state is an unsustainable institution."[46] Similarly, Bernd-Otto Kuper's candid analysis of the EU's 1993 Green Paper on European Social Policy and White Paper on Growth Competitiveness and Employment notes that both of these reports recommend the reduction of social benefits because "the level of public expenditure, particularly in the social field, has become unsustainable." Kuper is struck by the extent to which these two reports time and again refer to the social welfare systems in the United States and Japan as models for the basic principles of national policies in the EU. He suggests that the European public is insufficiently aware of the conclusions expressed in these reports from Brussels because their form and content constitute "a serious bar to readability and comprehensibility."[47]

The Emerging Paradigm

To suggest that the welfare state as we knew it is being left behind somewhere along the path of institutional evolution does not signify the end of social welfare programs. No one imagines that social security, health insurance, disability benefits, public assistance, unemployment insurance, day care, and the rest will be jettisoned. But the social policy environment in which they evolve will be constrained by a set of demographic and market conditions and informed by normative assumptions that are fundamentally different than those underlying the development of social welfare programs through the early 1980s. These structural conditions and social norms give rise to a new institutional framework that subordinates social welfare policies to economic considerations, such as the need for labor force flexibility, the opening of new markets for the private sector, the pressures of international competition, and the imposition of limits on deficit spending. Within this new framework, social welfare policies are increasingly being designed to enable more people to work and to enable the private sector to expand its sphere of activity.

Although public support for private responsibility is the governing principle of this approach to social protection, concerns for private effort and responsibility of citizens and nongovernmental organizations are embedded in a larger foundation of ideas and preferences, which differentiates the enabling state from the conventional welfare state paradigm. As formulated here, the conventional paradigm is represented by the Scandinavian, or social democratic, model.[48] Setting a high standard for other welfare states to emulate, the social democratic model has been widely considered the most generous and comprehensive arrangement for social protection. According to findings by Robert Goodin and his colleagues, the social democratic model— at least as practiced in the Netherlands—is also the most effective arrangement,[49] although there is a serious question of how closely the Dutch system of the 1990s reflects the social democratic model. As it happens, the same year this study appeared (identifying the Netherlands as a social democratic regime according to Esping-Andersen's classification) Esping-Andersen's reexamination of the regime typologies also appeared—concluding that when social service delivery and the role of the family are taken into account "the Netherlands becomes squarely a member of the conservative, Continental European fold."[50]

The most prominent characteristics of the social democratic welfare state model can be summed up as an emphasis on *universal* access to *publicly* provided benefits that offer strong *protection* of labor as *social rights* of citizenship. As James Midgley confirms, these characteristics are often identified with an institutional approach to social policy exemplified by the Scandinavian welfare states.[51] As an alternative paradigm, the enabling state emphasizes a market-oriented approach that targets benefits that promote labor force participation and individual responsibility. In a comparison of the central tendencies of these models, the picture that emerges (in table 2.1) illustrates the direction of some of the main trends in values and practice that frame the transformation of the welfare state.[52]

To begin with, the enabling state advances a market-oriented approach to social welfare along several avenues. The most obvious and direct line involves financing the private delivery of social welfare goods and services through purchase-of-service contracts, on the assumption that the private sector performs more efficiently and offers greater consumer choice than the public sector. At the same time, the market-oriented approach favors social welfare transfers in the form of cash and vouchers over in-kind provisions. Cash and vouchers are

Table 2.1 Shift in Central Tendencies from Welfare to Enabling State

Welfare State	Enabling State
Public Provision	Privatization
Delivery by public agencies	Delivery by private agencies
Transfers in the form of service	Transfers in cash or vouchers
Focus on direct expenditures	Increasing indirect expenditures
Protecting Labor	Promoting Work
Social support	Social inclusion
Decommodification of labor	Recommodification of labor
Unconditional benefits	Use of incentives and sanctions
Universal Entitlement	Selective Targeting
Avoiding stigma	Restoring social equity
Solidarity of Citizenship	Solidarity of Membership
Cohesion of shared rights	Cohesion of shared values and civic duties

seen as stimulating competition in the market to provide the goods and services that the government might otherwise produce or purchase through contracts; this empowers individual recipients to exercise consumer sovereignty and to profit from competitive market forces. Benefits in the form of cash can also be provided indirectly through tax credits (sometimes called tax expenditures) such as childcare credits and the Earned Income Tax Credit in the United States, which support consumer choice and restrict the amount of direct government expenditure (more by shifting social transfers through tax rebates than by reducing their size).[53]

By promoting a market-oriented approach to social protection, the enabling state seeks to check the rise of direct public expenditure and to foster an increased sense of fairness in how public funds are spent. Reversing the proliferation of social provisions that underwrote the expansion of the welfare state, policies implemented in recent times have been designed to restrict the access to benefits. One of the strongest checks on public expenditures for social welfare is exercised by targeting eligibility, which involves allocating benefits to the most needy and the most deserving rather than to all citizens as a universal right.

In line with efforts to contain direct public expenditures and promote private activities, the enabling state places less emphasis on providing income supports to people out of work than does the welfare state and more weight on fostering social inclusion, mainly through active participation in the labor force. Although social inclusion involves helping people to participate in the mainstream of community life through various measures, which encompass education, deinstitutionalization, and voluntary service, paid employment is a major, if not the central, concern.[54] The heightened emphasis on employment-related measures in the enabling state has been accompanied by the development of social provisions aimed to enhance human capital and to help the unemployed adjust to modern labor market requirements. Benefits are increasingly linked through incentives and sanctions to behavioral requisites, such as accepting work, performing community service, and attending training sessions and clinics. Unemployment compensation, for example, is conditioned on fulfilling "activation" contracts or is repackaged to incorporate such provisions as grants for traveling expenses incurred in quest of work and lump-sum allocations to help the unemployed finance new enterprises. Reviewing these measures, one analyst even suggests that unemployment insurance should stress provisions that facilitate reintegration into the labor force, with cash payments to be considered a measure of last resort.[55] By providing a source of income outside of market exchanges, welfare benefits in the past have contributed to the decommodification of labor—making it less like a commodity bought and sold purely in response to market forces. To the extent that social welfare benefits are now tied to incentives and packaged in ways that increase the compulsion to work in order to meet one's basic needs, the recent policy reforms can be said to promote the recommodification of labor.

Finally, the movement toward privatization, the curb on public spending, and the intensified efforts to encourage employment affect the character of social cohesion traditionally associated with the welfare state. That is, the kind of solidarity that is attributed to universal claims to social rights of citizenship is being diluted, and the form of cohesion based on shared values about civic duties and affiliations of group membership is being reinforced. As the promotion of private activity and the tightening of public expenditure delimit the state's role in the provision of social welfare and as demands on individuals to work and be independent are intensified, the grounds for social cohesion are shifting away from the state and toward the private market and civil society, made up of voluntary organizations and informal networks of family and friends. This development can be described in reference to the different levels and mechanisms of solidarity illustrated in the classic works of the British sociologist T. H. Marshall and the French sociologist Émile Durkheim. According to Marshall, the status of citizenship endows residents of a nation with social rights "to a modicum of economic welfare and security," which reinforces a sense of affiliation to the larger polity.[56] In contrast, Durkheim was interested in the formation of secondary groups, which created a sense of solidarity based on the social and moral homogeneity of their members. In his view (expressed long before the advent of women's liberation), "where the State is the only environment in which men can live communal lives, they inevitably lose contact, become detached, and society disintegrates. A nation can be maintained only if between the State and the individual, there is intercalated a whole series of secondary groups near enough to the individuals to attract them strongly in their sphere of action and drag them in this way into the general torrent of social life."[57] Whereas the erosion of social rights to welfare abrades the sense of belonging that unites citizens in the public sphere, the transfer of social welfare functions to private enterprise and civil society thickens the social glue of secondary group affiliations—shifting the basis of social cohesion from Marshallian citizenship to Durkheimian membership.

It should be obvious that the enabling state does not exist in a pure form. Even in the United States where the system of social protection has most evolved in this direction, many social policies do not coincide exactly with those that would be derived from the pattern of change noted above. That is, on all of the dimensions of change in table 2.1, there are areas of overlap between the welfare state and the enabling state. Both dispense social rights through transfers in the form of cash and services, which are financed by direct and indirect expenditures and delivered through public and private vehicles; both forge social policies that target benefits and seek to achieve varying degrees of equity. But in each case, the central tendencies advanced by the welfare state and the enabling state point in different directions. Social policy reforms over the last decade have moved strongly, almost uniformly, toward the enabling state.

It should also be obvious that although shaped by these central tendencies, the enabling state will not take one distinct form. Just as there have been different types of welfare states, variations within the basic pattern of the enabling state are likely to emerge in response to historic and cultural differences among the advanced industrial nations. For example, there may be an Anglo-Saxon version and a Scandinavian version. The Dutch will probably design policies that promote privatization and selective eligibility differently than the French. Although their bearings may vary (even clustering into distinct regimes) when examined closely and they may land at different points along the coast, these nations are sailing toward the same shores of the enabling state.

The enabling state, of course, is an analytic construct—a pattern of institutional functioning within the framework of values, objectives, and practical measures summarized in table 2.1. I submit this framework in the Weberian spirit as the conceptual foundation of an ideal-type model of the enabling state, which rests on policies that promote work, subsidize private activity, target benefits, and emphasize individual responsibility in ways that alter the basis of social cohesion.[58] As the new institutional arrangements for social welfare build on this foundation, many questions arise about the real meaning of social inclusion, the best design of work-oriented measures, the costs and benefits of privatization, the targets for the receipt of social benefits, and the maintainence of social solidarity under policies driven by market-oriented concerns. Addressing these questions requires a closer look at the development and implications of each cornerstone. But first, let us put a new frame on the overall picture of social expenditures.

The New Social Accounting

The emergence of an alternative framework for social protection advances fresh lines of thought and stimulates the discovery of new social facts. There are incontrovertible facts, such as the number of registered births and deaths last year, for which there are reasonably definitive measurements (although modern medical technology some-time confounds the exact determination of death). And there are social facts, such as the official unemployment rate, which can be measured in many ways, including the number of claimants who register for unemployment benefits or the number of people in a representative population survey who respond that they are out of work and looking for a job (even if they are only looking with their "third eye");[59] in both of these cases, unlike birth and death, unemployment is opera-tionally defined according to social criteria that can change over time. Direct public expenditure on social welfare as a percentage of GDP is a social fact that has been widely used by policy analysts, researchers, and journalists to represent the generosity of welfare states and to compare welfare efforts made by different countries.[60] This standard accounting, however, is deeply flawed.

It has long been recognized that in addition to the checks written directly by the government, comprehensive measures of generosity and welfare effort should include other sources of social expenditure that promote individual and family welfare. Consider, for example, the hypothetical case of Edith and Alva, citizens of Americana and Nordica, respectively. They both owe their governments $9000 in taxes. Alva pays her taxes and then receives a child-care grant in the form of a $1000 check from the government. Edith's government gives her a $1000 child-care tax credit, which reduces the taxes she pays by this amount. Which country is more generous in the provision of social benefits or is making the greater welfare effort? By the standard accounting of direct expenditures, Nordica rates $1000 higher on gen-erosity and welfare effort than Americana, which gives an equivalent child-care subsidy through special deductions in the tax code, re-ferred to as tax expenditures. As early as the 1930s, special tax de-ductions and exemptions were identified as a form of government transfer in Arthur Pigou's classic text, *Economics of Welfare,* an idea later elaborated on by Richard Titmuss, the founding director of the Department of Social Administration at the London School of Eco-nomics. Although the idea was bandied about for several decades, it was not until the mid-1970s that data on tax expenditures became available and were introduced as a regular component of the presi-dent's budget in the United States, which was among the first coun-tries to collect this information.[61]

But tax expenditures are not the only measures that need to be weighed into a comprehensive calculation of welfare effort. Taxes also count. What if Alva's $1000 government subsidy was included as part of her annual income and taxed at a rate of 30 percent, whereas Edith's subsidy was tax free? On the scale of direct expenditures Nordica still rates $1000 higher on generosity and welfare effort, although at the end of the day Edith ends up with more money in her pocket to pay for child care. In addition to direct taxes, there are considerations of indirect taxes, which also reduce the amount of cash subsidies that beneficiaries actually consume for goods and services; thus, many governments claw back significant parts of the benefit through both direct (income) taxes and indirect (sales and value added) taxes. In this regard, Willem Adema notes that when the value added tax was extended to cover domestic fuel in the United Kingdom, policymakers adjusted cash payments to low-income recipients to compensate for the loss in real value of these benefits.[62]

Beyond spending and taxing, governments can also create and manage social expenditures through their powers of regulation. Thus, for example, if Edith received neither a cash grant nor a tax credit for child care but her employer was required by federal legislation to give employees $1500 worth of child care services annually, she would receive subsidized child-care valued at more than twice the amount of Alva's child-care grant after direct taxes. Yet, Nordica would still appear to offer a more generous child-care benefit since the value of mandatory private benefits does not show up on the conventional ledger of direct public expenditures. Mandatory private social benefits have been enacted in many countries, such as Belgium, Denmark, the Netherlands, Germany Sweden, Norway, the United States, and the United Kingdom. These off-the-ledger arrangements for social protection usually include employer payments for absence from work because of sickness and maternity leave, as well as required pension contributions to employer-based or individual pension plans.

Finally, the OECD defines the full range of social expenditures to include all transfers, cash and in kind, by public and private institutions that provide support and protection against the risks of modern life. This definition excludes transfers between households.[63] Unlike the quid pro quo of exchange in the market economy, these transactions are unilateral transfers from public and private sources. If we accept the OECD definition of social expenditures, voluntary private social benefits form another component in the comprehensive measure of welfare effort. From an individual recipient's point of view, it does not much matter whether, for example, Edith's employer is statutorily required to provide child-care services or whether such a benefit is granted voluntarily (as long as her salary is not affected).

Thus, in addition to public and publicly mandated private benefits, a comprehensive ledger of social expenditure would incorporate the value of voluntary, private social benefits. These voluntary benefits involve a range of provisions—such as employer-provided pensions, health insurance, child care, unemployment compensation, severance pay, and sickness benefits—that are not legally mandated. However, the government can still affect the behavior of private institutions by granting tax advantages that encourage them to offer these benefits. Voluntary, private benefits also include many in-kind social supports allocated by private, nonprofit organizations, which are stimulated by government tax concessions for charitable purposes.

Taking into consideration social welfare transfers through these various channels, Adema and his colleagues have developed a new ledger for social accounting that controls for the effects of direct and indirect taxes—introducing the most rigorous and comprehensive analyses of social spending to date.[64] As illustrated in figure 2.3, this ledger allows us to compare how nations measure up on three distinct indicators of social spending as a percentage of GDP: (1) "gross public social expenditure," the usual yardstick of direct government spending, which offers the crudest estimate of welfare effort; (2) "net publicly mandated social expenditure," which represents the cumulative value of benefits distributed through direct public expenditures, tax expenditures, and publicly mandated private expenditures, reduced by direct and indirect taxes on these benefits; and (3) "net total social expenditure," which adds the value of voluntary private expenditures, reduced by direct and indirect taxes, to the total for net publicly mandated expenditures.

There are several notable results from this comparison. First, how nations rank on social spending changes considerably as the operational definition becomes more inclusive. For example, measured by gross public social expenditure as a percentage of GDP, Denmark, with 36.7 percent, stands first in welfare effort, and the United States, with 17.1 percent, comes in at the bottom of the list. However, ranked on the most comprehensive measure—net social expenditure—the order of their standing is reversed, as the United States moves up to sixth place and Denmark drops into seventh place. Second, when the impact of the tax system is taken into account, the net value of public social expenditure (including tax expenditures and mandated private benefits) declines in every country except the United States. The sharpest declines are registered in Sweden, Norway, Denmark, the Netherlands, and Finland, which claw back significant proportions of their public expenditures through high taxes on benefits. Finally, when the impact of the tax system is taken into account, along with the value of all public and private social welfare transfers, the large differences in gross public expenditure are washed out, leaving the high public social spenders such as Denmark, Finland, and the Netherlands with a net social expenditure equivalent to that of the United Kingdom and the United States. (As indicated in figure 2.3, this re-

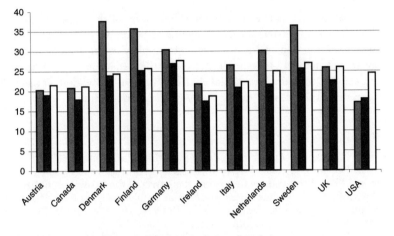

■ Gross Public Social Expenditure

■ Net Publicly Mandated Social Expenditure

□ Net Total Social Expenditure

Gross Public, Net Publicly Mandated, and Net Total Social Expenditures as a Percentage of GDP at Factor Costs, 1995

	Gross Public Social Expenditures	Net Publicly Mandated Social Expenditures	Total Net Social Expenditures
Mean	27.51	21.73	24.01
S.D.	7.10	3.39	2.75
Coefficient of Variation	25.81	15.60	11.45

Figure 2.3 Social Expenditure Indicators: Percentage of GDP at Factor Costs, 1995. *Source:* Willem Adema, *Net Social Expenditure*, Labour Market and Social Policy Occasional Paper No. 39 (Paris: OECD, 1999), table 7.

markable convergence in welfare transfers is reflected visually in the leveling of the bars and arithmetically in the decline of the variation coefficient from 25.8 to 11.5 as we move from gross public social expenditure to net total social expenditure.) In this comprehensive ledger of social accounting, there is much greater correspondence in the overall proportion of the GDP transferred as social benefits by public and private institutions in advanced industrialized societies than appears when judged by the conventional measure of gross public spending. According to this comprehensive measure, the countries have allocated roughly equivalent proportions of their resources to social welfare transfers, but in somewhat different ways. In analyzing the transformation of the welfare state, the following chapters will show that not only is there similarity in the net social expenditures but also the advanced industrial societies are converging in their basic approach to the design and delivery of social protection.

NOTES

1. OECD, *The Future of Social Protection* (Paris: OECD, 1988).

2. For an analysis of early retirement in Europe, see Susan Devereux, "Pension Systems Reform in Response to the Growth in Retired Popluations," in Dalmer Hoskins, Donate Dobbernack, and Christiane Kuptsch, eds., *Social Security at the Dawn of the 21st Century* (New Brunswick, N.J.: Transaction Publishers, 2001).

3. Board of Trustees of the Social Security and Medicare Trust Fund, *2000 Annual Report of the Board of Trustees* (Washington, D.C.: U.S. Government Printing Office, 2000).

4. Eugene Steuerle and Jon Bakija, *Retooling Social Security for the 21st Century: Right and Wrong Approaches to Reform* (Washington D.C.: Urban Institute, 1994).

5. Craig Whitney, "In Europe, Too, Social Security Isn't So Secure," *New York Times*, August 31, 1997, p. E4.

6. One set of projections estimates that between 1995 and 2050, the average percentage of GDP spent on old-age pensions in 16 of the wealthiest OECD countries (excluding the United States and Canada) will increase by more than two-thirds, from 8 percent to 13 percent. See Deborah Roseveare, Willi Leibfritz, Douglas Fore, and Eckhard Wurzel, "Population, Pension Systems, and Government Budgets: Simulations for 20 OECD Countries," OECD, Economics Department Working Paper, No. 168, table 3, Paris, 1996.

7. Changes in the standard age of entitlement to pensions are reviewed by Devereux, "Pension Systems Reform."

8. UN Population Division, *Replacement Migration: Is It a Solution to Declining and Ageing Populations? Executive Summary* (New York: United Nations, 2000).

9. The mean increase in numbers over the decade represents a range from −10 percent in Sweden to +83 percent in France. OECD, *A Caring World: The New Social Policy Agenda* (Paris: OECD, 1999).

10. Valeria Fargion, "Current Social Service Regimes in Europe: The Rise and Development (1965–1995)," paper presented at ISA Research Committee Meeting on Welfare State Challenge, Marginalization and Poverty, Copenhagen, August 21–24, 1997.

11. R. Lesthaeghe, "The Second Demographic Transition in Western Countries: An Interpretation," in K. Oppenheim Mason and A. Jensen, *Gender and Family Change in Industrialized Countries* (Oxford: Clarendon, 1995).

12. This point is nicely documented in Bea Cantillon, "Socio-Demographic Changes and Social Security," *International Social Security Review*, 43:4 (1990), 399–425.

13. The coefficient of variation—(S.D./x) (100)—allows us to compare the degree of dispersion around the mean for groups with different means. See Wayne Daniel, *Biostatistics: A Foundation for Analysis in the Health Sciences,* 6th ed. (New York: Wiley, 1995).

14. OECD, *Revenue Statistics: 1965–1998* (Paris: OECD, 1999), pp. 65–67.

15. Douglas Besharov with Jennifer Ehrle and Karen Gardiner, "Social Welfare's Twin Dilemmas: 'Universalism vs. Targeting' and 'Support vs. Dependency,' " paper presented at the International Social Security Association Research Conference, Jerusalem, January 25–28, 1998.

16. See David Prychitko, "The Welfare State: What Is Left?" *Critical Review,* 4:4 (Fall 1990), 619–32.

17. Maurice Chittenden and Will Peakin, "French Tax Exiles Flock to Britain," *Sunday Times,* February 13, 2000, p. 30.

18. This advanced period of capitalism is also referred to as post-modernity or post-Fordism and includes new information technologies and mass cultural consumption. See, for example, B. Jessop, "From Keynesian Welfare to the Schumpeterian Workfare State," in R. Burrows and B. Loader, eds. *Towards a Post-Fordist Welfare State?* (London: Routledge, 1994); and Peter Leonard, *Postmodern Welfare: Reconstructing an Emancipatory Project* (London: Sage, 1997). Leibfried and Rieger trace the different phases of globalization back to the turn of the twentieth century in Stephan Leibfried and Elmar Rieger, "Conflict Over Germany's Competitiveness: Exiting from the Global Economy?" Occasional Paper, Center for German European Studies, University of California, Berkeley, 1995. For a view of globalization as more of a new form than a modern phase of capitalism, see Robert Reich, *The Work of Nations* (New York: Knopf, 1991); and Jeremy Rifkin, *The End of Work: The Decline of the Global Labor Force and the Dawn of the Post-Market Era* (New York: Putnam, 1995).

19. Guy Standing, *Global Labour Flexibility: Seeking Distributive Justice* (London: Macmillan, 1999), pp. 62–63.

20. Thus, for example, McKenzie counsels that public spending on redistributive social benefits should be contemplated with the utmost care: "Otherwise, officials and policy makers can expect to find their fiscal troubles mounting as capital moves elsewhere or is created elsewhere in the world. Those who are concerned about the plight of the poor must realize that there are economic limits to how much society can do for the poor, given the mobility of capital." Richard McKenzie, "Bidding for Business," *Society,* 33:3 (March–April 1996), pp. 60–69.

21. Standing, *Global Labour Flexibility,* p. 68.

22. According to his analysis, the continental welfare states (e.g., France, Germany, Italy, the Netherlands, Belgium, and Austria) face a greater challenge in making these policy adjustments than the welfare states in Scandinavian and Anglo-Saxon countries. See Fritz Scharpf, "Globalization and the Welfare State: Constraints, Challenges, and Vulnerabilities," in *Social Security in the Global Village: The Year 2000 International Research Conference on Social Security, Helsinki, September 25–27, 2000* (Geneva: ISSA, 2000), pp. 12–45.

23. Werner Sengenberger, "Globalization: Guarantee of Welfare or Threat to Solidarity?" paper presented at the International Social Se-

curity Association Conference on Demographic Trends and Globalization: Challenges for Social Security, p. 2, Bratislava, Slovak Republic, October 14–15, 1999).

24. Elmar Rieger and Stephan Leibfried, "Welfare State Limits to Globalization," *Politics and Society*, 26:3 (September 1998), 361–85, quote at 379.

25. Helen Bolderson and Simon Roberts, "Social Security Across Frontiers," *Journal of International and Comparative Social Welfare*, 13 (1997), 7–23.

26. Robert Rector, "A Retirement Home for Immigrants," *Wall Street Journal*, February 20, 1996, op. ed. page.

27. For an analysis of the reforms and their implications, see Tanya Broder, "Preserving Services for Immigrants: State and Local Implementation of the New Welfare and Immigration Laws," *Clearinghouse Review*, January–February 1997), pp. 964–87. These reforms precipitated a surge of applications for citizenship by legal immigrants. In California, for example, the number of naturalized citizens doubled between 1995 and 1996.

28. OECD, *Economic Survey: Netherlands* (Paris: OECD, 1991).

29. These reforms were initiated under the Reduction Requirement on Industrial Disability Act of 1993, which introduced a stricter medical evaluation of disability and a reduction of benefits over time, and the 1996 reform of the Dutch Social Assistance Act. For discussion of these reforms see Hans Ariens, "To Rigorously Combat the Dutch Disease," *World: APB Annual Report 1996* (Heerlen, N.D.: APB Corporate Communication, 1997); and Romke van der Veen and Willem Trommel, "Managed Liberalization of the Dutch Welfare State," paper presented at the Society for the Advancement of Socio-Economics (SASE) Conference on Rethinking the Welfare State, Montreal, July 5–7, 1997.

30. Mary Collins, "A Guaranteed Minimum Income in France," *Social Policy and Administration* 42:2 (1990); Tony Eardley, Jonathan Bradshaw, John Ditch, Ian Gough, and Peter Whiteford, *Social Assistance in OECD Countries: Synthesis Report* (Paris: OECD, 1996); and David Kalish. "The Active Society," *Social Security Journal*, August, 1991, pp. 3–9.

31. For a discussion of concerns about the "poverty trap" in relation to various groups, see Jonathon Bradshaw and Jane Miller, "Lone-Parent Families in the U.K.: Challenges to Social Policy," *International Social Security Review*, 43:4 (1990); Alain Euzeby, "Unemployment Compensation and Unemployment in Industrialized Market Economy Countries," *International Social Security Review*, 41:1 (1988); and OECD, *The Future of Social Protection* (Paris: OECD, 1988).

32. OECD, *Shaping Structural Change: The Role of Women* (Paris: OECD, 1991).

33. Richard Stevenson, "Swedes Facing Rigors of Welfare Cuts," *New York Times*, March 14, 1993.

34. Charles Murray, *Losing Ground: American Social Policy: 1950–1980* (New York: Basic Books, 1989).

35. Joseph Schumpeter, *Capitalism, Socialism and Democracy*, 3rd ed. (New York: Harper & Row, [1942] 1950), p. 63.

36. Francis Fukuyama, *Trust: The Social Virtues and the Creation of Prosperity* (New York: Free Press, 1995), p. 17.

37. For a less assured view of the prospects for economic liberalism, see David Henderson, *The Changing Fortunes of Economic Liberalism* (London: Institute of Economic Affairs, 1999).

38. Albert Hirschman, *Shifting Inovlvements: Private Interest and Public Action* (Princeton, N.J.: Princeton University Press, 1982), p. 11.

39. John Stephens, "The Scandinavian Welfare States: Achievements, Crisis, and Prospects," in Gosta Esping-Andersen, ed., *Welfare States in Transition* (London: Sage, 1996), p. 46.

40. The movement toward privatization in the United States and Europe has been widely documented; for example, see Mimi Abramovitz, "The Privatization of the Welfare State," *Social Work*, 34:4 (1986), 257–64; Neil Gilbert, *Capitalism and the Welfare State* (New Haven Conn.: Yale University Press, 1983); Norman Johnson, ed., *Private Markets in Health and Welfare* (Oxford: Berg Publishers, 1995); Sheila Kamerman and Alfred Kahn, eds., *Privatization and the Welfare State* (Princeton, N.J.: Princeton University Press, 1989).

41. Neung Hoo Park and Neil Gilbert, "Social Security and the Incremental Privatization of Retirement Income," *Journal of Sociology and Social Research*, 26:2 (June 1999), 187–202.

42. Axel Pedersen, "Do Generous Public Pensions Crowd Out Private Pensions? Comparative Analysis of Time Series Data for Denmark and Norway," Center for Welfare State Research Working Paper 7, Copenhagen, Denmark 1997.

43. For a discussion of the middle course being charted by the New Left, see John Vinocur, "On the New European Road Map, There's Not Much Left of the Left," *International Herald Tribune*, November 24, 1998, p. 4.

44. OECD, *Future of Social Protection.*

45. OECD, *Shaping Structural Change.*

46. Henri Lepage, "A Liberal Socio-Economic Scenario for the Early Twenty-first Century," in *Societal Cohesion and the Globalization of the Economy: What Does the Future Hold?* (Paris: OECD, 1997). He suggests that socialized care has lost its moral and financial legitimacy because the system serves the interests of the early generations, who contributed a little and gained a lot, at the expense of the current generation, which can expect to pay a lot and receive much less.

47. Bernd-Otto Kuper, "The Green and White Papers of the European Union: The Apparent Goal of Reduced Social Benefits," *Journal of European Social Policy*, 4:2 (1994), 131, 137.

48. The tendencies identified with the conventional paradigm are not exclusively associated with the social democratic systems since, for example, all welfare states' allocations have primarily involved direct expenditures; even in the United States, publicly financed social benefits were delivered almost entirely by public agencies, and there was considerable expansion of social rights from 1960 through the early 1980s. See, for example, Gilbert, *Capitalism and the Welfare State.*

49. Based on a detailed comparison of the United States (liberal regime), Germany (corporatist regime) and the Netherlands (social

democratic regime), they conclude that on a range of outcome criteria the "social democratic regime is the best of all possible worlds.' " See Robert Goodin, Bruce Headey, Ruud Muffels, and Henk-Jan Dirven, *The Real Worlds of Welfare Capitalism* (Cambridge: Cambridge University Press, 1999), p. 260.

50. Gosta Esping-Andersen, *Social Foundations of Postindustrial Economies* (New York: Oxford University Press, 1999). For views of the Dutch welfare state as other than a social democratic model, see Anton Zijderveld, The Wanning of the Welfare State: The End of Comprehensive State Succor (New Brunswick, N.J.: Transaction, 1999); Frits Bolkestein, "The Dutch Model: The High Road That Leads Out of the Low Countries," *Economist*, May 22, 1999, pp. 97–98; and van der Veen and Trommel, "Managed Liberalization of the Dutch Welfare State."

51. James Midgley, "The Institutional Approach to Social Policy," in James Midgley, Martin Tracy, and Michelle Livermore, *The Handbook of Social Policy* (Thousand Oaks, Calif.: Sage, 2000), pp. 365–76.

52. My thinking about the fundamental characteristics of the enabling state has evolved from an initial study in 1989, in which the main line of analysis traced the increasing use of indirect expenditures, such as tax deductions and credit subsidies, and of the private sector to finance and deliver social welfare transfers in the United States. At that time, the basic functions of the enabling state were seen as subsidizing private activity, shaping expectations about social responsibility, regulating private activity, and providing an adequate level of social protection. These functions were analyzed in relation to U.S. experience. In 1995, the framework broadened to include the role of the state in promoting social equity and emphasizing social benefits linked to productivity and economic growth. Although that study also focused mainly on developments in the United States, there were glimmers of similar changes underway among all the advanced industrialized welfare states, which have grown much sharper on closer examination. See Neil Gilbert and Barbara Gilbert, *The Enabling State: Modern Welfare Capitalism in America* (New York: Oxford University Press, 1989); and Neil Gilbert, *Welfare Justice: Restoring Social Equity* (New Haven, Conn.: Yale University Press, 1995).

53. For an analysis of the range and expansion of tax expenditures and their impact on the enabling state in the United States, see Gilbert and Gilbert, *Enabling State.*

54. For a detailed examination of the complex relation between unemployment and social exclusion, see Tony Atkinson, "Social Exclusion, Poverty, and Unemployment," in A. B. Atkinson and John Hills, eds., *Exclusion, Employment, and Opportunity* (London: Center for the Analysis of Social Exclusion, London School of Economics, 1998).

55. Alain Euzeby, "Unemployment Compensation and Unemployment in Industrialized Market Economy Countries," *International Social Security Review* 41:1 (1988).

56. T. H. Marshall, *Class, Citizenship and Social Development* (New York: Anchor Books, 1964).

57. Émile Durkheim, *De la Division du Travail Social* (*The Division of Labor in Society*) George Simpson, trans. (New York: Free Press, [1893] 1933).

58. Weber's ideal type was not "ideal" in the sense of achieving perfection or representing exemplary values; it was an analytic construct that captured the essential tendencies of a phenomenon. There were, as Weber explained, ideal types of brothels, as well as of religions. For a discussion of Weber's method, see S. M. Miller, *Max Weber: Selections from His Work* (New York: Crowell, 1963), p. 31.

59. If two mothers stay home to care for their own preschool-aged children, they are counted as being out of the labor force; but if they switched children and paid each other $6.00 per hour to perform the same activity for the other's children, they would both be counted as employed (and at $6.00 per hour would probably qualify for a federal subsidy via the Earned Income Tax Credit).

60. See, for example, Spencer Rich, "Social Welfare Spending," *Washington Post*, April 11, 1989; Robert Moroney, *Social Policy and Social Work: Critical Essays on the Welfare State* (New York: Aldine de Gruyter, 1991); Harold Wilensky, *The Welfare State and Equality* (Berkeley: University of California Press, 1975); and Goodin et al., *Real Worlds of Welfare Capitalism*.

61. For a discussion of this development in the United States, see Stanley Surrey, *Pathways to Tax Reform* (Cambridge, Mass.: Harvard University Press, 1974); and Richard Goode, "The Economic Definition of Income," in Joseph Pechman, ed., *Comprehensive Income Taxation* (Washington, D.C.: Brookings Institution, 1977).

62. These indirect taxes vary by country. Average indirect tax rates in the United States are in the 5.3 percent to 7.5 percent range, compared to indirect rates of 13.5 percent to 20.5 percent in most European countries. Willem Adema, *Net Social Expenditures: Labour Market and Social Policy Occasional Papers No. 39.* (Paris: OECD, 1999).

63. *OECD Social Expenditure Database, 1980–1996* (Paris: OECD, 1999)

64. See Adema, *Net Social Expenditures*; Willem Adema and Marcel Einerhand, *The Growing Role of Private Social Benefits: Labour Market and Social Policy Occasional Papers No. 32* (Paris: OECD, 1998); and Willem Adema, Marcel Einerhand, Bengt Eklind, Jorgen Lotz, and Mark Pearson, *Net Public Social Expenditure: Labour Market and Social Policy Occasional Papers No. 19* (Paris: OECD, 1996); for one of the earliest attempts to reformulate the operational measure of social expenditure by including the impact of taxes and tax expenditures, see Neil Gilbert and Ailee Moon, "Analyzing Welfare Effort: An Appraisal of Comparative Methods," *Journal of Policy Analysis and Management*, 7:2 (1988), 326–40.

PART II

LINES OF CONVERGENCE

3

Protection to Inclusion

Promoting Work

Over the last decade, policies for social protection of the unemployed, originally formulated to provide income maintenance in times of duress, were recast into schemes for getting people back to work as soon as possible. One could see the coming change in the late 1980s when the International Social Security Association's review of major trends in social protection noted an increasing awareness that policies should be designed to reinforce "the social factors that underlay productivity"; at almost the same time, the OECD was calling for social policies that improved economic performance and the "effective functioning of the supply side of the economy."[1] Changes in the framework of social protection, which followed these pronouncements, are manifested rhetorically in a new discourse and substantively in a wave of policy reforms that has swept through the advanced industrialized world. As for the rhetoric, three tightly connected themes characterize the new discourse on assisting the unemployed: a shift from *passive* to *active* policies, an emphasis on *responsibilities* over *rights*, and a redefinition of objectives from *income maintenance* to *social inclusion*.

Apotheosis of Work

First, it has become almost universally accepted that social policies heretofore providing "passive" income supports, such as unconditional, exclusively cash benefits to the unemployed, should be replaced by measures designed to stimulate employment and other responsible behaviors—promoting what the Organization for Economic Cooperation and Development terms an "active society."[2] These measures encompass a wide range of reforms that link cash benefits under disability, unemployment, and public assistance programs to work-oriented incentives—a trend commonly referred to as "welfare to workfare" (not always with a positive connotation). Stretching across the political spectrum from Sweden to the United States, policies to activate the unemployed have created new incentives and strong pressures for welfare beneficiaries to find work. In the United States, the extensive reform of public assistance programs since the late 1980s has introduced an array of incentives linking benefits, for example, to attendance at school, work requirements, and the establishment of paternity for child-support payments.[3] Surveying Sweden, Staffan Marklund observes that "the idea of welfare according to need has at least partly been replaced by incentive-oriented policies."[4] In Denmark, the social reform of 1997 substituted the activation-workfare principle, that people should work in return for state benefits, for the early 1970s principle of "income disappearance," which held that cash benefits should be allocated to prevent the distress associated with loss of income. Jorn Loftager suggests that although the recent changes represent dramatic reductions in and tightening of earlier social policies, Danish policymakers responsible for the reforms have put a positive spin on these measures, presenting them as important social improvements.[5] Along these lines, Per Jensen interprets Denmark as an enabling state, in which the new labor market reforms represent a strategy that "enables individuals to gain control over their own lives rather than a strategy of workfare."[6] One might observe, however, that the main thrust of these reforms is to enable people to get back to work, which, depending on the job, may not always translate into gaining control over one's life.

Seeking to place the surge of work-oriented initiatives on a progressive (social democratic)–conservative (laissez-faire liberalism) axis, Jacob Torfing draws a distinction between what he terms *neostatist* and *neoliberal* strategies.[7] According to this view, the neostatist approach, found in Scandinavian countries, emphasizes positive incentives to seek employment rather than the reduction of benefits for those who do not comply with work requirements, aims to empower rather than punish and control beneficiaries, and favors training over "forced labor." In contrast, the neoliberal approach, with which he associates the Anglo-American nations (particularly the United States and the United Kingdom), relies more on economic sanctions, offers limited training, and applies coercive measures narrowly targeted on the unemployed.

This distinction, however, draws too sharp a line among the mix of carrots and sticks administered through work-oriented policies in different countries. Coercion and benefit reductions are found in countries identified with the neostatist approach, whereas those associated with neoliberal policies offer education, training, and positive incentives. In Denmark, for instance, welfare recipients who reject a fair offer of training, educational activities, and placement in jobs can have their benefits reduced by up to 20 percent;[8] in the Netherlands, Piet Keizer reports that guiding public assistance recipients in their search for jobs includes "both carrots—the delivery of relevant information on jobs and training possibilities—and sticks—the threat of sanctions for those who do not make sufficient efforts."[9] At the same time, the requirement for mandatory employment of welfare recipients in the United States is modified by a 20 percent waiver for those unable to work. Moreover, the coercive sticks of welfare reform in the United States are often combined with supportive services. Findings from 10 major studies of welfare-to-work programs in the United States showed that the most successful projects, in terms of the participants' earnings and rates of employment, delivered a mix of supportive services, such as education, training, and child care, along with mandatory work requirements.[10] In the United Kingdom, participants in the New Deal program for young people who do not find unsubsidized jobs after a four-month "gateway" period are offered several options, including subsidized employment for six months, a job with an environment task force, and a course of full-time education or training; more than half of the 42,000 participants enrolled in these options at the end of 1998 were in a full-time course of education or training.[11] If the distinction between progressive and conservative approaches to *active* policies tends to blur on close inspection, the effort to differentiate these alternative models nevertheless raises an important question about the best mix of public investments, economic sanctions, and social incentives in schemes to activate the unemployed.

Second, along with the transition from *passive* to *active* policies, the dominant discourse on social protection of the unemployed has migrated from the elaboration of citizens' *rights* to social benefits to the articulation of their *responsibilities* to work, to be self-sufficient, and to lead an active life. From the 1960s up through the mid-1980s, all the advanced industrial welfare states spawned a proliferation of claims to a range of increasingly generous social benefits—with little discussion of social responsibilities. In the wake of the Great Depression, the main causes of unemployment and poverty were attributed to structural factors, such as the international business cycles, not to individual idleness. Indeed, to hold those in poverty responsible for their circumstances or to suggest that welfare benefits created disincentives to work (which recipients consciously calculated) smacked of "blaming the victim," at least to supporters of the welfare state.[12] In the United States, this perception began to change in the mid-1980s.[13] Welfare critics such as Charles Murray made serious charges about the debilitating effects of welfare benefits.[14] At the same time that Murray's *Losing Ground* was gaining play in the media, Lawrence Mead's analysis of the social obligations of citizenship launched the American debate about the extent to which rights to welfare should be balanced by explicit expectations about the recipients' civic responsibilities.[15] By the early 1990s, this debate was joined and amplified by the communitarian movement under the leadership of Amitai Etzioni, which sought to carve out a centrist position that refined the moral symmetry between rights and responsibilities.[16]

In the 1990s, a notable emphasis on individual responsibilities entered the policy discourse on social protection of the unemployed in other OECD nations—although often expressed in more tentative language than in the United States. Unemployment rose among European nations after 1990, at the same time that new ideas were filtering into the social policy arena. Assessing the changes in the Scandinavian unemployment benefit schemes, Aksel Hatland notes, "Arguments that generous social benefits affected the recipients' economic behaviour in an undesirable way, had previously belonged to the conservative critique of the welfare state. Now this kind of critique also gained ground on the centre and left side of politics."[17] Policy changes in response to this development have imposed strong duties on the unemployed, which according to Hatland have been widely accepted. Similarly, Romke van der Veen recounts how the duties of beneficiaries have been expanded and more sharply defined under social assistance and unemployment reforms in the Netherlands, where after 1996 obligations related to job searches increased and single mothers were expected to find employment.[18] Analyzing these measures, Dick Vink sees the emphasis on individual responsibility as a central element of the Dutch reforms, one that creates unaccustomed financial risks for citizens who are experiencing illness and disability.[19] A little farther north, the 1992 *White Paper on Rehabilitation* introduced what Norwegians termed the "work approach" to social welfare policy, a basic premise of which was "that individual rights are not exclusively tied to cash benefits; each individual has, as far as possible, a right and a duty to work, to participate in rehabilitation programs or enter education."[20] And several years later, the New Labour government in Britain published a *Green Paper on Welfare Reform*, articulating eight principles that would guide the future course of the welfare state, the first of which is to encourage people to work. On this point, the report does not equivocate. "The Government's aim is to rebuild the welfare state around work." This is to be done through active work-oriented policies, supportive services, tax measures that make work pay, and "ensuring that responsibilities and rights are fairly matched."[21]

On first glance, the rhetoric of rights and responsibilities appears to be thoroughly uncontentious. No one is opposed to balancing rights and responsibilities—until we specify whose rights and what responsibilities are on the scale. The social obligations of community membership go well beyond the traditional charge to pay one's own way in life. In addition to caring for dependent kin, the more general charge to assist the weakest and protect the most vulnerable members of the community is widely considered a civic duty of all who are able. In many countries nonpoor homeowners and college students benefit immensely from tax-related subsidies and publicly subsidized loans—social transfers that allow them to accumulate considerable assets over a lifetime.[22] One can imagine several ways through which these beneficiaries might discharge their obligations to the community for the financial advantages gained from social transfers. Students subsidized by publicly supported universities or low-interest college loans, for example, could be expected upon graduation to perform some type of national service, such as working in nursing homes, on environmental protection projects, or in inner-city schools. Those who benefit from tax subsidies for home ownership might be assessed a special 1 percent or 2 percent transfer tax on profits from the sale of their property, which would go toward financing housing vouchers for low-income tenants. But the discourse on balancing rights and responsibilities has not concentrated on the diverse obligations that might attend the full spectrum of benefits derived from social rights. Rather, the moral calculus of this equation has been applied almost exclusively to the unemployed poor—whose rights to social benefits are being weighed against the recipients' efforts to be financially self-supporting.

Indeed, from official government documents to scholarly analyses of recent reforms throughout the OECD countries, one continually finds discussions about the importance of "active work-oriented" measures, complemented by the discourse on the need to balance rights and responsibilities. And these two themes are habitually joined with a third—the desire to promote *social inclusion*. Thus, the basic premise of social policy expressed in the Norwegian 1992 White Paper goes on to say, "Social insurance schemes should be designed so as to make the 'Work Approach' the first choice for all affected parties, and to prevent unnecessary exclusion or expulsion of vulnerable groups from the labor market." In the United Kingdom, the 1998 *Green Paper on Welfare Reform* identifies social exclusion as one of the three key problems that plagues the existing system.[23] In France, responses to the problem of social exclusion are embedded in the discourse on "insertion," a concept that is broadly interpreted to encompass a range of services directed toward the socially excluded; these services involve health and housing counseling and facilitating access to benefits, "as well as counselling, training and employment schemes explicitly linked to the labour market."[24] In the French context, the discussion of exclusion is connected to the state's responsibility to forge social cohesion. Following this line of analysis, some scholars see the response to social exclusion as leading to a new entitlement, "the right to insertion (le droit à l'insertion), in order to reconcile the French tradition of solidarity with the rise of individualism."[25] The international organizations have also joined in battle against social exclusion. By the late 1990s, to champion social inclusion had become "a main objective of the World Bank's mission."[26]

Social exclusion is a problem that requires more than a public transfer of money to those in need. In the past, cash benefits for people who were out of work for one reason or another—mainly disability, sickness, loss of job, and single parenthood—were commonly referred to as "income maintenance" programs. As the name suggests, they were based on policies designed to protect people against the loss of income and the inability to earn a salary. The objective was to provide basic financial support at a level that kept people above the poverty line (an objective rarely met in the United States).[27] Allowing the unemployed to survive without being forced to take the first job offered to them, these policies promoted what was referred to in chapter 1 as the decommodification of labor. In the 1960s and 1970s, the discourse surrounding income maintenance programs focused on the problem of poverty and the need for levels of support that afforded a decent standard of living. There was a burgeoning literature on poverty and its causes, conditions, functions, solutions, and measurements.[28] Today, poverty per se is a much less fashionable topic of discourse. In the United States studies of welfare recipients from the 1990s onward tend to focus less on conditions of poverty and levels of support than on the recipients' relations to the labor market and the dynamics of welfare dependency, which reveal that many people are poor for relatively brief periods of time because of divorce and unemployment.[29]

In much of Europe, analyses of poverty have been replaced by the broader, more diffuse problem of social exclusion.[30] The socially excluded are usually poor, but they suffer from more than just a shortage of money; they endure multiple deprivations, the cumulative impact of which leaves them detached from the mainstream of society. Christoph Badelt sees the problem, broadly defined, as involving exclusion from the labor market, goods and services, security, human rights, and land, particularly in developing countries.[31] If social exclusion is measured more narrowly as the proportion of households located simultaneously in the bottom 20 percent of the national distribution of employment, education, and income, one estimate concludes that 2.7 percent of households in Germany, 3.8 percent in the United States, and 4.4 percent in the Netherlands are socially excluded.[32] Other aspects of social exclusion involve lack of participation in community life and insufficient access to social benefits. However it is defined, exclusion from a decent-paying job rests at the core of this multidimensional concept. Indeed, labor force participation is so central to the concerns about social exclusion that analysts often go out of their way to stress other aspects of this concept so that it is not read merely as synonymous to unemployment.[33]

More Than Just Rhetoric

As social welfare policies from the Left and Right converge, they are increasingly wrapped in the elaborate rhetoric of social inclusion (in the labor force), empowerment (to earn wages), activation (to find a job), and responsibility (to take the job). Cutting through the rhetoric, however, one finds substantive expression of what it all means in a multiplicity of work-oriented reforms. These policies center on unemployment, disability, and public assistance programs—with measures devised for the reform of public assistance in the United States among the most far-reaching.

The United States's experience is notable in that it embodies an unequivocally qualitative change in policy. Public welfare for families with dependent children was initially designed under the Social Security Act of 1935 as an income maintenance program to assist needy, deserving widows and their children.[34] Originally entitled Aid to Dependent Children (ADC), the program provided financial support for women who were single parents so they could stay home and care for their children without regard for work-oriented sanctions and incentives. The monthly ADC grants in the mid-1930s, $18 for the first child and $12 for each additional child, were based on the amount for each child received by families of servicemen who lost their lives in World War I.[35] As the name changed to Aid to Families with Dependent Children (AFDC) in 1961 and finally to Temporary Assistance for Needy Families (TANF) in 1996, so did the program and its orientation to work. To analyze the conversion from income maintenance to work-oriented policy in the United States, let us examine why it occurred, how it was implemented, and what were its results.

The New Deal planners did not expect to be planting the seeds of work training, incentives, and sanctions for welfare mothers. Rather, they hoped the public assistance program would wither away as widows became eligible for survivors' insurance and were absorbed into the newly formed social security system.[36] But that was not to happen. Instead the program grew in response to increases in the divorce rate and out-of-wedlock births to teenage mothers, which started climbing in the 1960s. Between 1940 and 1960, unmarried women gave birth at a low and fairly stable rate, rising from 3.8 percent to 5.3 percent of all births.[37] During that period, from 1 million to 3 million recipients received welfare benefits annually.[38] From 1960 to 1996, however, the rate of births to unmarried women increased sixfold, rising from 5.3 percent to 32.4 percent of all births, with teenagers accounting for almost one-third of all the births to unmarried women.[39] Between 1960 and 1996, the ratio of annual divorces to marriages doubled, from about 25 percent to 50 percent. After 1960, the number of welfare recipients among families with dependent children climbed significantly, reaching a high of 14.2 million people in 1994; after the mid-1990s, the national caseload began a sharp decline.[40]

An unprecedented shift of women's labor from the household to the market economy accompanied the explosive growth and changing characteristics (a rising number of young, unwed mothers along with the increasing participation of minorities) of public welfare recipients. Between 1960 and 1997, the labor force participation rate of married women with children under the age of 6 multiplied from 18.3 percent to 63.6 percent[41]—a normative shift in the role of motherhood that dulled public sympathy for programs that paid women to stay at home and care for their children. These demographic and normative developments gave impetus to the move from income maintenance to work-oriented provisions—from welfare to workfare. But workfare as we know it did not arrive overnight. Implementation was an extended process, which evolved through a series of increasingly rigorous reforms crafted over a period of more than three decades. The four landmark reforms on the road to workfare involved the 1962 "service" amendments, the 1967 Work Incentive (WIN) Program, the Family Support Act of 1988, and the 1996 program of Temporary Assistance for Needy Families (TANF).

The Social Security Amendments of 1962 are often referred to as the "service" amendments because they provided substantial federal funding for social services to accompany the cash benefits dispensed to public welfare recipients in the AFDC program. The objective was to rehabilitate the poor through intensive social casework that would change their behavior in ways that would help them become economically independent.[42] The assumption here was that poverty stemmed largely from individual deficiencies that could be remedied through social casework.[43] But efforts to provide welfare recipients with high-level professional services were seriously hindered by the dearth of trained social workers, large caseloads, and high turnover rates of professional staffs in departments of public assistance.[44] In practice it was not uncommon for social workers to visit their clients less than once a month for 30 minutes.[45] Although the promise of high-quality clinical services was never realized, it is doubtful whether social casework at its professional best could resolve problems of poverty and unemployment. Whatever its powers, the implementation of these services was accompanied by continued growth of the public assistance rolls, which climbed by 1 million recipients from 1962 to 1966.[46]

The failure to reduce economic dependency, combined with the intangible quality of casework made these services a prime target of congressional dissatisfaction, which was expressed in the 1967 Social Security Amendments. As these amendments wended their way through Congress, "the old slogans—service instead of support, rehabilitation instead of relief—were abandoned and work and work incentives became the new thing in the continuing search for relief from relief costs."[47] Policymakers began to form a distinction between "soft," talking services, such as advice and counseling, and more tangible services, such as day care, drug treatment, and work training, which were "harder" and soon became emphasized.[48] Converting from a "soft" service orientation to a "hard" work-oriented approach, the 1967 amendments established WIN, which provided employment training, day care, and a financial incentive for welfare recipients to seek work (the first $30 of monthly earnings plus one-third of the remainder were exempted from determination of eligibility for public assistance).[49] Although the 1967 amendments did not require mothers to take work training or jobs, this program marked the first significant shift in emphasis from welfare services to workfare.

The results of WIN were not greatly encouraging. Of the 167,000 people who enrolled in WIN through March 1970, more than one-third dropped out of the program, and all told, only 25,000 got jobs. Those who moved on to work were "creamed" from the pool of applicants; that is, they were those best prepared for jobs, a high percentage of whom would probably have found employment sooner or later without social assistance. In light of the program's "conspicuously unspectacular performance," Sar Levitan and Robert Taggart concluded, "the wisdom of expanding WIN is questionable, and the theoretical arguments for such a move are even more dubious."[50] It appears that the program's shortcomings endured to the end. A study in 1982 found that only 3 percent of the AFDC clients registered for the WIN program in New York State were placed in a job; an additional 5 percent found employment through their own efforts. As in the earlier findings, the 1982 study showed that the clients served were generally from a low-risk group who were most likely to get jobs without the help of WIN.[51]

In 1981 a series of welfare-to-work demonstrations were initiated. Based in part on the encouraging results of these demonstrations, WIN was replaced by the workfare provisions of the Family Support Act of 1988.[52] This 1988 legislation differed from WIN in several respects. The most important difference, perhaps, was the mandatory directive for the participation of welfare mothers. Under the Family Support Act, federal regulations required AFDC recipients with children over 3 years of age to participate in the Jobs Opportunities and Basic Skills (JOBS) programs operated by each state and then to seek employment. States had discretion to go even further and lower the age of exemption to mothers with 1-year-old children. The act imposed no time limits on how long one may receive welfare, but those who did not participate in the work-training and job search efforts could have their AFDC grants reduced or eliminated. In addition to requiring participation in work-training programs, the Family Support Act offered AFDC recipients incentives to take paid employment by extending child-care services and Medicaid health coverage for 12 months after a family was no longer eligible to receive public assistance grants because of increased income from employment.[53] The initial results of the JOBS program were generally positive but not compelling. A summary of findings on 10 programs evaluated through experimental designs shows earnings and employment increasing and AFDC receipt and payments decreasing in most of the programs.[54]

On the whole, mandatory participation in workfare programs, educational demands, social controls, and requirements for the establishment of paternity imposed by the Family Support Act of 1988 delivered a forceful message to welfare recipients. Heretofore, public assistance agencies had occasionally paid lip service to this message, but now bureaucratic behavior had become seriously devoted to implementing the work-oriented legislative mandate. The old mold of entitlement to welfare as income maintenance was broken. States followed with a rush of work-oriented demonstrations and reforms, which culminated in the passage of the Personal Responsibility and Work Opportunity Reconciliation Act of 1996—achieving President Clinton's campaign promise to "end welfare as we know it," if not exactly along the lines he envisioned. This act eliminated the AFDC program, creating in its place the Temporary Assistance for Needy Families (TANF) program. Under TANF states receive a fixed level of federal funding to provide income support to poor families with children. The total federal allocation to all states—$15.3 billion a year, plus a $2 billion contingency fund—was based on the amount states spent on AFDC in 1994. As it turned out, this sum was considerably more than adequate to cover the costs of welfare caseloads into at least 2001 since these caseloads had already declined by almost 48 percent between 1993 and 1999. It is axiomatic, however, that good times do not afford the best test of welfare reform. Since the federal grant is unconnected to changing levels of need, during a period of recession, when welfare caseloads tend to rise, a state could run out of federal funds, and eligible applicants for public aid would have to be denied assistance unless the state had the fiscal resources and political will to provide supplementary funding (or Congress passed emergency legislation to deal with the shortfall). Thus, by substituting the TANF block grant for the open-ended funding arrangement under AFDC, Congress effectively eliminated the federally guaranteed entitlement to public assistance.

Although capping the level of federal funding, TANF gives the states considerable discretion on the use of these grants to provide cash aid, emergency assistance, child care, job training, education, and job subsidies. States also have wide latitude in designing incentives and sanctions to motivate welfare recipients; in California, for example, benefits are linked to school attendance, and in Michigan absent fathers who do not make required child-support payments lose their driver's license and other professional licenses. Wisconsin initiated Wisconsin Works (W2), based on the premise that to help people find a job programs should function as much like work as possible, making a seamless transition from public assistance activities to self-supporting employment. At intake to the W2 program, welfare applicants are assigned to meet with a financial and employment planner to explore various avenues to becoming economically self-sufficient. For those who cannot immediately be placed in jobs, three avenues of support are available: remedial activities for clients least prepared to function in a work setting; placement in community service jobs provided by local public and nonprofit agencies; and placement in time-limited, subsidized jobs in private and public organizations. The W2 participants are eligible for child-care subsidies, health insurance, and full child-support payments, which mirror the general conditions of low-wage workers.[55]

Although TANF gives substantial authority to the states, the program remains firmly framed by a number of federal rules. The use of federal funds is prohibited for assistance to varying categories of potential welfare recipients (teenage mothers who are living in their own homes, mothers who are uncooperative in establishing paternity, and individuals convicted of drug crimes). States are required to meet strict timetables for employment. According to the federal mandate, welfare recipients must be engaged in some kind of work-related activity to continue to receive benefits under TANF after their first two years of support. (However, the rules fail to specify how the work requirements must be satisfied. It is not clear, for example, whether self-employment, work for family members, or volunteer or other unpaid work would count as a job.[56]) Arguably, the most stringent regulation involves the 60-month limit on assistance, which bars states from providing federally funded cash benefits to families for more than a total of 5 years during their lifetime. States may exempt, because of family hardship, up to 20 percent of TANF recipients from the federal 5-year limit. Policymakers are challenged to define the nature and severity of "family hardship" as advocates for needy groups—such as victims of AIDS/HIV and other chronic disabilities, battered women, and grandparents who are providing kinship foster care—mobilize to protect their constituencies.[57]

What are the preliminary results of TANF? As noted, the exacting work-oriented welfare reforms that began as demonstration projects in the early 1990s and concluded with the establishment of TANF were accompanied by a remarkable and unprecedented decline in the welfare caseload, which plunged by 48 percent from the historic high of 5.1 million families in March 1994 to 2.68 million families in March 1999. Precisely how much of the caseload reduction was due to the pressures of reform and how much to the draw of employment opportunities is hard to untangle. The 1990s were a booming period, when the unemployment rate fell to a 30-year low of 4.3 percent. One estimate suggests that between 1993 and 1996, the falling unemployment rate accounted for almost 50 percent of the caseload reduction.[58] Studies in the later years conclude that in 1996 to 1999 only about 10 percent to 20 percent of the decline could be attributed to the strong economy.[59] But the work-oriented reforms also exerted powerful stimuli toward caseload reduction on at least three fronts. First, incentives and sanctions encourage unemployed welfare recipients to search for jobs and to accept those offered. On this front, initial findings suggest that the most promising efforts to move recipients from welfare to work involve a mix of strategies that emphasizes intensive job search and quick employment—the "work first" approach—joined to on-the-job training and continued education to upgrade skills.[60] Second, the time limits and work requirements discourage new applications for welfare from people who might well be able to find employment in times of economic expansion. Finally, the stringent demands to pursue training and job search activities, coupled with the 2-year work rule and 60-month time limit, place heavy pressures to exit the welfare rolls on the many recipients already engaged in unreported work. A number of studies has clearly established that a significant proportion of welfare recipients regularly worked for pay that was not reported.[61]

Many of the welfare recipients who left the rolls entered low-paying, minimum-wage jobs. It is widely believed that people in these jobs remain poor. Yet Robert Lerman shows that when the full range of benefits is taken into account, those who exit welfare to work at the minimum wage have a net income above the poverty level. Examining 12 large states in 1997, Lerman calculated the net income for a family of three that included the minimum wage plus any benefits from TANF or food stamps and the earned income tax credit minus payroll taxes and income taxes. The results demonstrate that in every state, welfare recipients who work 35 hours a week would have a net income well above the official poverty line ($10,610 for a family of two and $13,330 for a family of three in that year); in five of these states (including California and New York), the family's net income would rise above the poverty line for those who worked only 20 hours a week at the minimum wage.[62]

At the same time that many recipients who left the rolls went to work full time, a surprising number of mothers seemed to be leaving welfare without taking regular jobs. Douglas Besharov and Peter Germanis conclude that only about 50 percent to 60 percent of those who left and stayed off welfare appeared to be working regularly. Those who left without working drew on other sources of public support, including social security, supplemental security income, and food stamps; in Alabama the $329 food stamp allotment for a family of three in 1999 was almost twice as high as the welfare benefit. They could also draw support from preexisting coresidency arrangements. Before the decline in welfare caseloads, at least 37 percent of welfare mothers lived with other adults.[63]

This brief foray into the reform of public assistance in the United States illustrates a course of change punctuated by four distinct phases. First, counseling services to rehabilitate welfare recipients were injected into a program originally designed to provide income maintenance. Second, the emphasis shifted to more utilitarian services, such as day care for children, and work-related incentives, along with opportunities for voluntary participation in work-training programs. Third, voluntary work-training and job search activities became mandatory. Fourth, incentives for engaging in work-related activities were joined with sanctions for those who failed to cooperate, going to work within 2 years became mandatory, and the duration of benefits was capped by a 60-month lifetime limit. As the objective of moving welfare recipients into paid employment became increasingly well focused and widely accepted, new policies introduced more forceful incentives and social controls, which were strictly implemented by line-workers in the public assistance bureaucracies.

Although the U.S. welfare reforms are the most stringent in the extent to which they employ lifetime limits and firmly administer incentives and sanctions, they have moved in a direction that closely parallels the growing emphasis on work-oriented measures in the public assistance policies of most other industrialized welfare states.[64] In Denmark, the Social Assistance reform of 1997 marked a significant step in the transition from welfare to workfare. Emphasizing the "activation" of welfare recipients, the Danish scheme requires all persons who are receiving social assistance to participate in formulating individual action plans, which are designed to improve their working skills and to facilitate gainful employment. Activation entails job placements, training, and educational opportunities. And all recipients under the age of 30 are expected to be activated within their first 13 weeks on welfare. Those who reject a fair offer of activation can have their welfare benefits reduced by up to 20 percent.[65]

After the 1994 elections in the Netherlands, "Work, work, and work again!" was the motto of the "purple coalition" (red Social Democrats and blue Liberals) that formed the new government.[66] True to its words, the purple cabinet's 1996 reform of the Social Assistance Act advanced measures to restrict access to welfare, to alter the level of benefits, and to activitate those on the rolls. Thus, persons younger than 21 are no longer eligible for social assistance, and recent graduates between the ages of 21 and 27 who are looking for work (and would not qualify for unemployment insurance because they have no labor history) cannot claim welfare benefits for the first six months of their unemployment. The standard level of benefits has been lowered by 20 percent, at the same time that local agencies have increased discretion to supplement, based on individual circumstances, the reduced payments by up to 20 percent. This flexibility supports an activating strategy that allows local agencies to incorporate incentives and sanctions into the design of individual reintegration plans. The law prescribes a reduction in benefits for participants who do not comply with these plans. This reform not only reinforces the duty to seek gainful employment for those unemployed but also extends this obligation to single mothers, who are now expected to become active on the labor market when their children reach the age of 5.[67]

In France, the *Revenu Minimum d'Insertion* was introduced by Prime Minister Michel Rocard in 1988 as a "veritable revolution in welfare entitlement." Designed to aid the poor, in 1996 this program provided monthy allowances ranging from 2077 francs (about $290) for a single claimant to 5902 francs (about $825) for a couple with three children, amounts that are reduced by income from other sources. But to receive the cash benefits, recipients must meet certain requirements. According to the law, participants are obliged to sign a contract of rehabilitation worked out with a local committee, which embodies a plan of action and a timetable of specific steps to be taken toward "insertion"—a concept that, as previously noted, includes a range of activities.[68] This contract is the linchpin in a reciprocal scheme, which the French designed to unite public entitlement to financial aid with the duty to exercise individual responsibility. Allowances are supposed to be reviewed quarterly and can be withdrawn if recipients fail to discharge their contractual obligations.[69]

In the early 1990s, versions of workfare were introduced to social assistance schemes in Scandinavia. The Social Services Act of 1991 gave local administrations in Norway authority to institute work requirements as a condition of eligibility for welfare benefits. After Swedish welfare expenditures nearly doubled in the first half of the 1990s, similar reforms were initiated that qualified the long-standing social right to public assistance. Although it was not adopted everywhere, the Uppsala model (named after Sweden's fifth-largest municipality) required public assistance applicants to develop individual career plans in consultation with welfare officers and employment counselors and to search actively for work.[70]

Just as public assistance reforms are forging tighter links between benefits and work-related activities, unemployment and disability policies have been reframed to incorporate robust behavioral incentives and work requirements.[71] The changes in unemployment policies are more evident in Europe than in the United States because European unemployment compensation schemes typically offer benefits that are comparatively higher, last longer, and are often available to teenagers with no work record. Thus, according to one's previous work record, the period of coverage by unemployment insurance ranges from around 5 months to 2 years in Germany, between 3 months and 5 years in France, and 6 months to 5 years in the Netherlands.[72] These relatively generous arrangements provide less of an incentive for recipients to seek work than in the United States, where benefits are usually limited to 6 months (with an extension of 13 weeks in states where the unemployment rate is high) and provide a relatively low replacement rate, with an average weekly benefit around 35 percent of the average weekly wage.[73]

Recasting the Policy Mold

Designs for social protection of unemployed people in the advanced industrialized nations have been substantially reshaped by a new policy mold that alters the basic features of entrance and exit and what happens to participants along the way. The four most prominent dimensions of change are these:

1. Restricting entrance and accelerating exit
2. Segmentation of participants
3. Introduction of contractual obligations
4. Formulation of work-oriented incentives and services

Beginning with access and exit, we see that whereas young people who never held a job could once acquire unemployment benefits with a simple application and those who lost their jobs were entitled to benefits for years, if not for a lifetime, various measures over the last decade have tightened requirements at the point of entry and limited the duration of benefits.[74] Countries such as Denmark, the United Kingdom, Finland, Spain, and the Netherlands have extended the period of paid employment required to qualify for benefits; from another angle Sweden, Finland, Belgium, and France have narrowed access to unemployment benefits by introducing or lengthening waiting periods.[75] New Zealand raised the minimum age to qualify for unemployment benefits.[76] Other countries, such as the United Kingdom, have conditioned the receipt of unemployment benefits to teenagers upon participation in some form of employment-related activity. To speed up exit from these programs, a number of countries, including Denmark, Norway, Italy, the Netherlands, and Germany, have shortened the maximum duration for receiving unemployment benefits, (although the duration of benefits in these countries is still quite long by U.S. standards). In 1999, the Swedish government was debating proposals to limit the duration of unemployment benefits.

The doorway to disability programs has also been narrowed in many, perhaps most, of the industrialized countries.[77] In some instances, the definition of what constitutes a disability has been delimited, as in the United States where 1996 policy reforms eliminated alcoholism and drug addiction as conditions that qualified for disability benefits (under both the SSI and the disability insurance programs). In 1998, Canada extended the period of contribution required to qualify for a disability pension. Norway intensified the requirement to demonstrate a causal link between the claimant's medical condition and the reduced capacity to earn a living.[78] In 1991, the Dutch cabinet initiated one of the most extensive and widely cited reforms of disability insurance. At that time, the number of people who were receiving disability payments had climbed to 14 percent of the Dutch labor force, with absences because of illness claiming another 6 percent. Altogether, one in five members of the labor force received benefits, the cost of which amounted to 7 percent of the Dutch GDP[79] (not that the Netherlands is an unhealthy place—despite much higher disability claims, the Dutch live longer, consume less alcohol, have fewer traffic accidents, and visit a doctor less often than their neighbors in Germany and Belgium).[80] In response to this situation, a series of 18 reforms were designed to lower financial disincentives to work, encourage reentry to the labor force, and broaden opportunities for employment. These reforms included a more rigorous definition of the degree of disability. By 1996, after almost a decade of growth from 1983 to 1993, the number of recipients of disability benefits had declined, the percentage of recipients on partial disability had increased, and the disability expenditure as a proportion of GDP had dropped by almost 25 percent.[81] Much of the initial decline in the number of recipients from 1993 to 1996 is attributed to the effect of sudden medical reexaminations under the new definition of disability, which resulted in moving many people off the disability rolls and into unemployment schemes. After the initial drop, however, the number of recipients climbed back up and by 1999 had surpassed the previous high of 1993.[82]

Concurrent with the efforts launched to tighten access to disability benefits, many countries, including the United States, Norway, and the Netherlands, introduced measures to accelerate exits by increasing the frequency of reexaminations of claimants, sometimes assessing their status in light of new, more rigorous criteria of degrees of disability. Beginning in the year 2000, disability payments in Germany were awarded as temporary benefits rather than permanent pensions. Investigation of fraudulent claims to disability pensions in Italy between 1992 and 1997 resulted in discontinuation of benefits to almost 20 percent of the cases examined.[83]

The new design for social protection not only constricts passage into unemployment, disability, and social assistance programs but also substantially reforms what happens to claimants who cross the threshold. Upon entering these programs, recipients are increasingly being segmented according to characteristics, such as age and length of unemployment, that forecast their service needs and employability. In the United States, for example, programs to assist dislocated workers sort through unemployment insurance recipients to distinguish between those who are likely to find work without assistance and those in need of early reemployment services. Each state is developing a Worker Profiling and Reemployment Services system, which uses statistical models based on unemployed workers' characteristics (such as education, job tenure, local unemployment rate, and previous changes in employment) to identify permanently separated workers with reemployment difficulties who would benefit from immediate referral to services. From October 1985 to June 1996, 87 percent of workers who were receiving their first unemployment insurance payments were profiled, and 11 percent of those profiled were referred to services.[84] The Blair government in the United Kingdom has initiated a large-scale welfare-to-work program that offers New Deals tailored to the needs of five main groups: young, unemployed people; long-term unemployed people; single parents; people with disabilities or long-term illnesses; and partners of the unemployed.[85]

In programs for disabled persons, the general trend has been to differentiate recipients more precisely according to degrees of incapacity for work, particularly the potential for part-time employment and work in occupations other than those in which they were originally employed. The 1999 Pension Reform Act in Germany distinguishes among claimants unable to work more than three hours a day; those capable of working between three and six hours a day; and those who can work more than six hours in the general labor market, not necessarily in a job related to their previous occupation.[86] The same trichotomous classification of capacity for work, based on in-depth assessments by specialists, was introduced in New Zealand in the late 1990s.[87] The Dutch Disability Law of 1967 distinguished among seven degrees of disability between 15 percent and 100 percent. The benefit rate ranged from 10 percent of last earnings in the case of 15 percent disability to 80 percent of last earnings in the case of 100 percent disability. But in practice these distinctions were rarely applied with rigor, and claimants were awarded the full benefit. This changed in 1993 with the passage of the Disability Benefit Claims Reduction Act, which introduced compulsory reexaminations with an exacting medical assessment of disability and broadened the interpretation of "suitable employment" that partially disabled people were required to accept. About 60 percent of the reexamined people were judged to have a lower degree of disability than granted in their initial assessment.[88]

The processes of differentiating among claimants are closely linked to what is perhaps the most crucial development in reshaping the daily practices of administrative agencies in social assistance, unemployment, and disability programs—the introduction of quasi-contractual arrangements, sometimes referred to as activation plans. These contracts are formulated by mutual agreement between clients and administrative officials. Activation plans typically specify the clients' obligation and right to participate in education, training, job search, subsidized work, and other activities to improve their chances for paid employment, along with the agency's obligation to provide a range of supports and opportunities aimed at facilitating the movement of clients from welfare to work.

Many countries, including Denmark, Britain, Finland, France, the Netherlands, New Zealand, Sweden, and Australia, have adopted policies that require individualized action plans, which stipulate the steps that will be taken toward reemployment. Tony Eardley sees the traditional entitlement to unemployment benefits in Australia being nullified as eligibility is increasingly dependent on compliance with individual contractual agreements.[89] The unemployment policies in Australia dictate intensive interviews with long-term clients and individualized case management. In an effort to create a broad-based, open market, the case management services are contracted out to local private providers, who compete with one another and with public providers. Believing that the employment-oriented case management process requires a new set of skills for civil servants, the Dutch train "activation officers" to help them better understand their clients' life situations and to work with people who may express hostility under the pressures of activation. In Denmark, a needs-oriented individual plan is drafted and signed by both an official from the labor exchange and the unemployed person. Overall, the advent of individually tailored social contracts in unemployment, disability, and social assistance programs has converted the allocation of benefits from administrative procedures based on the impartiality of social rights framed by bureaucratic formulas to highly individualized and discretionary dispensations based on case-by-case assessments.

Finally, the new dimensions of policy for the unemployed are marked by an array of work-oriented incentives and services. To be sure, the general idea of work incentives in social policy is hardly new. Almost one-quarter of a century ago the 1967 amendments to the U.S. Social Security Act established the Work Incentive Program, which offered supportive services and financial inducements to work. Indeed, one could glance back even further to Edward Bellamy's nineteenth-century classic, *Looking Backward*, about a utopian society that includes an elaborate scheme of status-enhancing work incentives.[90] Thus, efforts to design work incentives have been around for as long as people have thought about the provision of welfare benefits. What distinguishes the current stream of work-oriented measures are the remarkable convergence of liberal and conservative opinion that these incentives are necessary; the assortment of incentives and range of program areas in which they are employed; and the conviction that the proper mix of incentives will produce the desired results, a heightened regard for the efficacy of social engineering.

Work-related incentives fall into four broad categories designed to (1) increase the availability of work; (2) reinforce the capacity for work by upgrading the skills of unemployed people, raising their level of motivation and helping them to overcome tangible barriers to employment; (3) augment the rewards of work efforts; and (4) heighten the cost of refusing to participate in work-related activities. First, there are numerous initiatives to increase the availability of work, both directly through the creation of public employment opportunities and indirectly through tax credits, wage subsidies, and other financial incentives for employers to hire recipients of welfare, disability, and unemployment benefits. In the United States, for example, a business that employs a welfare client at the minimum wage in the state of Florida can be subsidized by the amount of the client's welfare check, and for companies that provide on-the-job training the state offers to reimburse up to 50 percent of a client's wages during the training period. In addition to subsidizing public and private work opportunities, France has invoked the regulatory powers of government to spread the current work by limiting the number of hours in the work week and restricting overtime.

Second, efforts to strengthen the capacity for work draw on a variety of direct measures, such as education, training, and work-experience programs, to enhance practical skills. On the psychological plane there are motivational programs aimed at raising self-esteem and confidence. In Australia, for example, the Special Intervention Program provides therapeutic intervention for the long-term unemployed who do not respond to the standard case management services.[91] In addition to overcoming psychological impediments, work-related incentives include supportive services to help surmount tangible obstacles to employment, such as the need for child care, transportation, and extended medical coverage.

The third category of incentives involves ways to ensure a decent standard of living to very low-paid workers, who are disproportionately represented among those on the track from welfare to work. Several methods have been advanced to "make work pay"—as expressed in the current vernacular—through tax-code reforms. One approach uses tax expenditures to subsidize low-income employment in such schemes as the Working Families Tax Credit in the United Kingdom, the Family Tax Credit in New Zealand, and the Earned Income Tax Credit (EITC) in the United States. Under the EITC, the value of the refundable tax credit rises by 40 cents for every dollar of income until earnings reach $9,390, and it only begins to decline after earnings go above $12,250. Since the EITC is a refundable credit, workers with two or more children who are earning $9,390 to $12,250 (and do not benefit from the normal tax deductions available to middle-income citizens) are eligible for the maximum $3,756 refund from the federal government.[92] The French version of public support for low-paid workers is called a "job bonus." Established in 2001, this subsidy is paid by tax authorities to those earning less than 140 percent of the minimum wage, adjusted for household income and number of dependents.[93]

Subsidies such as the EITC are a way for governments to mediate between the individual and the market, providing an adequate income to those who work by topping up earnings with a social transfer. These income tax–related benefits may also help to shrink the underground economy since they offer an incentive for people being paid off the books to report their income. Although tax credits can be seen as a response to the market's failure to provide an adequate standard of living for workers with families, they can also create a form of market failure by oversubsidizing low-wage jobs—dampening political pressures to raise the minimum wage when an increase would not reduce the level of profit in low-wage occupations to the point that many jobs would be lost. In France, the unions favored a rise in the minimum wage rather than the job bonus for low-income earners.[94] Political tensions between the EITC and minimum-wage legislation were also evident in the United States.[95] Here the EITC, combined with the value of food stamp benefits, lifts the income of minimum-wage earners in a family of three to about 20 percent above the federal poverty level. However, raising the wage rate about 75 percent from the $5.15 federal minimum to $9.00 an hour returns only a 16 percent increase in income because the other subsidies decline.[96]

If we look at taxes from another angle, low-paid workers' take-home pay can be increased by reducing the effective tax rate on their earned income—discounting or eliminating, for example, social security taxes. In addition, the financial rewards for welfare recipients who are moving into the paid labor force (and facing withdrawal of their social benefits) can be raised by adjustments that slow the rate at which benefits are withdrawn as earned income increases. This approach, however, spawns perverse incentives that tempt people currently at work in low-paid positions to leave their jobs long enough to establish eligibility for social benefits.[97] Slowing the withdrawal rate of welfare benefits can also encourage people to move into part-time jobs, which yield the best combination of earned income and social assistance, while creating a disincentive for full-time employment or, in a more positive sense, an incentive for part-time work—if part-time employment is seen as a desirable way to spread jobs among the population and increase the volume of working hours.

Then the issue arises: how many hours constitute part-time work that would qualify for benefits? In Europe many of those who are officially counted as part-time workers are employed 30 to 34 hours a week.[98] Finally, another way to elevate the rewards of work vis-à-vis social benefits is to cut the level of social benefits.

The fourth category of incentives, those that heighten the cost of nonparticipation in work-related activities, is a tactful way of describing sanctions. Almost every program to activate the unemployed includes a codicil that imposes some degree of financial penalty on those who might reject fair offers of work, training, or community service. Even in Bellamy's Utopia, mild incentives to work were backed by sanctions: those who persistently refused to do their duty were sentenced to solitary confinement on bread and water.[99]

The policy options outlined above pose an important choice about the degree to which work-oriented incentives emphasize what might be termed strategies of public investment versus private inducement in relation to both individuals and the market. As they bear on individuals, public investment strategies seek to improve chances for employment by providing education and training programs, typically construed as the basic means to enhance human capital. There is an assumption here that education and training enhance human capital more than it might be enhanced by immediate employment, which even in the simplest jobs usually involves some kind of training and development of work skills, like dress codes, customer relations, and punctuality. In contrast, private inducements focus on creating tax benefits (as well as financial penalties) designed to encourage movement into the labor force at the individual's current level of skill, which exerts no upward pressure on wages. Of course, the option between education and work need not be a zero-sum choice since many people are able to attend school part-time while working. In the United States, for example, almost 40 million employed people participated in work-related adult education classes in 1995.[100] As these strategies bear on the market, public investment schemes create new jobs for the unemployed through public works, whereas private inducements rely on tax credits and other benefits and sanctions aimed at encouraging private enterprises to hire welfare recipients. But the results of these policies do not always comport with their intentions. Public works can morph into contrived jobs that add little value and even undermine morale, and state-subsidized private employment can end up paying for jobs that otherwise would have been filled without public subsidies.

Implementation: To the Letter of the Law?

To say that this surge of work-oriented policies has remolded the basic legislative framework for social protection of unemployed people, is not to imply that the implementation of these measures has been smooth or everywhere the same. The course of implementation must sail a difficult passage between the Scylla of defining what constitutes work and work-related activities and the Charybdis of deciding what to do about participants who fail to develop or fulfill activation plans. The first challenge is how to determine what ultimately qualifies as work and work-related activities. This is no trivial matter since eligibility for social benefits increasingly requires recipients to engage in work-related activities. Is voluntary community service a work-related activity? Although one might assign vocational education to the work-related category, what about the more general liberal arts education? How should self-employment be viewed, particularly for artists, writers, and street corner musicians whose work may generate little or no income? Should caring for children, the elderly, and infirm relatives qualify as a form of work or active participation?[101] How should part-time work be weighed in relation to unemployment benefits? How long does one count looking for work as a work-related activity?

One of the debates in the United States concerns the difference between regular public employment and on-the-job training by performing community service. At issue here is the discrepancy between the levels of compensation for participating in a program that requires community service in exchange for a welfare grant and the salary received by city employees for rendering essentially the same service. For example, more than 1400 workfare participants in San Francisco performed such work as janitorial duties in public buildings, sweeping city streets, and cleaning public transit vehicles for grants that amounted to less than one-half the hourly wage paid to union employees who were sometimes engaged side-by-side in similar jobs. Welfare advocates claimed that the city was taking advantage of needy applicants, forcing them to work at below union scale. City officials responded that the workfare recipients were doing community service in a program designed to teach basic work habits: showing up on time, working in a team, and accepting supervision. The issue, in part, revolves on the nature of the activity and the length of time a recipient spends in the program. That is, after a year or so of sweeping city streets, one would not expect much more to be gained in the way of developing basic work habits (or sweeping skills).

The debate in California took place within the context of a robust economy with the lowest unemployment rates in more than a decade. Questions about the meaning of work and the place of public employment schemes take on even greater weight in societies with high unemployment and future growth of joblessness, where the public sector may find itself the employer of last resort. In Italy, "socially useful jobs" created by public agencies were supposed to avoid routine activities and place the unemployed in special innovative projects, dealing with, for instance, environmental protection and urban renewal. However, in practice, most of those enrolled in these publicly subsidized jobs ended up engaged in routine paper-pushing administrative activities.[102] A similar issue appears in Denmark, where unemployment was halved from 12 percent in 1993 to 6 percent in 1998; but during this period only 1,000 jobs were added in the private sector compared to 15,000 jobs in the public sector.[103] One criticism of the Danish success is that too many of these public jobs leave participants stranded in artificial work, without access to regular employment in the private sector.[104]

Also at issue is the interpretation of part-time work. Some see this trend as a problem of substandard employment, which should not be promoted by social policies. Others argue that for many it is a positive choice, representing a functional adaptation to the family life cycle and educational needs, which subordinates work to other life interests. In either case, the rise of part-time work accounted for most of the additional jobs created during the 1980s in the northern states of the European Community; these positions were held disproportionately by women.[105] In the Netherlands, part-time employment has climbed from 5 percent to 37 percent of total employment over the last 25 years—becoming in the process a " 'normal' form of gainful activity."[106] Reading the decline in unemployment from a high of 14 percent in the summer of 1983 to under 3 percent in the winter of 2000—the so-called Dutch miracle—as largely a redistribution from full-time to part-time work, Uwe Becker deems the record "still impressive, but less miraculous."[107]

Once work and other gainful activities are defined, the question arises of what to do about participants who refuse to engage in these activities. (A related question of what to do about recipients of public aid who may lack the basic capacity for work in modern society is not yet as salient as the issue of how to activate the recalcitrant unemployed.)[108] By their very nature, contracts and activation plans that specify clients' obligations provide tangible criteria for monitoring their behavior and for imposing sanctions when this behavior is not consistent with administrative rules. But sometimes in moving from policy to practice, the plans themselves do not materialize according to legislative intent. Case-by-case contractual agreements on activation plans have expanded the sphere of administrative discretion, leaving "street-level bureaucrats" considerable room for shaping pol-

icy through local interpretation.[109] In France, for example, the legislative requirement for a *contrat d'insertion*, an agreement between
claimants and their local authorities (specifying the work and
training-related activities that would be undertaken by claimants),
was a major innovation of the Revenu Minimum d'Insertion (RMI)
program. It appears, however, that local officials are not too keen on
drawing up these contracts. Thus, since the program's inception, almost 50 percent of RMI beneficiaries have not signed a *contrat
d'insertion*, and only 5 percent to 6 percent have been sanctioned for
noncompliance.[110]

Even when activation contracts are drawn up and signed, participants are rarely sanctioned to the letter of the law for failure to comply
with the agreement. In the Netherlands, research indicates that in the
majority of cases, public assistance recipients who fail to fulfill their
part of the activation contract are not penalized by a reduction of
benefits. Seeking to maximize the rate of employment in their caseloads, activation officers concentrate their efforts on clients who are
cooperative and appear likely to profit from supportive services. The
imposition of penalties is avoided as a costly and troublesome process. Supervisors exert little pressure from above to assess penalties
because, as Piet Keizer observes, they are not motivated to buy costly
units of justice that require distinguishing between an impartial administration of tough policies and subjective assessments of civil servants who may be biased or having a bad day.[111] There is some evidence, however, that in the realm of unemployment insurance,
sanctions are being delivered more frequently to clients who exercise
insufficient efforts to find work.[112]

With time limits for the receipt of welfare benefits and firm work
requirements, the United States is widely perceived as having the
stiffest sanctions on the books and, perhaps, the firmest resolve to
apply them according to the letter of the law. Yet even here the data
suggest that either compliance is remarkably high or the administration of sanctions is not quite as pronounced as the laws prescribe—
laws that vary considerably among the states.[113] According to figures
released by the General Accounting Office, in an average month in
1998 less than 1 percent of the families receiving public assistance
had their entire benefit cut for failure to comply with welfare rules,
and slightly more than 4 percent of the families had their cash assistance partially reduced under sanction policies.[114] Along similar lines,
Italy's law 223 of 1991 introduced express limits on eligibility for
unemployment benefits and their duration. However, in the process
of implementation, the new measures that bind the unemployed to a
more active orientation have been substantially loosened, if not completely unfastened. Despite the attenuation that marked the law's

course from policy to practice, Valeria Fargion notes that it represents an important change in the framework of Italian social policy, the implications of which have not yet been fully realized.[115]

Recommodification of Labor

Whatever slippage has occurred in practice, steering people back to work as soon as possible has become the guiding principle for the social protection of the unemployed. The advent of work-oriented policies represents a reformulation of income maintenance programs, which marks a notable break with the immediate past. Analyzing welfare-to-work initiatives in Great Britain, the Netherlands, and the United States, Dan Finn concludes that despite differences in approach these countries "are engaged in major organizational and programmatic reforms to 'activate' their benefit systems. The governments are institutionalizing the assumption that *all* people of working age who receive benefits should take jobs if they are able to do so."[116] Not only that, but the range of jobs they are expected to be available for—the definition of "suitable employment"—has broadened well beyond the occupational status and functional borders of the previous position held. Overall, this development signifies a move toward the recommodification of labor—which some would interpret as a pivotal shift in the conventional welfare state paradigm based on a social democratic model.

This movement inverts the *de*commodification of labor, predicated on policies that emancipate citizens from dependency on wage labor, a principle firmly identified as one of the preeminent attributes of the modern social democratic regimes of Nordic welfare states. One crucial dimension of decommodification policies involves the rules that govern entry to and exit from programs that provide income supports. Gosta Esping-Andersen explains that "a program can be seen to harbor greater de-commodification potential if access is easy, and if rights to an adequate standard of living are guaranteed regardless of previous employment record, performance, needs-test or financial contribution."[117] The duration of benefits and the extent to which they replace normal earnings also affect how quickly recipients will be driven back to work.

In judging the significance of work-oriented measures, the ways in which Nordic welfare states have experienced these policies and the interpretations given to this experience are instructive. Norway may be taken as a case in point. An analysis of eight programs serving the unemployed confirms that the main trends in the 1990s have been toward tightening eligibility, reducing the duration of benefits, and introducing behavioral requirements that condition the right to benefits on work-related activities—all of which reinforce what Norwegians term the "work approach" to welfare policy. Only the level of benefits has remained constant in most programs and has increased in two programs, which at the same time have reduced their duration.[118] But does this change qualify as a qualitatively new development or merely a consistent extension of the Nordic model? The question is fraught with political and ideological implications.

Let us assume for a moment that policies initiated in Norway over the last decade, which emphasize the citizen's obligation to be an active participant in the labor market while introducing work-oriented rules and regulations that firmly press in that direction, embody a movement toward the recommodification of labor, which represents a qualitative break with past measures. In that case, one can no longer assert that a policy emphasis on the decommodification of labor is one of the essential distinguishing features of the social democratic–Nordic model at the dawn of the twenty-first century. Indeed, when seen as a qualitative break with past policies, the shift toward work-oriented initiatives might well lead one to conclude that the Nordic model of the welfare state is being reshaped in line with the emerging paradigm of the enabling state. On the other hand, if the shift to work-oriented policies is interpreted as a consistent extension of the social democratic–Nordic model, the presumed emphasis on the decommodification of labor was highly overrated and this model retains its integrity and continuity (while relinquishing one of the dominant characteristics that lent a socialist flavor that distinguished its blend of policies).

Which of these explanations prevails? When assessing the significance of the contemporary wave of work-oriented reforms, there is a tendency among many, though not all, scholars of the Nordic welfare state to tread a fine line between the interpretation of a qualitative change and a consistent extension of the Nordic model. As noted earlier, Loftager's analysis marks activation measures in Denmark as a clear break with the past, representing a paradigm shift in welfare policy thinking.[119] In contrast, in examining the Norwegian experience, for example, Espen Dahl and Jon Dropping observe that policy reforms in the 1990s generated many small adjustments, all in the same direction, the sum of which lend support to the "overarching ideology of the Work Approach" and "reflect a committed political will to change the profile of the programs and emphasize the obligations of the citizens." But does fostering the ideology of the work approach and altering the profile of programs for social protection of the unemployed constitute a major transformation? Dahl and Dropping interpret these developments as neither a qualitatively new approach nor an immediate extension of current policies—but rather as a return to first principles of the Nordic welfare state articulated 40 to 50 years ago. "The Work Approach of the 1990s," they explain, "amounts to a resurrection of ideas which served as ideological underpinnings of the legislation in the 1950s and 1960s."[120] Anders Nordlund submits a parallel interpretation of the course of social policy in Denmark, Finland, Norway, and Sweden. To the question of whether the frequent reforms in recent decades have "pushed Nordic social policy qualitatively in the direction of an achievement model," Nordlund responds, "yes in the sense that there are indications of an increased emphasis on labour market performance in rules governing income protection." He goes on to explain, however, that this apparently new direction does not signify so much a break with the tradition of the Nordic model as a return to its earlier roots. "Thus, the tendency toward an increased emphasis on labour market performance must be regarded as a strengthening of an old intention rather than a fundamental shift away from the overarching goals of Nordic social policy."[121]

How do these explanations of the original intentions of promoting active labor market participation square with the view that the Nordic model has been distinguished by a policy emphasis that champions the decommodification of labor?[122] The answer may be that it depends on the time frame under consideration. The decommodification thesis gained considerable force and academic legitimacy from Esping-Andersen's empirical analysis, based largely on comparative data that reported the status of welfare programs in 1980. During the period from 1960 to 1980, often referred to as the golden era of welfare state expansion, government spending on social welfare in the Western democracies took a dramatic leap (as noted in chapter 1). In the course of this growth, enlarged rights to social benefits increased the protection of the unemployed through an array of income supports that were easily accessed, had a lengthy duration, and made limited demands on recipients. The decommodification of labor ocurred to varying degrees in all of the industrialized welfare states—a development led by the Nordic countries (according to Esping-Andersen's analysis). It is difficult to judge the extent to which this development was a deviation from original principles that supported the obligation to work or an overextension of good intentions to protect workers from being held in bondage by the market. In either case, at the time there was no discernable outcry that the welfare state (in Nordic countries and elsewhere) had gone off course. In the 1990s, the trend toward policies in support of decommodification has been reversed—a development led by the Anglo-American countries. Whether this turn of events is described, in Dahl and Dropping's words, as "an effort to reshape the welfare state in accordance with its original principles" set down 40 to 50 years ago or as the transformation of the welfare state, the evidence points to the emergence of a new institutional framework for social protection that rests, in part, on the promotion of work.[123]

NOTES

1. ISSA, "Developments and Trends in Social Security 1978–89," *International Social Security Review*, 3 (1989), 258; OECD, *The Future of Social Protection* (Paris: OECD, 1988), p. 24.

2. David Kalisch, "The Active Society," *Social Security Journal*, August 1991; OECD, "Editorial: The Path to Full Employment: Structural Adjustments for an Active Society," *Employment Outlook*, July 1989.

3. See, for example, Michael Novak, "Welfare's New Consensus: Sending the Right Signal," *Public Interest*, 89 (Fall 1987), 26–30; Robert Greenstein, "Cutting Benefits vs. Changing Behavior," *Public Welfare*, 50:2 (1992), 22–23.

4. Staffan Marklund, "The Decomposition of Social Policy in Sweden," *Scandinavian Journal of Social Welfare*, 1:1 (July 1992).

5. Jorn Loftager, "Solidarity and Universality in the Danish Welfare State—Empirical Remarks and Theoretical Interpretations," paper prepared for the 7th BIEN International Congress 1998, Amsterdam, September 10–12, 1998.

6. Per Jensen, "Activation of the Unemployed in Denmark Since the Early 1990s. Welfare or Workfare?" Centre for Comparative Welfare State Studies Working Paper No. 1/1999, p. 14, Department of Economics, Politics, and Public Administration, Aalborg University, Aalborg Denmark, 1999.

7. Jacob Torfing, "From the Keynesian Welfare State to a Schumpeterian Workfare Regime—the Offensive Neo-Statist Case of Denmark," paper presented at the 9th International Conference on Socio-Economics, Montreal, July 5–7, 1997.

8. Ibid.

9. Piet Keizer, "From Welfare to Work Fare: Dutch Policies in the Nineties," in Neil Gilbert and Rebecca Van Voorhis, eds., *Activating the Unemployed: A Comparative Appraisal of Work-Oriented Policies* (New Brunswick, N.J.: Transaction Publishers, 2001).

10. U.S. General Accounting Office, *Welfare Reform: Assessing the Effectiveness of Various Welfare-to-Work Approaches* (Washington, D.C.: U.S. General Accounting Office, 1999).

11. Ken Judge, "Evaluating Welfare to Work in the United Kingdom," in Neil Gilbert and Rebecca Van Voorhis, eds., *Activating the Unemployed: A Comparative Appraisal of Work-Oriented Policies* (New Brunswick, N.J.: Transaction 2001).

12. This view was elaborated in the early 1970s in William Ryan's popular book *Blaming the Victim* (New York: Random House, 1971). By the 1990s, a more critical view was developing on the claims of victimhood; see, for example, Charles Sykes, *A Nation of Victims: The Decay of the American Character* (New York: St. Martin, 1992).

13. For further discussion of this development in the United States, see Neil Gilbert, *Welfare Justice: Restoring Social Equity* (New Haven, Conn.: Yale University Press, 1995).

14. Charles Murray, *Losing Ground: American Social Policy 1950–1980* (New York: Basic Books, 1984).

15. Lawrence Mead, *Beyond Entitlement: The Social Obligations of Citizenship* (New York: Free Press, 1986). This book was among the most influential works that initiated the social rights vs. responsibilities debate; see also Mary Ann Glendon, *Rights Talk* (New York: Free Press, 1991).

16. Amitai Etzioni, "What Community? Whose Responsiveness?" *Responsive Community*, 1:2 (1991), 5–8; for a delineation of the communitarian principles, see "Responsive Communitarian Platform," *Responsive Community*, 2:1 (1992), 4–20.

17. Aksel Hatland, "The Changing Balance Between Incentives and Economic Security in Scandinavian Unemployment Benefit Schemes," paper presented at the International Social Security Association Conference on Social Security, p. 6, Jerusalem, January 25–28, 1998.

18. Romke van der Veen, "An Organized Future? A Review and Analysis of the Reform of the Dutch Welfare State, 1985–1997," paper presented at the International Social Security Association Conference on Social Security, Jerusalem, January 25–28, 1998.

19. Dick Vink, "Will Wisconsin Works (W2) Fit into the Dutch 'Poldermodel'?" *Focus*, 19:3 (Summer–Fall 1998), 41–48.

20. Espen Dahl and Jon Anders Dropping, "The Norwegian Work Approach in the 1990s: Rhetoric and Reform," in Neil Gilbert and Rebecca VanVoorhis, eds., *Activating the Unemployed: A Comparative Appraisal of Work-Oriented Policies* (New Brunswick, N.J.: Transaction Publishers, 2001).

21. *Green Paper on Welfare Reform* (London: HMSO, 1998).

22. For an excellent discussion of the differences between social benefits for the poor, which are for immediate consumption, and benefits for the middle classes, which contribute to the accumulation of assets, see Michael Sherraden, *Assets and the Poor: A New American Welfare Policy* (Armonk, N.Y.: M. E. Sharpe, 1991).

23. The establishment of the Center for Analysis of Social Exclusion at the London School of Economics and Political Science in 1997 guarantees a proliferation of research into and publication on this problem.

24. Jean-Claude Barbier and Bruno Theret, "Welfare-to-Work or Work-to-Welfare: The French Case," in Neil Gilbert and Rebecca Van Voorhis, eds., *Activating the Unemployed: A Comparative Appraisal of Work-Oriented Policies* (New Brunswick, N.J.: Transaction Publishers, 2001).

25. Bernard Enjolras and Ivar Lodemel, "Activation of Social Protection in France and Norway: New Divergence in a Time of Convergence," in *Comparing Social Welfare Systems in Nordic Europe and France: Copenhagen Conference* (Paris: MiRe-DRESS, Research Mission—The Centre of Research, Studies, and Statistics, Ministry of Employment and Solidarity, 2000), vol. 4, p. 484.

26. Robert Holzmann and Steen Jorgensen, "Social Risk Management: A New Conceptual Framework for Social Protection and Be-

yond," Social Protection Discussion Paper No. 0006, p. 21, World Bank, Washington, D.C., February 2000.

27. Under the Aid to Families with Dependent Children's program, state departments of public welfare were required to define a level of income maintenance support that would provide a decent standard of living for AFDC recipients, but few if any departments supplied welfare grants at the defined levels of adequacy. See Neil Gilbert, Harry Specht, and Paul Terrell, *Dimensions of Social Welfare Policy*, 3rd ed. (Upper Saddle River, N.J.: Prentice Hall, 1993), pp. 54–55.

28. In the 1960s, Michael Harrington's *The Other America: Poverty in the United States* (New York: Macmillan, 1962) was followed by a flurry of works on the culture, functions and incidence of poverty; within a few years two major anthologies, both entitled *Poverty in America*, along with other collections on *Poverty as a Public Issue*, *New Perspectives on Poverty*, *Poverty in Affluence*, and *Poverty Amid Affluence*, were added to the literature.

29. For an example of the path-breaking research on the dynamics of welfare use conducted by Bane and Ellwood, see Mary Jo Bane and David Ellwood, *Welfare Realities: From Rhetoric to Reform* (Cambridge, Mass.: Harvard University Press, 1994).

30. An International Labour Organization report suggests that the concept of social exclusion can be seen as a replacement for poverty, which provides a multidimensional view of the processes of impoverishment—a concept that "points particularly to the links between poverty and employment, and the ways in which particular types of citizenship rights enable social and occupational participation." International Institute for Labour Studies, *Social Exclusion and Anti-Poverty Strategies* (Geneva: International Labour Organization, 1996).

31. Christoph Badelt, "The Role of NPOs in Policies to Combat Social Exclusion," Social Protection Discussion Paper No. 9912, World Bank, Washington, D.C., 1999.

32. Robert Goodin, Bruce Headey, Ruud Muffels, and Henk-Jan Dirven, *The Real Worlds of Welfare Capitalism* (Cambridge: Cambridge University Press, 1999).

33. Thus, for example, in the opening chapter of A. B. Atkinson and John Hills, eds., *Exclusion, Employment, and Opportunity* (London: Centre for Analysis of Social Exclusion, London School of Economics, 1998), Tony Atkinson asserts, "Social exclusion is not just concerned with unemployment." Yet with three of the five chapters that follow in this volume devoted to issues of labor market flexibility, skills acquisition, and employment and social cohesion, one might guage the centrality of unemployment to analyses of social exclusion.

34. Although public assistance covers additional categories of welfare recipients—the blind, aged, and disabled—assistance to families with dependent children is the largest and most controversial program.

35. James Leiby, *History of Social Welfare and Social Work in the United States* (New York: Columbia University Press, 1978).

36. For a first-person account of these events by the executive director of the staff of the Committee on Economic Security, which drafted the Social Security Act, see Edwin E. Witte, *Development of the Social Security Act* (Madison: University of Wisconsin Press, 1962).

37. U.S. Census Bureau, *Statistical Abstract of the United States: 1981* (Washington, D.C.: U.S. Government Printing Office, 1981).

38. U.S. Department of Health, Education, and Welfare, *Social Security Bulletin* (Washington, D.C.: U.S. Government Printing Office, 1974).

39. U.S. Census Bureau, *Statistical Abstract of the United States: 1998* (Washington, D.C.: U.S. Government Printing Office, 1998).

40. U.S. Department of Health and Human Services, *Indicators of Welfare Dependence and Well-Being: Interim Report to Congress* (Washington, D.C.: U.S. Department of Health and Human Services, 1996); "Data File," *Welfare to Work*, 6:16 (August 25, 1997).

41. Overall, 71.1 percent of married women with children under 17 years of age were in the labor force in 1997. U.S. Census Bureau, *Statistical Abstract of the United States, 1998* (Washington, D.C.: U.S. Government Printing Office, 1998).

42. Although the 1962 amendments also provided for other forms of service such as homemakers and foster-home care, the provision of casework by a trained social worker was the centerpiece of efforts to reduce welfare. For a detailed analysis of the 1962 and 1967 amendments, see Martha Derthick, *Uncontrollable Spending for Social Service Grants* (Washington, D.C.: Brookings Institution, 1975).

43. A different view of welfare recipients prevailed up through the 1950s, a time in which they were considered to be "victims of external circumstances such as unemployment, disability, or death of the family breadwinner," who "needed to be relieved—not treated or changed." See Davis McEntire and Joanne Haworth, "Two Functions of Public Welfare: Income Maintenance and Social Services," *Social Work*, 12:1 (January 1967), 24–25.

44. Gilbert Steiner, *The State of Welfare* (Washington, D.C.: Brookings Institution, 1971); Lawrence Podell, "Attrition of First-Line Social Service Staff," *Welfare in Review*, 5:1 (January 1967), 9–14.

45. Joel Handler and Ellen Hollingsworth, "The Administration of Social Services and the Structure of Dependency," *Social Service Review*, 43:4 (December 1969), 409–14.

46. Gilbert et al., *Dimensions of Social Welfare Policy*.

47. Steiner, *State of Welfare*, p. 25.

48. Derthick, *Uncontrollable Spending*.

49. The program was dubbed WIN because the right acronym for the Work Incentive Program—WIP—had an unseemly sound.

50. Sar Levitan and Robert Taggart III, *Social Experimentation and Manpower Policy: The Rhetoric and the Reality* (Baltimore: Johns Hopkins Press, 1971, p. 53.

51. Mary Bryna Sunger, "Generating Employment for AFDC Mothers," *Social Service Review*, 58:1 (March 1984), 25–32.

52. For a review of the findings on these demonstrations, see Judith Gueron, *Reforming Welfare with Work*, Ford Foundation Project on Social Welfare and the American Future Occasional Paper 2 (New York: Ford Foundation, 1987). The extent to which these studies contributed to the development of the Family Support Act is examined by one of the program's architects; see Erica Baum, "When the Witch Doctors Agree: The Family Support Act and Social Science Research," *Journal of Policy Analysis and Management*, 10:4 (Fall 1991), 603–15.

53. Beyond requirements and incentives for work-training and job search activities, the act imposed other regulations aimed at tightening social controls and balancing social obligations and the social right to welfare. Teenage mothers with children under the age of 3 were required to complete their high school education or to acquire a high school equivalency diploma; single mothers applying for AFDC were obliged to help establish paternity in order to hold absent fathers accountable for child-support payments; unwed teenage mothers had to live with a parent or other adult relative or reside in a foster home or some other adult-supervised living arrangement.

54. U.S. General Accounting Office, *Welfare to Work: State Programs Have Tested Some of the Proposed Reforms*, (Washington, D.C.: U.S. General Accounting Office, 1995). Although the differences between experimental and control groups were statistically significant, they were not usually substantively large.

55. Michael Wiseman, "Welfare Reform in Wisconsin," *Poverty Research News*, 1:3 (Summer 1997), 13–15.

56. Eugene Smolensky, Erik Evenhouse, and Siobhan Reilly, *Welfare Reform a Primer in 12 Questions* (San Francisco: Public Policy Institute, 1997).

57. Rachel Swarms, "Welfare Family Advocates, Once Allies Become Rivals," *New York Times*, March 27, 1997, p. A1.

58. Sheldon Danziger, Robert Moffitt, and LaDonna Pavetti, *Is Welfare Reform Working? The Impact of Economic Growth and Policy Changes: A Congressional Briefing* (Washington, D.C.: Consortium of Social Science Associations, 1998)

59. Douglas Besharov and Peter Germanis, "Welfare Reform—Four Years Later," *Public Interest*, 140 (Summer 2000), 17–35.

60. Julie Strawn, *Beyond Job Search or Basic Education: Rethinking the Role of Skills in Welfare Reform* (Washington, D.C.: Center for Law and Social Policy, 1998).

61. In a study of welfare recipients in Illinois between 1988 and 1990, Edin and Jencks found that almost 80 percent of their sample worked (in both legal and illegal activities) without reporting their income. Kathryn Edin and Christopher Jencks, "Welfare," in Christopher Jencks, *Rethinking Social Policy* (Cambridge, Mass.: Harvard University Press, 1992), pp. 204–36. Other studies reveal significant employment rates, though not quite as high as in the Edin and Jencks work: for example, Maureen Marcenko and Jay Fagan, "Welfare to Work: What Are the Obstacles?" *Journal of Sociology and Social Welfare*, 70:3 (1996), report 27 percent; Dave O'Neill and June O' Neill, *Lessons for Welfare Reform: An Analysis of the AFDC Caseload and Past Welfare-to-Work Programs* (Kalamazoo, Mich.: Upjohn Institute for Employment Research, 1997), report 49.4 percent; and Kathleen Harris, "Work and Welfare Among Single Mothers in Poverty," *American Journal of Sociology*, 99:2 (1993), reports 51 percent. As illustrated in the following table, Kathryn Edin and Laura Lein, "Work, Welfare, and Single Mothers' Economic Survival Strategies," *American Sociological Review*, 62:2 (1997), provide strong corroborating evidence of large discrepancies between the amount of work AFDC recipients reported to their local welfare offices in four cities and the rates of employment revealed through in-depth interviews.

Percentage of Welfare Mothers Involved in Various Work Activities
in Four U.S. Cities.

	Boston	Chicago	Charleston	San Antonio
Total	44	60	36	41
Reported work	2	2	9	6
Unreported work	36	52	32	35
Underground work	7	19	2	3

Note: Percentages for subcategories will not sum to total percentages because of mothers engaged in multiple work activities.

Source: Kathryn Edin and Laura Lein, "Work, Welfare, and Single Mothers' Economic Survival Strategies," American Sociological Review, 62:2 (1997), table 3.

62. Robert Lerman, "Carrots and Sticks: How Does the New U.S. Income Support System Encourage Single Parents to Work?" Paper presented at the 2nd International Conference on Social Security, Jerusalem, January 25–28, 1998.

63. Besharov and Germanis, "Welfare Reform."

64. Tony Eardley, "From Safety Nets to Spring Boards? Social Assistance and Work Incentives in the OECD Countries," Social Policy Review, 8 (1996), 265–85.

65. Torfing, "From the Keynesian Welfare State." As this reform took shape, more than half of the activation opportunities involved participation in educational programs.

66. Vink, "Wisconsin Works."

67. Romke van der Veen and Willem Trommel, "Managed Liberalization of the Dutch Welfare State," paper presented at the SASE Conference on Rethinking the Welfare State, Montreal, July 5–7, 1997.

68. Merrien explains that the concept of social insertion was invented to forge a consensus between French politicians who supported an unconditional right to a minimum income and those who favored some form of workfare policy. Francois X. Merrien, "Reforming French Social Policies: Between Solidarity and Rhetorics," paper delivered at the 1999 Annual Meeting of the American Political Science Association, Atlanta, May 2–5, 1999.

69. Mary Collins, "A Guaranteed Minimum Income in France," Social Policy and Administration, 42:2 (1990); Barbier and Theret, "Welfare-to-Work or Work-to-Welfare."

70. Sven Hort, "From a Generous to a Stingy Welfare State? Targeting in the Swedish Welfare System in the 1990s," in Neil Gilbert, ed., Targeting Social Benefits: International Perspectives and Trends (New Brunswick, N.J.: Transaction Publishers, 2001).

71. Here, too, one finds a changing discourse. In Australia, for example, passive "unemployment benefits" became a "job search allowance."

72. Jef Van Langendonck, "The Social Protection of the Unemployed," International Social Security Review, 50:4 (1997), 29–43.

73. Between 1980 and 1996, the average duration of unemployment benefits ranged from 13.2 to 16.2 weeks and the benefits ranged from 36.6 percent to 34.5 percent of the weekly wage. U.S. Census Bureau, Statistical Abstract of the United States: 1998, p. 386.

74. Some evidence indicates that restrictive measures introduced in the United Kingdom and the Netherlands have resulted in a shift of public expenditures from insurance-related unemployment benefits to social assistance. See Mark Knight, "Restrictive Measures in Unemployment Schemes; Impact on Other Social Security Schemes," in *Harmonizing Economic Developments and Social Needs: ISSA Technical Conferences, 1997, 1998* (Geneva: ISSA, 1998).

75. For a more detailed review of these changes, see Mary Daly, "Welfare States Under Pressure: Cash Benefits in European Welfare States Over the Last Ten Years," *Journal of European Social Policy*, 7: 2 (May 1997), 128–46; Hatland, "Changing Balance Between Incentives and Economic Security."

76. Ross Mackay, "Work Oriented Reforms: New Directions in New Zealand," in Neil Gilbert and Rebecca Van Voorhis, eds., *Activating the Unemployed: A Comparative Analysis of Work-Oriented Policies* (New Brunswick, N.J.: Transaction Publishers, 2001).

77. Over the last decade, almost every industrialized country has experienced steep growth in their disability rolls, often among young workers. For an analysis of this development and the policy responses, see Christine Kuptsch and Ilene Zeiter, "Public Disability Programs Under New Complex Pressures," in Dalmer Hoskins, Donate Dobbernack, and Christiane Kuptsch, eds., *Social Security at the Dawn of the 21st Century: Topical Issues and New Approaches* (New Brunswick, N.J.: Transaction Publishers, 2000).

78. Dahl and Dropping, "Norwegian Work Approach."

79. Organization for Economic Cooperation and Development, *Economic Surveys: The Netherlands* (Paris: OECD, 1991).

80. Reink Prins, *Sickness Absence in Belgium, Germany (FR) and the Netherlands: A Comparative Study* (Amsterdam: Netherlands Institute for the Working Environment, 1990).

81. Piet Keizer, "Targeting Strategies in the Netherlands: Demand Management and Cost Constraint," in Neil Gilbert, ed., *Targeting Social Benefits: International Perspectives and Trends* (New Brunswick, N.J.: Transaction Publishers, 2000).

82. Although the number of recipients increased, the disability rate remained fairly constant when adjusted for the level of disablement. See Sabine Geurts, Michiel Kompier, and Robert Grundemann, "Curing the Dutch Disease? Sickness Absence and Work Disability in the Netherlands," *International Social Security Review*, 53:4 (October–December 2000), 79–101.

83. Kuptsch and Zeitzer, "Public Disability Programs."

84. Stephen Wander, "Early Reemployment for Dislocated Workers in the U.S.," *International Social Security Review*, 50:4 (1997), 95–112.

85. For a more detailed assessment of these New Deals, see Judge, "Evaluating Welfare to Work."

86. Kuptsch and Zeiter, "Public Disability Programs."

87. Mackay, "Work-Oriented Reforms."

88. Keizer, "Targeting Strategies in the Netherlands."

89. Tony Eardley, "New Relations of Welfare in the Contracting State: The Marketisation of Services for the Unemployed in Australia," Social Policy Research Center Discussion Paper 79, SPRC, University of New South Wales, Sydney, Australia, 1997.

90. Edward Bellamy, *Looking Backward* (New York: New American Library, [1888] 1960).

91. Eardley, "New Relations of Welfare." A study of psychological services in Britain suggests that cognitive-behavioral therapy may have beneficial effects in helping the long-term unemployed find work. See J. D. Proudfoot, J. Guest, J. Carson, G. Dunn, and J. Gray, "Effect of Cognitive-Behaviorial Therapy Training on Job-Finding Among the Long-Term Unemployed," *Lancet*, 305 (July 12, 1997), 96–100.

92. In addition to the federal program, which treats all working families the same regardless of local taxes and costs of living, seven states have initiated refundable state EITCs, which are calculated as a percentage of the federal credit and range from 10 percent to 43 percent of the federal EITC. Nicholas Johnson and Ed Lazere, "State Earned Income Tax Credits," *Poverty Research News*, Winter 1999, pp. 23–25.

93. "France: Help the Poor," *Economist*, January 20, 2001, pp. 30–31.

94. Ibid.

95. For a discussion of these tensions, see Christopher Howard, *The Hidden Welfare State: Tax Expenditures and Social Policy in the United States* (Princeton, N.J.: Princeton University Press, 1997), pp. 150–52.

96. Norma Coe, Gregory Acs, Robert Lerman, and Keith Watson, *Does Work Pay? A Summary of the Work Incentives under TANF* (Washington, D.C.: Urban Institute, 1998).

97. Mickey Kaus, "The Work Ethic State," *New Republic*, July 7, 1986, pp. 27–28, describes a classic case of a worker who left her job to go on welfare in order to receive child-care and health insurance benefits when she returned to work.

98. For a breakdown of how definitions of part-time work vary within and between countries, see Catherine Hakim, "A Sociological Perspective on Part-Time Work," in Hans-Peter Blossfeld and Catherine Hakim, eds., *Between Equalization and Marginalization: Women Working Part-Time in Europe and the United States of America* (Oxford: Oxford University Press, 1997).

99. Bellamy, *Looking Backward*.

100. U.S. Census Bureau, *Statistical Abstract of the United States, 1999* (Washington, D.C.: U.S. Government Printing Office, 1999), p. 439.

101. Examining social policy from a life course perspective, Scherer argues that child care should be considered a form of "active participation and supported in its own right"; see Peter Scherer, "Socio-Economic Change and Social Policy," in *Family, Market and Community: Equity and Efficiency in Social Policy* (Paris: OECD, 1997), p. 55.

102. Valeria Fargion, "Creeping Workfare Policies: The Case of Italy," in Gilbert and Van Voorhis, eds., *Activating the Unemployed*.

103. In fact, there has been almost no increase in private sector employment in Denmark since 1948. In addition to the increase in public sector employment, the substantial decline (sometimes referred to as "miraculous," as with the Dutch experience) in Danish unemployment is explained by such measures as early retirement incen-

tives and special leave arrangements (sabbaticals, educational, and parental). For a detailed analysis, see Jorgen Goul Andersen, "Welfare Crisis and Beyond: Danish Welfare Policies in the 1980s and 1990s," in Stein Kuhnle, ed., *Survival of the European Welfare State* (London: Routledge, 1999), pp. 69–87.

104. Karl Hinrichs, "Combating Unemployment: What Can Be Learned from Whom?" paper presented at the International Social Security Association Research Conference, Helsinki, September 25–27, 2000.

105. Hakim, "Sociological Perspective on Part-time Work."

106. Ulrich Walwei and Heinz Werner, "Employment Problems and Active Labour Market Policies in Industrialized Countries," in Dalmer Hoskins, Donate Dobernack, and Christaine Kuptsch, eds., *Social Security at the Dawn of the 21st Century: Topical Issues and New Approaches* (New Brunswick, N.J.: Transaction, 2000).

107. Uwe Becker, "Welfare State Development and Employment in the Netherlands in Comparative Perspective," *Journal of European Social Policy*, 10:3 (August 2000), 233.

108. As welfare recipients most able to work are drawn or pushed out of the recipient pool, those remaining will increasingly represent the least competent and most difficult to employ—posing a challenge beyond the conventional scope of incentives and sanctions. In the United States, an analysis of the National Adult Literacy Survey, which tests an individual's ability to apply math and reading skills to everyday situations, indicates that 35 percent of public assistance recipients score in the lowest of five levels of literacy; people in this category are unable to perform such tasks as locating an intersection on a street map, filling out a government benefits application, and totaling the costs from an order. Similarly, findings from the Armed Forces Qualifying Test, which measures the application of math and reading skills in an academic context, show that 33 percent of the welfare recipients have very low basic skills, scoring at or below the tenth percentile. Alec Levenson, Elaine Reardon, and Stefanie Schmidt, "Welfare Reform and the Employment Prospects of Welfare Recipients,"*Jobs and Capital*, 6:3 (Summer 1997), 36–41. In addition, research suggests that 25 percent to 33 percent of clients who remained on the welfare rolls in 1999 had serious mental health problems. Eileen Sweeney, *Recent Studies Indicate that Many Parents Who Are Current or Former Welfare Recipients Have Disabilities* (Washington, D.C.: Center on Budget and Policy Priorities, 2000).

109. For a cogent analysis of how social policy is shaped by line workers in welfare bureaucracies, see the widely cited work by Michael Lipsky, *Street-Level Bureaucracy* (New York: Russell Sage Foundation, 1980).

110. Barbier and Theret, "Welfare-to-Work or Work-to-Welfare."

111. Keizer, "From Welfare to Workfare."

112. Between 1987 and 1994, the use of sanctions by unemployment insurance agencies in the Netherlands more than doubled, from 7 percent to 17 percent of the cases. See van der Veen, "An Organized Future?"

113. Only about 25 percent of the states impose a full benefit reduction the first time a welfare recipient is out of compliance with work requirements, whereas more than 75 percent of the states impose

a full benefit reduction for varying durations after a subsequent instance of noncompliance. For a detailed analysis of the variance among states, see L. Jerome Gallagher, Megan Gallagher, Kevin Perese, Susan Schreiber, and Keith Watson, *One Year After Federal Welfare Reform: A Description of State Temporary Assistance for Needy Families (TANF) Decisions as of October 1997* (Washington, D.C.: Urban Institute, 1998).

114. U.S. General Accounting Office, *Welfare Reform: State Sanction Policies and Number of Families Affected* (Washington D.C.: U.S. Government Printing Office, 2000).

115. Fargion, "Creeping Workfare Policies."

116. Dan Finn, "Welfare to Work: The Local Dimension," *Journal of European Social Policy*, 10:1 (February 2000), 53.

117. Gosta Esping-Andersen, *The Three Worlds of Welfare Capitalism* (Princeton, N.J.: Princeton University Press, 1990), p. 47.

118. Dahl and Dropping, "Norwegian Work Approach."

119. Loftager, "Solidarity and Universality in the Danish Welfare State."

120. Dahl and Dropping, "Norwegian Work Approach," p. 270.

121. Anders Nordlund, "Social Policy in Harsh Times: Social Security Development in Denmark, Finland, Norway and Sweden During the 1980s and 1990s," *Journal of International Social Welfare*, 9: 1 (January 2000), 40–41.

122. Nordlund's response is "that the degree of 'decommodification' has been high for those who have had a solid labour market record. Those with weak labour market histories have been dependent on less generous programs or social assistance" (ibid., p. 36). This is not persuasive, in part because Esping-Andersen's definition of decommodification emphasizes easy access and a wide range of entitlements. Nordlund's view suggests a form of decommodification that protects mostly those who need it least, whereas people who are most in need of support remain highly vulnerable to market forces.

123. Dahl and Dropping, "Norwegian Work Approach," p. 287.

4

State to Market

Subsidizing Private Activity

Since the mid-1980s, a pervasive movement toward the privatization of social welfare activity has redrawn the boundaries and redefined the relations between state and market, not only in the United States, but also across Europe from London to Stockholm. The increasing use of private alternatives has been extensive and most widely documented in the United States. In the 1980s Robert Reich was already proposing that a significant part of the public welfare system be replaced by government grants to businesses to hire the chronically unemployed and to provide day care and other social services.[1] By the 1990s, business schools around the country were training social entrepreneurs to apply commercial skills to the management of social welfare organizations.[2] The opportunity for business students to do well by doing good was advanced as state governments began to spend billions of dollars annually, contracting with private, nonprofit agencies and for-profit firms to deliver the entire range of social welfare services from day care to nursing homes. By the late 1980s, the purchase of service contracting in Massachusetts alone had multiplied threefold in 20 years, reaching $850 million.[3] On the federal level, $2.4 billion in tax credits were granted to individuals for the purchase of day-care services in 2000.[4] Other indirect public expenditures that subsidize individuals through the tax system, allowing them to make private arrangements for their financial security in old age, have increased dramatically in recent times. Tax expenditures on individual retirement accounts, for example, climbed from $6.5 billion in 1989 to $15.3 billion in 2000.[5]

In the United Kingdom, Margaret Thatcher's historic election to a third term in 1988 was the second-largest Conservative victory since World War II and the first consecutive three-term winning streak by a British prime minister since the 1820s. Mrs. Thatcher gained the day on a platform that included the privatization of social welfare. Her efforts toward this end were reflected in such initiatives as the sale of public (council) housing and the contracting out of ancillary hospital services.[6] The market-oriented approach to social provision advanced during the Thatcher decade of the 1980s, continues apace at the dawn of the twenty-first century under the New Labour policies of Tony Blair.[7]

In Sweden, the Conservative-led defeat of the Social Democrats in 1991 hinged in part on consumers' increasing dissatisfaction with social provisions, particularly the lack of choice or types of services and range of providers.[8] The Conservatives argued that as a basic principle, private agencies should be allowed to compete with public providers of services. After taking office, they introduced a system of educational vouchers under which parents who chose to send their children to private schools were entitled to a voucher equivalent to 85 percent of the cost of a public education. Although the Social Democrats had called for the abolition of educational vouchers, when they returned to office in 1994 the party revised its position, lowering the value of vouchers to 75 percent of the cost of a public education.[9] The Swedish government also requires private employers to pay sickness benefits, the cost of which amounted to about .06 percent of the GDP in 1993.

The march toward privatization is most broadly configured as a movement away from a purely public state of social welfare under which benefits are funded by tax revenues and directly provided by government agencies. Of course, no system of social protection among the Western democracies has ever been purely public. Even in countries where the government has been most deeply involved in the doings of the welfare state, other institutions—church, market, and family—have always contributed in some measure to the provision of social welfare. For over a hundred years, the Catholic Church has endorsed the principle of subsidiarity, which holds that welfare provisions by the state are appropriate only after private and voluntary sources have been exhausted. In Germany, as Jens Alber points out, the Protestant and Catholic churches established major welfare associations in the mid and late eighteenth century, which carved out a private realm of social services that to this day has resisted penetration by the state. These associations, the Catholic *Caritas* and the Protestant *Diakonie*, are currently Europe's largest employers, with a work force of 800,000.[10] This pluralistic arrangement for the finance and provision of social benefits is often referred to as the *mixed economy of welfare*.

With the private share of the mixed economy on the rise, it is becoming difficult to distinguish countries that are traditionally identified with the collectivist ideology that champions a strong and expansive role for the state. The political compass for privatization has lost its conventional bearings. Where is the Left? In the U.S. 2000 presidential campaign, Republicans wanted to expand private activity through educational vouchers and a shift in Social Security financing that would allow individuals to invest 2.5 percent of their contributions in private equity accounts. Democrats opposed these measures, although 60 percent of all African-Americans and 70 percent of those under age 35 (predominantly Democrats) support educational vouchers.[11] At the same time, the privatization of 2.5 percent of social security contributions and the use of educational vouchers have been approved in Sweden under a Social Democratic regime that is traditionally to the left of both parties in the United States.[12]

Paths to Privatization

These illustrations of various public policies, from vouchers to tax credits, that enable private financing and delivery of social welfare in the United States, the United Kingdom, and Sweden are all over the map, geographically as well as conceptually. They are offered not as firm evidence of a trend toward privatization but as an indication of the varied measures that will advance this trend. Before taking a closer look at the substantive evidence, it will be useful to mark the immediate course of change and to survey the conceptual terrain, tracing the main avenues to privatization.

In recent years the long-standing debate about the proper blend of public and private provisions of social welfare has favored enlarging the private contribution to the mix. The meaning of *privatization* is thus defined as a change in the initial organization of state and market responsibilities for social welfare toward more market and less state. This course of change is guided by policies that aim to limit the direct role of the state and to increase private activity in the financing and provision of social benefits.[13] To map the conceptual terrain, we begin by exploring the several lanes that branch off these two main avenues of finance and provision, along which the movement toward privatization is accelerating at different speeds.

Concerning financing, one alternative to a purely public social welfare system paid for entirely by tax revenues involves private charitable contributions to voluntary agencies, which deliver social services to those in need. Although they are voluntary in nature, it is important to note that these private benefactions are often gently prodded by the invisible hand of the state, which returns a portion of the contributions through tax deductions to the donors. Another alternative to public tax-and-spend financing draws on individual out-of-pocket payments for social provisions, such as child care and health insurance. But here, too, public incentives enable private financing through such measures as tax credits for child care and other tax benefits that partially subsidize private spending on health insurance and pension savings. Finally, a less noticeable route to private financing follows the course of publicly mandated, private social welfare expenditures, which rely on government interventions to smooth the surface and point (some would say, force) the way forward. In the Netherlands, for example, the sickness insurance scheme was privatized in 1994, when reforms were introduced that required employers to assume the responsibility of paying at least 70 percent of their workers' salaries for 6 weeks of sick leave; in 1996, the period of private coverage was extended to 52 weeks, after which workers could qualify for public disability benefits.[14] Along each of these paths the state plays a direct or indirect role in stimulating private financing. All social welfare benefits are to some degree subsidized or mandated by the state; in part it is the public intervention by fiscal or legal means that makes these benefits "social."[15]

The other main avenue to privatization is the provision of social welfare—the actual production and delivery of goods and services—by the private sector. Benefits can be publicly financed but purchased on the private market either by government agencies or by the individual beneficiaries. In the former instance, privatization is fostered through purchase-of-service contracts, sometimes referred to as *outsourcing*, under which government agencies pay voluntary and for-profit organizations to provide goods (such as low-cost housing and meals-on-wheels to the elderly) and social services. Privatization is also advanced when the government elects to offer benefits in the form of cash or vouchers, such as food stamps, which allow recipients to purchase the goods and services they need in the private market.

This brief summary suggests four broad approaches to increasing private involvement in the finance and provision of social welfare—tax benefits for voluntary private activity; government regulations that mandate private provisions, public purchase-of-service contracts; and allocation of public benefits in the form of cash or vouchers, which are consumed on the market.[16] All of these approaches may be pursued simultaneously in the allocation of social benefits. The case of child-care services is illustrative. In the United States, for example, an exacting gauge of the major funding streams—the Child Care and

Development Fund, Social Services Block Grant, Temporary Assistance for Needy Families, Head Start, and Child Care Food Program—indicates that spending on child care nearly doubled, from $8.5 billion in 1994 to $15.9 billion in 1999 (both in 1999 dollars).[17] A large portion of these funds goes to support a purely public arrangement under which child-care services are delivered through state-owned and-operated centers supported by tax revenues. But much of the support from these sources is also channeled to private providers through purchase-of-service contracts between government agencies and local day-care establishments, as well as through vouchers to parents, which expand the private market by allowing parents to purchase child-care services from friends, neighbors, family members, and licensed centers. The provision of private child care is also financed indirectly through tax benefits. In 2000, for example, the child- and dependent care tax credit and the exclusion of taxes on employer-provided child care subsidized approximately $3.9 billion of voluntary, private spending.[18] Finally, although government regulations rarely mandate private provisions of day care in the United States, in some cases this approach is employed. In San Francisco, for example, the City Board of Supervisors requires developers of large downtown office buildings to construct a child-care facility on the property or to pay $1 per square foot of office space into a child-care fund.

Whether voluntary or mandatory, it should be immediately recognized that the extent to which social welfare benefits are privately financed has yet to approach the scale of public financing. On the level of private financing, change is measured against a low baseline. The most comprehensive measure of social accounting reveals that in 1995 private spending ranged from 4 percent to 17 percent of social expenditures in Denmark, Sweden, the Netherlands, and the United Kingdom. Only in the United States did the private share rise to more than one-third of all social spending. However limited it may be, there has still been a palpable increase in private financing in all of these countries. As shown in table 4.1, since 1980 private spending accounts for a growing proportion of the total gross social expenditure. There are good reasons to anticipate that this trend will continue, sustained in large measure by private initiatives in the realm of old-age pensions.

Private Accretion and Public Erosion of Retirement Income

A major portion of the private share of social expenditures comes from the increasing privatization of old-age pensions through both

Table 4.1 Private Share of Gross Social Expenditure:
1980–95

	1980	1990	1995
Denmark	1.04	1.94	4.1
Sweden	4.01	4.12	6.9
Netherlands	—	11.67	16.0
United Kingdom	10.24	14.78	16.8
United States	28.01	36.60	34.7

Source: Willem Adema and Marcel Einerhand, "The Growing Role of Private Social Benefits," table 4, Labour Market and Social Policy Occasional Paper No. 32 (Paris: OECD, 1998); Willem Adema, "Net Social Expenditure," table 2, Labour Market and Social Policy Occasional Paper No. 39 (Paris: OECD, 1999).

employer-based and individually based schemes. Between 1980 and 1993, for example, private old-age benefits rose from 18 percent to 28 percent of all old-age pensions paid in the United States and almost doubled, from 12 percent to 23 percent, in the Netherlands and, from 15 percent to 27 percent, in the United Kingdom.[19] These private schemes are publicly cultivated through tax advantages and legal mandates. Many of the private pensions are new programs that have not yet fully matured. Among 24 of the most industrialized nations of the Organization for Economic Cooperation and Development, the aggregate value of financial assets held by private pension funds climbed from 28 percent of the GDP in 1987 to 39 percent in 1996.[20] These aggregate figures, of course, mask considerable variation, ranging from lows of 0.2 percent to 4.1 percent of the 1996 GDPs in Austria, Belgium, and Hungary to highs of 74.7 percent to 117 percent in the United Kingdom, Netherlands, and Switzerland. The private share of social expenditure in all of these countries is expected to grow as the private retirement schemes mature.

The rise of participation in private retirement schemes is related to numerous measures that have been advanced to reform public social security systems (usually based on the universal pay-as-you-go model). On the one hand, policy initiatives sought to restore the fiscal integrity of the existing systems—through either a decrease in benefits or an increase in revenues—by raising the age of retirement or the years of contribution required for the maximum benefit, reindexing benefits, taxing benefits, altering the coverage of dependents, and increasing contributions.[21] In France's major program covering all private sector employees, for example, the period of contributions required to qualify for the maximum old-age pension was increased in 1993 from 37.5 years to 40 years, and the calculation of pension benefits was changed from the average income over the best 10 years to the best 25 years. In 2000, reform efforts were well underway to extend the 40-year coverage requirement for pensions into the public sector.[22] On the other hand, there were reforms explicitly designed to incorporate private schemes, to varying degrees, as a source of funding in an overall plan for retirement income. Touting such potential benefits as higher earnings, greater savings, economic growth, and diversification of risk, the World Bank, among other institutions, stands in the forefront of those promoting the increased privatization of old-age pensions.[23]

The World Bank recommends a multipillar system of old-age pensions, under which a minimum, public, pay-as-you-go scheme would be heavily supplemented by a compulsory second pillar of fully funded, individualized, and privately managed accounts, as well as a third pillar of voluntary savings.[24] Without much effort, the compulsory private accounts could be seen as an opening move to insert the camel's nose of market-oriented interests into the government's tent of public pensions. The Bank's views on the benefits of privatization did not go unchallenged. Although this is not the place to recount the details of the lively debate that ensued, some of the principal responses that weighed into the fray are worth noting. In the mid-1990s, Roger Beattie and Warren McGillivray argued, for example, that rather than diversifying risk, increased privatization heightens it;[25] Ajit Singh detected little evidence that privatization will enhance economic growth;[26] in a major project initiated by the International Social Security Association, Lawrence Thompson found, among other things, that empirical studies were unable to prove that privately financed schemes have a discernable impact on national savings rates;[27] and the difficulties of using private accounts to insure against the risk that retired workers would outlive their savings are examined in a discussion paper prepared by Larry Wilmore of the United Nations Department of Economic and Social Affairs.[28] By 1999 it looked as if the World Bank was beginning to hedge, if not backpedal, on the presumed advantages of privatization when its chief economist, Joseph Stiglitz, coauthored a paper that renounced most of the arguments in favor of expanding the privately managed second pillar as "based on a set of myths that are often not substantiated in either theory or practice."[29] It is unclear how much this paper signaled a shift in the Bank's position since shortly after it appeared, Stiglitz resigned from his post.

Among the reforms designed to privatize old-age pensions, the most sweeping measures were implemented in Chile, which introduced policies in 1981 that replaced the state-and-employer-supported public pension system with a new scheme of mandatory individual accounts, invested and managed through the private sector.[30] After the first decade's experience, during which high rates of return lent a favorable aura to the program's early years, the Chilean model spread to other Latin American countries.[31] Later, however, private pension fund returns declined from the 12 percent average registered during the first 15 years to gains of only 2.5 percent to 4.7 percent between 1994 and 1997; in 1998 the Chilean stock market lost 25 percent of its dollar value and the pension funds were down an average of 5 percent.[32]

Moving toward partial privatization, Britain, which has a two-tiered system of social security, introduced somewhat narrower measures—a basic, flat-rate, public pension that is topped up by a mandatory earning-related pension. The British Social Security Pensions Act of 1975 encouraged the contracting out of the earnings-related portion of pension benefits to private sources—a portion that is growing and is expected to amount to one-third of social security costs by 2030.[33] By the mid-1990s, over 60 percent of the households headed by a person aged 60 years or over were receiving income from private pensions in Finland, the Netherlands, Norway, and Sweden.[34] In 2000, Germany's Social Democratic–led government introduced a large-scale reform of its old-age pension scheme, which will offer $8.4 billion a year in tax breaks and subsidies designed to induce workers to deposit 4 percent of their earnings into a private pension fund (as part of a package that would also reduce state pension benefits from 70 percent to 67 percent of average gross earnings by 2030). In time, these private funds could amount to as much as 40 percent of the employee's total pension.[35] In March 1997, the Juppé government in France passed the Thomas Law, authorizing companies to establish pension funds on behalf of their employees, although enabling legislation was not immediately issued. Seen as a threat to the public, pay-as-you-go pensions, the move toward privatization was opposed by the Left, who promised to repeal the law if elected. However, later that year, when a left-wing coalition took office, the new government under Lionel Jospin had second thoughts. Instead of abandoning the idea of private pension funds, it proposed a new version, which ordained privatization with a twist to the Left. Under the alternative outlined by Jospin, private pensions would be managed jointly by employer and union organizations and contributions would not be deductible from those collected by the public system.[36]

Finally, as noted earlier, the Swedish pension system went even further down the road of partial privatization under legislative reforms in 1998. Swedish pensions are based on contributions of 18.5 percent of the individual's lifetime income, of which 2.5 percent is invested in a private account selected by the individual. Some may insist that this 2.5 percent is a trivial sum. Others may reason that it amounts to a palpable 14 percent of the total contribution. Whether the private accounts are considered relatively large or insubstantial, they represent a discernable breach in the public system. This is an important point because once the principle of private accounts is solidly established, the next step depends on what occurs in practice. One might well anticipate vigorous pressures for the expansion of these accounts if the average returns are fairly high over the next 5 to 10 years. The Swedish system now operates as a "defined contribution" scheme under which benefits are equal to the individual's contributions plus interest (in contrast to a "defined benefit" scheme that insures a specified level of retirement income). Workers may start to draw their pensions at any time after the age of 61, but up to age 70 the size of the pension will vary according to the lifetime contributions divided by the average life expectancy at the time of retirement. In the name of equality, the calculation of average life expectancy in Sweden does not distinguish between men and women. Since women live longer than men, however, on the average men can be expected to consume less of their contributions through the pension annuity than women.

Reexamining his models of welfare capitalism in 1999, Gosta Esping-Andersen argued that one can empirically distinguish the Scandinavian–social democratic welfare regime from the Anglo-American liberal regime, in part, on the index of private pensions as a percentage of total pensions in the countries represented by these welfare state models. However, the 1980 data used in his statistical calculations do not capture the current reality, and the cross-sectional analyses offer a static picture, which fails to reveal where things are headed.[37] In fact (as noted in chapter 2), after 1980 the private pension expenditures in Norway and Denmark rose as a share of total public and private pensions, and with the pension reforms of the late 1990s, Sweden will follow suit. Although the social democratic welfare regimes have been characterized as "statist" arrangements that drive out alternatives, Einar Overbye finds that "this is only half true, at least as far as pensions are concerned. Private pensions are alive and well in all the Nordic countries bar Finland."[38]

The rise of privatization is transparent in such countries as Chile, the Netherlands, Norway, Denmark, Sweden, Germany, and the United Kingdom, where private pensions are mandated either by legislation or collective agreement and partially incorporated into public schemes. A more circuitous and less apparent shift toward privatization occurs when reforms that erode public social security pension benefits are joined by policies that support the expansion of voluntary, private alternatives.[39] In the absence of an explicit design, these incremental measures produce a steady decline in the percentage of retirement income derived from public social security schemes relative to the percentage of retirement income derived from employer-provided pensions and individual retirement plans[40]—a process exemplified by reforms initiated in the United States since the late 1970s.

The reduction of benefits started in the United States with the 1977 social security amendments and advanced under the 1983 amendments. Introduced to restore the solvency of the public system, these reforms increased the retirement age from 65 to 67, raised the employer-employee tax rate and increased the taxable-earnings base, and imposed an income tax on social security benefits for retirees with a modest level of income from other sources.[41] Since 1980, the value of social security benefits has declined relative to the wages they replace at all levels of income, and so has the size of the positive net transfers.[42]

While the payoff on public pensions was being eroded by these reforms, the number of participants in private retirement schemes was increasing. Private pensions, of course, are not a recent invention. They were introduced well before the 1935 Social Security Act by employers that wanted to increase work force loyalty. According to one account, the American Express Company is credited with establishing the first private pension plan in 1875.[43] Before the 1940s, private pension plans were prevalent in only a few industries, primarily railroads, banking, and public utilities. After World War II, private pensions began to spread, rising to 489,000 plans by 1980. From 1980 to 1995, participants in private pension plans increased by over 50 percent, from 57.9 million to 87.5 million people.[44] By the mid-1990s, more than one-half of the civilian labor force participated in private, employment-based pensions. Although employers have much discretion in how they structure private plans, to receive favorable tax treatment these plans must meet both the terms of the Internal Revenue Code and the minimum standards of the 1974 Employee Retirement Income Security Act for participation, vesting, nondiscrimination against lower paid workers, and other criteria. Even with mandatory minimum funding standards, however, it is worth noting that private sponsors have considerable leeway in funding contributions, which leaves some schemes poorly funded.[45]

As wage replacement rates and net transfers decline—most rapidly for those in the middle-and upper-income categories—and the normal age of retirement rises under social security, an increasing proportion of the U.S. population is quietly coming to rely on private pensions as a primary source of retirement income. But the shifting mix of support from public and private pensions is quite different for people in the upper-, middle-, and low-income groups. By 1990, private retirement benefits accounted for more of the aggregate income than social security benefits of elderly people in the top 20 percent of the income level. The elderly in the bottom 40 percent of the income distribution remain highly dependent on social security, and reliance on private pensions is climbing for those in the middle and upper-middle levels.[46] Overall, estimates point to the emergence of a two-tiered system of pensions in the not-too-distant future. The first tier will consist of a whittled-down version of social security, which provides the main source of retirement income for low-wage earners within the framework of universal coverage and pay-as-you-go financing. The second tier will consist of private pension arrangements, which are proliferating and partially subsidized by tax preferences. This tier will provide increasing portions of retirement income for elderly persons in the middle- and upper-income groups, which are converging in their level of reliance on private schemes (as shown in figure 4.1). One result is to widen the inequality of retirement income.[47] Although the second tier is publicly subsidized indirectly through tax expenditures, unlike other countries in which measures for the partial privatization of old-age pensions are incorporated into a coherent system, there is virtually no coordination or integration between private pensions and public schemes in the United States.

In many, if not most, of the OECD countries, private financing of retirement income is slowly on the rise, whether it comes directly through the front door of compulsory schemes coordinated with public pensions or creeps in through the back door of voluntary, private

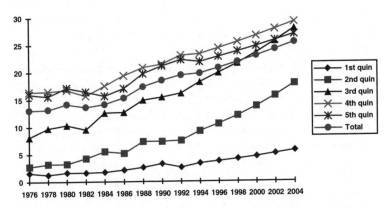

Figure 4.1 Private Pension as a Percentage of the Aggregated Income of Aged Units by Income Quintile: 1976–2004. *Source*: Neil Gilbert and Neung Hoo Park, "Privatization, Provision and Targeting: Trends and Policy Implications for Social Security in the United States," *International Social Security Review*, 49: 1 (1996).

arrangements that offset the erosion of public benefits. This does not mean that the state is being squeezed out of social protection for the elderly. For the foreseeable future, publicly funded pensions will still provide the main source of old-age security in the advanced industrialized countries where these schemes are already well established (if for no other reason than the immense transition costs of shifting to individual accounts).[48] However, in the movement toward privatization, the state has begun to play a more diversified role in providing for old-age security—one that involves less emphasis on the traditional approach of direct public financing through taxing and spending and more emphasis on enabling the development of private arrangements that are indirectly subsidized through tax expenditures and are publicly regulated.

Contracting for Welfare

Whereas private financing of social welfare is slowly but steadily expanding, the use of public funds to support contracts with voluntary and for-profit organizations for the delivery of social services has grown in leaps and bounds. The United States probably leads the field in contracting out all sorts of public services, even the management of correctional institutions. The number of privately run prisons has climbed from just a few in the mid-1980s to at least 168 in 1999.[49]

Contracting for social services accelerated in the mid-1970s under the Title XX amendments to the Social Security Act, which allowed donations from private agencies to qualify as part of the state's matching share of federal social service grants.[50] In the United States, particularly, advances have been made in purchase-of-service arrangements with profit-making organizations. By the mid-1990s, proprietary agencies were prominently represented as service providers in the fields of nursing-home care, homemaker aides, day care, child welfare, health care, and housing.[51] Since the 1996 welfare reforms, there has been an avalanche of multimillion-dollar contracting for welfare case management, training, and job search and placement services between human services agencies and private companies. In 1998 and 1999, for example, the Department of Labor awarded over half a billion dollars in competitive grants to community-based organizations, for-profit and nonprofit agencies, educational institutions, and local government units for the provision of job training, child care, transportation, and employment advice to hard-core welfare recipients. The development of electronic benefit-transfer systems that allow food stamp recipients to collect their vouchers at automated teller machines is a multimillion dollar service under contracts between state welfare agencies and major corporations like Lockheed Martin, Transactive Corporation and Citicorp. Social welfare has become big business.

The United States is not alone in its efforts to transform the role of government—less rowing and more steering is the metaphor that comes to mind—in the production and delivery of social services. Between 1979 and 1996, the proportion of all public expenditures on personal social services contracted out to the private sector in the United Kingdom more than tripled, from 11 percent to 34 percent. Most of this increase reflects a change in the provision of residential care, which shifted from facilities operated by local authorities to home care under private auspices.[52] Via reforms implemented in 1993, commercial firms are also moving into domiciliary care—such services as in-home meals, cleaning, home nursing, and emergency alarm systems—under contracts with local public authorities who are "expected to be enablers rather than providers."[53]

Since the early 1990s in Sweden, there has been substantial growth in child-care arrangements that are publicly financed and privately operated, mainly by parent cooperatives and other nonprofit organizations.[54] By 1995 these arrangements accounted for about 10 percent of the Swedish child-care placements. Tracing the changing mix in public and private provisions for child care since the 1980s in Denmark, France, Germany, the United Kindgom, and Sweden, Anna-Lena Almqvist and Thomas Boje find that although the public sector and private households are still the main providers, state-organized services have been reduced as the role of private firms and voluntary organizations expands. Social care for the elderly is moving in the same direction. According to Juhani Lehto's analysis, "The shift from traditional old age homes to modern service homes means in most Nordic countries a shift from mostly public providers to a more significant role for private nonprofit providers."[55]

Private, for-profit arrangements are also blossoming in several areas of service that are not like other commodities sold in the economic marketplace. In normal market transactions, consumers have knowledge about the commodities they are buying, and most important, they are usually willing to make a trade between cost and quality—accepting a slower car, a day-old loaf of bread, or a less attractive tie for a lower price. But if a child is seriously ill and needs an operation or some other medical intervention, few parents are willing to accept a lower quality of medical care or treatment in residential facilities. When stricken by a serious physical or mental illness, people want the best care and do not think it fair if wealth allows others to obtain better, quicker, more effective treatment. The sense of fairness that people expect from systems of health and social care is captured in

Richard Titmuss's poignant account of his experience with the National Health Service. Titmuss, a distinguished professor of social administration at the London School of Economics, was being treated for cancer. He compares his experience to that of a young West Indian from Trinidad who was being treated in the same office: "His appointment was the same as mine for radium treatment—10 o'clock every day. Sometimes he went into the Theratron Room first; sometimes I did. What determined waiting was quite simply the vagaries of London traffic—not race, religion, color, or class."[56]

Around the mid-1980s, Swedish counties that operated local health-care systems under which physicians were public employees began contracting for medical services with doctors in private practice. By the mid-1990s, observers reported that "what started out as a minor revival of private practice has become a boom."[57] On a larger scale, these counties are also farming out entire segments of their primary health-care systems. Although all of the country's 789 primary-care clinics were publicly operated in 1986, just six years later 11 of these clinics had been contracted out, with the number expected to rise. Market-oriented models of social service delivery for residential care gained impetus in the late 1980s. Thus, whereas the public sector provided almost 90 percent of the beds in residential care facilities for children and youths in the 1970s, by 1995 close to 60 percent of these beds had shifted over to private institutions, many of them medium-scale operations larger than foster-care homes but smaller than the traditional state-run institutions.[58] A similar trend is evident in contracting out beds in residential treatment homes for alcoholics. Here, as shown in figure 4.2, for-profit providers were almost absent from the picture until the mid-1980s, after which they have come to dominate the field. These data reflect what is seen more generally in Sweden as a steady trend toward privatization in health care and the personal social services.[59] In Norway, private for-profit providers are gradually enlarging their share of the residential homes for children and youths. In 1998, they accounted for 33.4 percent of the institutions in this field of service, a 10 percent increase over their share in 1995.[60]

On the Continent, Germany has experienced an extraordinary increase in for-profit providers in the realm of long-term care, a field of service from which they were virtually excluded by law until the mid-1990s. Once the introduction of a new long-term insurance scheme opened the door to commercial providers in 1994, they leaped at the opportunity and by 2000 accounted for about half of all services and one-third of the personnel in this field.[61]

After privatizing sick leave benefits for workers through a public mandate in 1996, the Netherlands came to the brink of completely

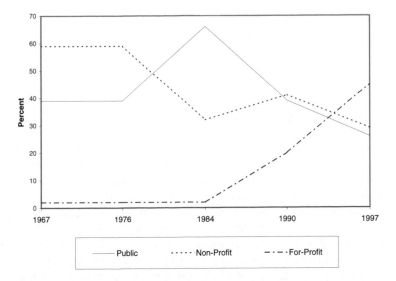

Figure 4.2 Residential Treatment Placement for Alcoholics. *Source:* Sune Sunesson, "Restructuring State Welfare," paper presented at the International Conference on Playing the Market Game? University of Bilefeld, Germany, March 9–11, 2000.

privatizing unemployment and disability insurance. The plan, forged in 1999 by the Socio-Economic Council, involved shifting the administration of employed persons' insurance schemes to commercial providers, who would run the day-to-day operations all the way from the collection of premiums to determination of eligibility to distribution of benefits to contracting for the delivery of employment counseling, training and other reintegration services. Prime Minister Kok's purple cabinet agreed with the general direction of this plan but proposed selling the public agencies to commercial providers, although retaining the assessment of claims as a function that should be performed only by public employees, who would be seconded to the private agencies. This proposal for the almost complete privatization of insurance plans, however, was rejected by the Dutch parliament. The elected officials were particularly resistant to the sale of the public agencies and were also concerned about how data on beneficiaries would be used by the commercial providers. In response, the purple cabinet did a complete turnaround and came back with a new proposal to keep the entire administration of the insurance schemes in the public sector, allowing for privatization of only the reintegration activities.[62] The Dutch reversal might be a general sign of rising discontent with the market (as Hirschman's public-private cycle has, perhaps, run its course) or just a notice that on the road to privatization, the outright sale of pubic social welfare agencies to commercial interests is a sharp curve, to be approached with caution.

Promoting Civil Society, Raising Social Capital, and Other Consequences

The contracting out of services from the public to the private sector is part of a larger trend in the devolution of responsibility for social welfare from central to local units of government and from local government to community-based private agencies. Although both large- and small-scale for-profit providers are penetrating the social service arena more and more, voluntary, community-based agencies continue to receive a significant proportion, if not the bulk, of purchase-of-service contracts.[63] These local private agencies are believed to be better able to meet the needs of their consumers because they reside closer to the people being served and are less bureaucratic than public institutions. Voluntary, community-based organizations are also seen as mediating structures that create a cushion of civil society between the individual and the state, which softens the power of government, bolsters the influence of individuals, and affirms the norms of communal life—an observation that draws heavily on the seminal works of Alexis de Tocqueville and Émile Durkheim, among others.[64] De Tocqueville found that "Americans of all ages, all conditions, and all dispositions constantly form associations." And he thought that was good because among "the laws that rule human societies there is one which seems to be more precise and clear than all others. If men are to remain civilized, or to become so, the art of associating together must grow and improve in the same ratio in which the equality of conditions is increased."[65]

Echoing the nineteenth century commentary on the brink of the twenty-first century, both liberals and conservatives trumpet the merits of voluntary association. "When civil society is strong," U.S. Senator Dan Coats asserts, "it infuses a community with its warmth, trains its people to be good citizens, and transmits values between generations. When it is weak no amount of police or politics can provide a substitute."[66] And the platform of the communitarian movement, whose initial signatories include a broad cross section of intellectual, political, and public leaders (e.g., Amitai Etzioni, Albert Shanker, Adlai E. Stevenson, Alice Rossi, Isabel Sawhill, and Lester Thurow), "recognizes that the preservation of individual liberty depends on the active maintenance of the institutions of civil society where citizens learn respect for others as well as self-respect; where we acquire a lively sense of our personal and civic responsibilities, along with an appreciation of our own rights and the rights of others."[67]

The popular appeal of strengthening the mediating structures of civil society generates much support for contracting with community-based agencies to deliver social welfare services. By shrinking the role of government and shifting responsibility for service delivery to local voluntary agencies, Charles Krauthammer suggests that these "mediating institutions will once again have the space to flower, reclaiming their rightful place at the center of a revitalized civil society."[68] But this outcome is not assured, for as long as the local voluntary agencies are heavily dependent on government funds, there will be a tension between the extent to which they are serving the interests of the state and the extent to which they are mediating the interests of local consumers.[69]

Along with providing a communal buffer between the individual and the state, voluntary associations are highly regarded as fertile space for civic engagements that cultivate what social scientists refer to as "social capital." This is a concept that lends itself to various interpretations and has stirred much debate in recent years—although reference to the term and its general idea have been traced back to the turn of the twentieth century.[70] In the early 1960s, social capital was identified by Jane Jacobs as a prerequisite of vibrant community life. Cohesive, well-functioning neighborhoods could remain strong and absorb newcomers as long as the change was gradual and did not disrupt the continuity of local networks formed by existing residents. "These networks," she explained, "are a city's irreplaceable social capital."[71] But it was not until the late 1980s that this idea was more fully explored in the pioneering work of James Coleman, who saw social capital as a kind of productive resource created through networks of interpersonal connections. These interpersonal networks forge norms, obligations, and trust and open channels of communication, all of which heighten the capacity of people to work together for common purposes.[72] Because it is not owned by individuals but inheres in the structure of interpersonal relations, social capital is not immediately fungible, though it can promote accumulation of economic resources. Coleman's analysis examined social capital at the level of family and community life. Applying his definition of this concept on a national scale in the mid-1990s, Robert Putnam's influential analysis warned of the deterioration of social ties and disengagement from civic life in the United States, a malaise neatly captured in the evocative title of his work—*Bowling Alone*.[73] Putnam marshaled convincing evidence of a serious decline in the U.S. stock of social capital, which sparked a lively academic debate since, of course, everyone was not convinced.[74] In the end, however, his argument stands. For the time being, at least, the need to revitalize civil society by strengthening the role of nongovernmental organizations in community life has become a tenet of political wisdom widely shared in the United States and Europe.[75]

The associations typically connected to the formation of social capital include a multitude of fraternal and ethnic societies, religious groups, committees for the arts, civil rights organizations, community chest agencies such as the Boy Scouts and YMCA (Young Men's Christian Association), and other nonprofit social service agencies. Still, one may question whether the so-called third sector of voluntary, nongovernmental, nonprofit organizations is the only seedbed for cultivating civil society.[76] A flexible view of the boundaries of civil society incorporates a range of activities under auspices of the state and market. From this perspective, civil society is not so much embedded in the third sector as linked to the processes that produce social capital.[77] If state-supported, nonprofit groups enlarge the social capital of civil society, then why not for-profit, company-sponsored bowling teams? Alan Wolfe's findings suggest that "work-related organizations are more common in American middle-class life than social and fraternal ones."[78] Yet he allows that the qualitative nature of work-based civic ties may be tinged with more of an instrumental character than civic ties developed within voluntary associations.

Thinking about the institutional spaces in which civil society might flourish suggests another consequence of shifting service delivery from the public domain to voluntary, community-based agencies, which has not been fully articulated, particularly in the United States. Standing between the individual and market forces, labor unions are in many ways an archetypical mediating structure and source of social capital in modern society. Over the last several decades, public bureaucracies have emerged as the last stronghold of the labor union movement in the United States. From 1983 to 1998, union membership fell by almost one-third, from 20 percent to 14 percent of all wage and salary workers. All of the decline was in the private sector, where union membership slid from 16.5 percent to 9.5 percent of all wage and salary workers—a drop of over 40 percent. At the same time, the percentage of union membership represented by the public sector slightly increased. In 1983 government workers accounted for 32 percent of all union membership, a figure that climbed to 44 percent by 1998.[79] One of the reasons for this holding power is that organized labor in government is largely in the service sector; unlike industrial production, these service jobs could not be shipped overseas to be performed at a lower cost. Instead, they are now being contracted out to local community organizations, which are relatively small, voluntary nonprofit units that have few ties to organized labor. One might argue that in the contracting out of services, the public benefits from lower costs and heightened flexibility of labor in community-based organizations, where the job security of civil service employment is almost unknown. But before suggesting that this shift to local voluntary agencies also advances the cause of civil society and generates a net gain in social capital, one ought to factor in the impact of this form of privatization on the membership and communal life of organized labor.

Moreover, some analysts argue that in efforts to reconstruct civil society, government funding of voluntary, nonprofit service providers tends to be more of a fatal embrace than a helping hand. According to Douglas Besharov, bottom-up funding of clients through cash, vouchers, and reimbursement of copaid services is preferable to top-down funding through government contracts with local providers. The former allows individuals to make the decisions about where the money goes and to support local organizations that best satisfy their needs. Under contracting for services, on the other hand, governments have a hard time cutting their losses because once funding starts community-based political constituencies make it difficult to withdraw support, even when agencies deliver low-quality care. He also suggests that government contracting is often accompanied by regulatory standards, such as proscribing religious activities, which may alter the nature of mediating structures.[80]

Commodification of Social Care

Before the drive for market-oriented reforms, public agencies produced and delivered the bulk of social services, although occasionally purchasing them from private providers in a context that relied on the good faith and charitable ethos of traditional voluntary organizations. Today public agencies are being asked to behave in a more "businesslike" manner and to duplicate the virtues of a competitive market by contracting with voluntary and commercial organizations to deliver social welfare services. But these third-party contracts fail to provide the kind of consumer signals that serve to regulate cost and quality in the competitive market. Under third-party contracts, the first-party buyer does not consume the services acquired, the second-party consumer does not pay for the services received, and the third-party producer stands in the highly advantageous position of dealing with a buyer who rarely sees what is purchased and a consumer who never bears the expense.

The competition, such as it is, that operates under purchase-of-service arrangements is usually among contractors vying for public funds to deliver social services. In the course of choosing among private firms, public administrators must exercise considerable skill to formulate contracts that deliver the best deal—a task that most of them were not required to perform 10 to 15 years ago and for which few have received adequate professional preparation. The most effective purchase of service contracts demand a precise specification of what it is that the public agency is buying—the units of social service—and how much each of these units costs. This is often complicated and difficult to determine. Unlike a highly standardized and discrete public service such as refuse collection, which has been contracted out to private firms in many cities in the United States and essentially entails emptying a certain number of trash cans into a large truck on a periodic basis, the delivery of social services often involves an operation that is highly variable. Some social services, of course, involve uniform procedures, for example, a drug abuse treatment program that periodically dispenses a prescribed dose of methadone to clients. The unit of service is discrete, and the cost can easily be appraised. However, many services are individually tailored and multifaceted, involving a package of social care that is holistic in nature. Group-home placement for emotionally disturbed children, for example, encompasses a 24-hour-a-day operation that includes food, shelter, care, and therapeutic counseling. Here the provision of services is a complex process that integrates diverse functions, and the determination of unit costs requires a careful analysis that divides the holistic service into relevant components. Social services may be ranged along a continuum from highly standardized and discrete provisions to highly complex and holistic forms of care. Somewhere in the middle, we might place day care for young children, which provides a service that encompasses food, shelter, education, socialization, and sometimes even health care.

The central challenge to purchase-of-service contracting involves computing the unit cost for complex and holistic forms of provision such as day care for children, group-home care for the emotionally disturbed, and community care for the elderly. The arithmetic is rudimentary: divide the total annual costs for a service component by the units of interest.[81] However, the denominator in this equation is often baffling. There are at least three ways to define units of interest in service contracts: the consumers served, the type and quality of provisions delivered, and the level of performance involved in achieving results. Consider the case of a group home for severely emotionally disturbed children, which can accommodate six residents. With the consumers as the unit of interest, the annual costs for providing this service (staff, rent, food, administration, insurance, utilities, furniture, transportation, etc.) are totaled and divided by the number of children in residence over the year. Costs often run in the range of $120,000 to $140,000 per year for a bed and mental health services in a group home facility for disturbed children, which may sound expensive until they are compared with the $200,000 to $250,000 annual costs of hospitalization—the other alternative for severely disturbed children.[82] Although using the number of consumers as the unit of interest is the easiest way to calculate the unit price of group-home care, from a purchase-of-service perspective it is the least effective method for contracting out complex services since it ignores the question of exactly what is being delivered in the way of care.

Performance contracting is an alternative and more demanding approach, which ties the level of funding directly to what the purchaser hopes to achieve—linking service costs to results. Results are relatively simple to assess for fixed services that are highly standardized, such as administering flu inoculations, but difficult to set and measure when dealing with complex, multifaceted services. What is the desired outcome of group-home care for emotionally disturbed children? One could say that just keeping these children out of harm's way in a group home and out of the considerably more expensive hospital care is a desirable outcome. "Warehousing," however, is an unseemly goal of social care—even prisons aspire to rehabilitation. A more agreeable goal would be to stabilize the children's emotional state and improve their behavior so that they can function well enough to be moved to a less restrictive environment, preferably returning home to their parents or going into foster care, within a specified period of time. In response to this outcome, the unit cost of service could be tied to performance measured by periodic evaluations of the children's social-emotional state or the rate of discharge from the group home. Discharge rates, of course, would have to be adjusted for the incidence of recidivism to ensure that the children were not just being ushered through a revolving door to meet the contractor's performance criteria. In both cases—periodic testing and tracking of children discharged from group care over time—it is costly to assess performance. Moreover, in the absence of a random-assignment, experimental study, one could not attribute improvements in the children's behavior to participation in the group-home program with a high degree of scientific confidence—maybe they would have improved anyway as they matured over time. Not only does pay-for-performance contracting involve measures that are costly, uncertain, and difficult to administer for comprehensive types of social care, but also a payment structure based on particular results may encourage the process commonly referred to as "creaming," through which service providers avoid the risk of failure by selecting clients at the top of the pool, those who are most likely to succeed, rather than those who are most impaired.

Given the limitations of pegging contract costs to the number of consumers who are receiving care and the difficulties and risks of the pay-for-performance approach, purchase-of-service arrangements are most often designed to pay contractors the actual costs incurred for their work. In practice, some contract arrangements are more complicated because of substantial variations in the level of services that clients will require, which neither the purchaser nor the provider can know in advance. The managed-care model in child welfare, for example, often provides a fixed amount of payment per client per month (the *capitation* fee), based on an estimate of the average cost of services to the enrolled client population. Contracting agencies able to deliver adequate services for less than the capitation amount can pocket the difference, and those who end up serving clients that cost more than the monthly payment are liable for the difference.[83]

The decisive task in designing contracts that reimburse costs is defining all the relevant components of service and the level of quality expected in each area. Consider how public officials might define quality for the most basic components of group-home care: daily adult supervision and meals. In regard to supervision, a purchase-of-service contract would be likely to specify the educational level of the staff; their professional training, and the staff-child ratio in the home at all times, probably on the order of one staff person for every three children during the day and a one-to-four ratio during the evening hours. As for meals, the contract would certainly specify the number of meals (three daily per child, plus an afternoon snack) and basic nutritional standards. However, for the provision of both staff and meals there is a range between minimal and optimal quality, which transcends the easily measured criteria of staffing ratios, education, days of training, number of meals, and nutritional standards. These measures fail to capture such essential qualities of group care as the maturity and warmth of the staff (and where they got their education) and the taste, texture, and presentations of food. Beyond the basics of food and supervision looms the more perplexing question of what constitutes all the relevant components of care: does the contract specify the nitty-gritty of how often the floors are swept and the bed sheets are changed, how high the thermostat is kept, how many square feet are allocated per child, and how other household amenities are maintained?

One might ask, does all this really matter that much? Why not have public administrators just prepare contracts that enumerate the basic components (e.g., ratio of staff to children and number of meals) of the service being purchased and leave the rest to the professional judgment and good intentions of the private service providers? Why not just trust them to do the right thing? The answer, in part, is illustrated by the experiences of welfare offices in the United States in contracting out employment services related to the 1996 policy reforms, which replaced Aid to Families with Dependent Children (AFDC) with the Temporary Assistance for Needy Families (TANF). A study of four urban areas reports considerable variation within and between the sites in the amounts paid to the private providers who were delivering similar types of services in job search, placement assistance, and case management. For components of service that sounded very much alike, the average per-person reimbursement across the four urban areas differed by as much as 130 percent, and very large differences, up to 400 percent, were also found on the price of services within each of the areas. The largest variations in cost appeared among the sites in which the public program administrators tended to accept the price set by the service providers.[84] These findings are hardly unexpected. In the ethos of market exchanges, the admonition that the customer is always right is countermanded by the advice of caveat emptor, a warning especially pertinent to third-party purchases in which service providers stand between the buyer and the consumer.

Privatization through contracting relies on the beneficial effects of competitive bidding from service providers to contain costs and foster quality of services. However, an adequate supply of service providers is not always forthcoming. Research suggests that there are geographic areas and fields of service in which few contracts are competitively bid, and once awarded they are generally renewed without careful review.[85] But even in a highly competitive environment, it is difficult to minimize cost and maximize quality in selecting among organizations that are bidding for service contracts. How are public officials to know whether those agencies that come in with the lowest bid are offering the best prices for the most effective delivery of services? Whenever a purchase-of-service contract contains some slack in the definition of service components and measures of quality, the best price from the provider's vantage point is one that offers minimal provisions and charges as much as the market will bear, particularly if one is interested in squeezing a profit out of the transaction.

Several studies that compared profit-oriented and nonprofit service providers, for example, reveal that for-profit providers charged less in both day-care programs for children and nursing homes for the elderly when calculated simply on the basis of cost per consumer. But this advantage quickly fades when considerations for the quality of care are introduced. Thus, for example, further analysis shows that whereas for-profit day-care centers charged a lower hourly fee per child than nonprofits, they had a higher child-to-staff ratio, a lower percentage of teachers with college degrees, and a higher rate of staff turnover.[86] In nursing homes, Burton Weisbrod and Mark Schlesinger found that for-profit providers employed fewer staff members, both professional and nonprofessional, per patient than nonprofit homes and that the staff in for-profit facilities administered considerably higher doses of sleeping medication to their clients than those in non-profit homes.[87] As voluntary, nonprofit providers are increasingly drawn into competition with profit-oriented providers for service contracts, they will come under growing pressure to cut service costs by reducing quality in the areas of service that are most difficult to quantify and least likely to be specified in contractual agreements.

To perform effectively in the purchase-of-service environment, public administrators must draw contracts that tightly frame the components of services offered and define quality standards with precision. But this demand for exactitude presents a dilemma. On the one hand, if the specifications for purchase of service are not well drawn, contracts will go to those providers who promise the lowest costs, and consumers will end up paying the price by receiving a diminished quality of social care. On the other hand, if the administrators are able to break down each component into its smallest segment, rationalizing services and leaving providers less room to manoeuver (and cut corners on provisions and quality of care), they also leave less room for professional discretion. Under this system, social care that heretofore involved a holistic process informed by professional values and expertise is transformed to a series of discrete procedures bridled by pressures to contain costs—changes that more closely align the production and delivery of social care to assembly-line commodities bought and sold on the market.

Purchase-of-service contracting is not the only approach to privatization that creates pressures for the commodification of social care, as seen in the increasing use of vouchers since the 1980s, primarily in the United States. This path is paved with huge blocks of state funds disbursed to purchase care for dependents, mainly children, from kith and kin. Under the Family Support Act of 1988, for the first time states were authorized to give welfare parents who were preparing to enter the labor force vouchers or cash to pay for private child-care arrangements. Initially, only a few states exercised this option. In the 1990s, additional programs were established, which required states to offer vouchers for child care contingent on copayments usually levied according to family income. The voucher system that has emerged mitigates some of the problems of third-party purchase-of-service arrangements by tightening the link between the purchase and the consumption of care. The vouchers also increase consumer choice, which provides an opportunity for low-income parents to pay licensed and unlicensed providers, including friends and other family members, to care for their children. Precise national data on these arrangements are difficult to aggregate. A conservative estimate placed 135,000 low-income children in the care of paid relatives at a total cost of $423 million in 1993. At the same time, almost twice as many low-income children were in unpaid care with relatives, which could have cost the government an additional $827 million.[88]

The appreciable use of state funds to remunerate relatives for daily child-care services is more than matched by the burgeoning growth of kinship foster-care benefits, which pay for children to live full time with members of their extended family. Payments for kinship care surged after the 1979 Supreme Court ruling in *Miller v. Youakim* made relatives who were caring for dependent children in approved homes eligible for the same level of benefits as foster-care providers who were unrelated to their wards.[89] One national survey suggests that about one-third of the children in foster-care arrangements are living with a member of their extended family, which extrapolates to more than 150,000 children in 1996.[90]

To what extent are people today expected to care for their dependent kin—young or old or disabled? This normative question gains saliency as state monies are increasingly made available to subsidize friends and relatives for the private provision of social care. Under these arrangements, time and effort hitherto invested in unpaid, informal care, both as a demonstration of mutual aid and an expression of the traditional norms of kinship obligation, are now converted into a contractual exchange of service for payment on an hourly rate. Ultimately the public provision of cash for care creates a situation in which relatives and friends who continue to assist kin and neighbors without pay will begin to feel exploited because everyone else is being compensated for these services. Until recently, remuneration for these services has been reserved for strangers who are licensed and professional caretakers. As payments are extended to kith and kin, the marketplace absorbs a large realm of social care that was previously in the domain of unpaid labor animated by compassion, obligation, and mutual aid. Of course, there is nothing sacred about the continuation of unpaid social care—work that has been performed largely by women. However, the commodification of this realm of care diminishes the opportunity and practice of voluntarily tending to the needs of others for reasons that transcend the immediate incentives of market exchanges. Different meanings can be attributed to this development. Some might interpret the trend as promoting equal opportunity and rewards, with women receiving greater financial compensation for their labors. Still others might associate the contraction of services that people perform for each other outside the market with a hardening of human relations. These views, of course, are not mutually exclusive.

Private Safety Nets: To Each His Own?

As privatization filters into every realm of social protection, the province of state activity continues to shrink and more room is allotted for measures that shift responsibility to the individual and the market. The final outcome of this movement is not yet in sight. Carried to the extreme, one could envision the principle of public support for private responsibility to result in a scheme that would replace almost all public provisions with a system of compulsory, private "safety-net accounts." The partial privatization of old-age pensions discussed earlier represents a tentative step in this direction. Staking individual safety nets on private savings, as Dennis Snower proposes, would involve earmarked accounts to cover losses of income due to unemployment, illness, disability, and retirement; the costs of health care; and even the costs of education.[91] The accounts would be financed by the huge tax savings to individuals, derived from the elimination of taxes normally collected to pay for the public programs—no longer needed for protection against the risks of unemployment, disability, illness, and the like. To ensure equity, government grants would be used to top up the accounts of those in the lowest income groups. To guarantee a minimal level of security, an individual would be entitled to pubic assistance benefits similar to those under current policies when all the funds in one of that person's accounts are consumed and allowable transfers from other accounts are exhausted. People would be able to select among a government agency and private financial institutions to manage their private accounts, and fund managers in the private sector would be publicly regulated.

Several advantages are associated with private safety-net accounts. They represent personal assets that can be drawn upon and consumed at various points in the life cycle. At the time of retirement, for example, remaining balances in an account earmarked for protection against unemployment could be transferred to an old-age pension account and ultimately bequeathed to one's successors. Unlike public unemployment benefits, for example, which are possessed only when drawn upon, the private accounts are a potential source of wealth that accumulates with contributions. Since wealth declines when private accounts are drawn upon, this system alleviates the moral hazard induced by access to public benefits. People who rely on their private

safety nets have a greater incentive to avoid the risks of unemployment, illness, and disability (to the extent that such risks can be
avoided) than those protected by the public tax and transfer system.
And if people who are banking on private safety nets behave more
responsibly, the overall long-term costs for loss of income due to unemployment, disability, and illness will be lower than those that
would accrue under the tax-supported, public safety net.[92] In the short
term, however, high transition costs pose a daunting problem for the
financing of private safety nets. People who are entering the new system would need time to accumulate enough in their accounts for a
minimal level of protection, while still being taxed to pay for the benefits of older workers who remain covered by the tax and transfer
system of social protection. And even when accounts are mature,
those earmarked for health care would rarely contain enough to cover
the costs of catastrophic illnesses or long-term care.

Individual "endowment accounts," proposed by Robert Kuttner, offer a variation from the Left on private safety nets. In this scheme,
every child would have $5000 at birth placed in an individual account
invested in stocks and bonds and administered by the Social Security
system. Low-income children would receive additional grants, and
middle-income families would get tax deductions to add to these accounts. Over the course of one's life, various proportions of the money
accumulated in these accounts could be used to purchase education,
homes, and job training, with the residue available at age 60 to supplement retirement. This proposal is designed as a supplement, not a
substitute, for the existing Social Security program.[93]

The development of safety-net or endowment accounts emphasizes
the role of individuals and privatizes the demand side of social protection to purchase education, housing, training, and the like. The
principle of public support for private responsibility also animates the
state's efforts to enlarge the market's role—not only through purchase
of services but also by reinforcing what might be called the "caring
workplace"—in privatizing the supply side of social protection. Many
commercial firms in the advanced industrial countries already provide a vast array of pensions; disability and health insurance benefits;
and child care and personal social services, some of which are mandated by the state—and many of these provisions are financially
subsidized through tax expenditures. Going beyond indirect subsidies
through tax incentives, public programs also directly subsidize businesses to employ welfare recipients and provide on-the-job training.
The caring workplace has a special attraction in that it joins social
protection to private enterprise, imbuing social welfare activities with
the legitimacy and values of the market economy.[94] As the caring
workplace assumes increasing responsibilities for social protection,

the public system becomes more narrowly centered on ministering to people who are outside the labor force.

Whether driven by schemes that give individuals greater command over the demand for social protection or by measures that shift responsibility to businesses for the supply of social protection, the state plays a direct role in fueling the movement toward privatization with tax incentives, direct purchases, and the exercise of its regulatory powers. But there is another way, somewhat less direct, through which social welfare policy reforms over the last several decades have expedited privatization. That is, by raising the thresholds of eligibility and targeting social benefits to those most in need, the state is quietly spurring citizens who can afford it to make their own private arrangements for social welfare.

NOTES

1. Robert Reich, *The Next American Frontier* (New York: Times Books, 1983), p. 247.

2. For a discussion of developments in social entrepreneurship programs, see Emily Mitchell, "Getting Better at Doing Good," *Time*, February 21, 2000, pp. B9–12.

3. Steven Rathgeb Smith and Michael Lipsky, *Nonprofits for Hire: The Welfare State in the Age of Contracting* (Cambridge, Mass.: Harvard University Press, 1993), p. 6.

4. U.S. Census Bureau, *Statistical Abstract of the United States: 1999* (Washington, D.C.: U.S. Government Printing Office, 1999), p. 352.

5. Ibid.; U. S. Census Bureau, *Statistical Abstract of the United States: 1992* (Washington, D.C.: U.S. Government Printing Office, 1992), p. 321.

6. See, for example, Julian LeGrand and David Winter, "The Middle Classes and the Welfare State," The Welfare State Programme, Suntory Toyota Center for Economics, London School of Economics, Discussion Paper No. 14 (March 1987); and Carol Steinbach, "Eight Lessons from Europe," *Entrepreneurial Economy*, 3:7 (January 1985), 4–14.

7. By the late 1980s, the increasing popularity of a market-oriented approach to social policy stirred even the Fabian Socialists to rethink the merits of market forces, briefly flirting with the idea of "market socialism"—a new label for the notion of worker-owned cooperatives that functioned in a competitive market. Raymond Plant, "The Market: Needs, Rights, and Morality," *New Statesman*, March 6, 1987, pp. 14–15; Julian LeGrand, "The Market: Workers, Capital and Consumers," *New Statesman*, March 6, 1987, pp. 16–18; Alan Ryan, "Socialism's Great Rethink," *London Times*, March 25, 1987, p. 14.

8. John Stephens, "The Scandinavian Welfare States: Achievements, Crisis and Prospects," in Gosta Esping-Andersen, ed., *Welfare States in Transition* (London: Sage, 1996), pp. 32–65.

9. Ibid.

10. Jens Alber, "Recent Developments in the German Welfare State: Basic Continuity or Shift of a Paradigm," paper prepared for the Conference on Continuities and Change in the Welfare State, Bellagio Study and Conference Center, Italy, August 7–11, 2000.

11. David Bositis, *1999 National Opinion Pool: Education* (Washington, D.C.: Joint Center for Political and Economic Studies, 1999).

12. Myrdal offers one of the clearest statements of the Swedish perspective on the virtues of having in-kind social welfare benefits financed and produced by the government. See Alva Myrdal, *Nation and Family* (Cambridge, Mass.: MIT Press, 1968), pp. 141–43.

13. The division between finance and provision (or delivery) of social benefits is a basic distinction drawn in analyses of social policies. See, for example, Neil Gilbert and Paul Terrell, *Dimensions of Social Welfare Policy*, 4th ed. (Boston: Allyn & Bacon, 1998).

14. The Dutch reforms are reviewed by Renee van Wirdum, "The Context of Change: Social Security Reform in the Netherlands," *International Social Security Review*, 51:4 (October–December, 1998), 93–103; and Sabine Geurts, Michiel Kompier, and Robert Grundemann, "Curing the Dutch Disease? Sickness Absence and Work Disability in the Netherlands," *International Social Security Review*, 53:4 (October–December 2000), 79–103.

15. For elaboration of this point, see Willem Adema, "Net Social Expenditure," Labour Market and Social Policy Occasional Papers No. 39, p. 9, Organization for Economic Cooperation and Development, Paris, 1999.

16. For a more elaborate conceptualization of the different avenues to privatization, which adds loci of decision making to finance and provision, see Tania Burchardt, *Boundaries Between Public and Private Welfare: A Typology and Map of Services* (London: Center for Analysis of Social Exclusion, London School of Economics, 1997). In other contexts, "privatization" would also include the selling off of publicly owned enterprises, such as railroads, automobile factories, and so on.

17. Douglas Besharov and Nazanin Samari, "Child Care After Welfare Reform," Washington, D.C.: American Enterprise Institute, 2000.

18. U.S. Census Bureau, *Statistical Abstract of the United States: 1999* (Washington, D.C.: U.S. Government Printing Office, 1999), p. 352. The $3.9 billion tax expenditure is not entirely for child care, since the portion from the child and dependent-care tax credit also includes day-care services for adult dependents.

19. In the Netherlands, the United Kingdom, and the United States, for example, private pension payments as a percentage of GDP from 1988 to 1993 grew faster than public pension expenditures. Willem Adema and Marcel Einerhand, "The Growing Role of Private Social Benefits," Labour Market and Social Policy—Occasional Papers No. 32, OECD, Paris, 1998.

20. OECD, *Maintaining Prosperity in an Ageing Society* (Paris: OECD, 1998), p. 64.

21. International Social Security Association, "Developments and Trends in Social Security 1993–1995: Broad Based Retrenchment Developments," *International Social Security Review*, 49:2 (1996), 17–32.

22. The French pension system is highly fragmented, with 538 regimes serving numerous categories of public and private employees, under different rules and levels of provision, which makes reform in this area a rather complicated affair. For a detailed analysis of this system, see Jean-Claude Barbier and Bruno Theret, "The French System of Social Protection: Path Dependencies and Societal Coherence," paper prepared for the Conference on Continuities and Change in the Welfare State, Bellagio Study and Conference Center, Italy, August 7–11, 2000 (rev. December 2000).

23. K. Borden, "Dismantling the Pyramid: The Why and How of Privatizing Social Security," The CATO Project on Social Security Privatization, SSP No.1, 1995; World Bank, *Averting the Old Age Crisis* (New York: Oxford University Press, 1994).

24. World Bank, *Averting the Old Age Crisis*; see also Robert Holzmann, "A World Bank Perspective on Pension Reform," paper prepared for the Joint ILO-OECD Workshop on the Development and Reform of Pension Schemes, Paris, December 15–17, 1997.

25. This debate was launched by Roger Beattie and Warren McGillivray, "A Risky Strategy: Reflections on the World Bank Report *Averting the Old Age Crisis*," *International Social Security Review*, 48:3/4 (1995), 5–22. For the rejoinders, see Estelle James, "Providing Better Protection and Promoting Growth: A Defence of *Averting the Old Age Crisis*," *International Social Security Review*, 49:3 (1996), 3–17, and the response by Roger Beattie and Warren McGillivray, 17–20.

26. Ajit Singh, "Pension Reform, the Stock Market, Capital Formation and Economic Growth: A Critical Commentary on the World Bank's Proposals," *International Social Security Review*, 43:9 (1996), 21–41.

27. Lawrence Thompson, *Older and Wiser: The Economics of Public Pensions* (Washington, D.C.: Urban Institute, 1998).

28. Larry Wilmore, "Public Versus Private Provision of Pensions," Discussion Paper of the United Nations Department of Economic and Social Affairs, No. 1 (1998).

29. Peter Orszag and Joseph Stiglitz, "Rethinking Pension Reform: Ten Myths About Social Security Systems," paper presented at the Conference on New Ideas About Old Age Security, p. 40, World Bank, Washington, D.C., September 14–15, 1999.

30. For example, see R. Meyers and P. Diamond, "Social Security Reform in Chile: Two Views," in P. Diamond, D. Lindeman, and H. Young, eds., *Social Security: What Role for the Future?* (Washington, D.C.: National Academy of Social Insurance, 1996); Martin Tracy and F. Pampel, eds., *International Handbook on Old-Age Insurance* (New York: Greenwood, 1991); John Turner and Noriyasu Watanabe, *Private Pension Policies in Industrialized Countries: A Comparative Analysis.* (Kalamazoo, Michigan: W.E. Upjohn Institute for Employment Research, 1995); Dimitri Vittas and Augusto Iglesias, "The Rationale and Performance of Personal Pension Plans in Chile," Working Paper, Financial Policy and Systems Division of the World Bank, Washington, D.C., 1992.

31. In 1993–94, private schemes based on the Chilean model were introduced in Peru, Argentina, and Columbia. In the late 1990s, Venezuela was planning to follow suit. However, in January 2000 the Ve-

nezuelan Council of Ministers changed course and eliminated the earlier plans to privatize the country's social security system. See Monkia Queisser, "Chile and Beyond. The Second-Generation Pension Reforms in Latin America," *International Social Security Review*, 3–4 (1995), 23–29; and International Social Security Association, *Trends in Social Security*, no. 3 (2000), 7.

32. C. Kraus, "Social Security, Chilean Style: Pensioners Quiver as Markets Fall," *New York Times*, August 16, 1998, p. 4.

33. See Howard Glennerster *Paying for Welfare* (Oxford: Basil Blackwell, 1985); Chrisotpher Daykin, "Occupational Pensions in the United Kingdom," in Zvi Bodie, Olivia Mitchell, and John Turner, eds., *Securing Employer-Based Pensions* (Philadelphia: University of Pennsylvania Press, 1995); Turner and Watanabe, *Private Pension Policies in Industrialized Countries*.

34. Christina Behrendt, "Private Pensions—A Viable Alternative? Their Distributive Effects in a Comparative Perspective," *International Social Security Review*, 53:3 (2000), 3–26.

35. "Germany: Radical Pensions," *Economist*, November 18, 2000, pp. 60–61; International Social Security Association, "2000 Pension Reforms: Key Elements of the Government Approach," *Trends in Social Security*, 4 (2000), 13.

36. Jonah Levy, "France: Directing Adjustment?" in Fritz Scharpf and Vivien Schmidt, eds. *From Vulnerability to Competitiveness: Welfare and Work in the Open Economy* (Oxford: Oxford University Press, 2000).

37. See Gosta Esping-Andersen, *Social Foundations of Post-Industrial Economies* (New York: Oxford University Press, 1999), p. 81. The source of the data given for the analyses conducted here by the author cites table 3.1 in his 1990 book, Gosta Esping-Andersen, *Three Worlds of Welfare Capitalism* (Cambridge: Polity Press, 1990). The data in that table were from 1980.

38. Einar Overbye, *Risk and Welfare: Examining Stability and Change in Welfare Policies* (Oslo: Norwegian Social Research, 1998).

39. Neil Gilbert and Barbara Gilbert, *The Enabling State: Modern Welfare Capitalism in America* (New York: Oxford University Press, 1989).

40. Under employer-related pensions, I would include those for government employees. Although partially financed by units of government, these pensions are not "private" in the literal sense. However, in their diversity they resemble more the private exchange of fringe benefits for labor negotiated between employer and employees in the private sector than standard, publicly mandated, intergenerational transfer under universal social security programs.

41. For a discussion of these reforms, see C. Eugene Steuerle and Jon Bakija, *Retooling Social Security for the 21st Century: Right and Wrong Approaches to Reform* (Washington, D.C.: Urban Institute, 1994).

42. The net transfer is the difference between lifetime benefits received and the social security taxes paid by recipients. Among those retiring in 2010, the net transfers are expected to become negative for average and high-earning single retirees and high-earning two-earner couples. Ibid.

43. B. Stein, *Social Security and Pensions in Transition: Understanding the American Retirement System* (New York: Free Press, 1980).

44. This figure does not include those covered by private individual plans, such as individual retirement accounts (IRAs)—the value of which multiplied from $200 billion to $1.3 trillion between 1985 and 1996—and Keogh plans. U.S. Census Bureau, *Statistical Abstract of the United States: 1999* (Washington, D.C.: U.S. Government Printing Office, 1999), p. 394.

45. According to the Pension Guarantee Corporation, underfunding among private pensions has more than doubled, from $18 billion in 1982 to about $40 billion in 1991, for single-employer plans. Another $11 billion in underfunding among multiemployer plans brought the 1991 total underfunding in the federally insured pensions to about $51 billion. Although most of the underfunding is concentrated in a relatively small number of companies, public liability is substantial and warrants reforms that strengthen the funding rules for private plans. Pension Benefit Guarantee Corporation, *Annual Report, 1992* (Washington, D.C.: Pension Benefit Guarantee Corporation, 1992).

46. Neil Gilbert and Neung Hoo Park, "Privatization, Provision, and Targeting: Trends and Policy Implications for Social Security in the United States," *International Social Security Review*, 49:1 (1996), 19–29.

47. Neung Hoo Park and Neil Gilbert, "Social Security and the Incremental Privatization of Retirement Income," *Journal of Sociology and Social Welfare*, 26:2 (June 1999). Similar results of privatization are found in other countries. See Behrendt, "Private Pensions."

48. For an analyses of these transition costs, see Thompson, *Older and Wiser*, pp. 124–30.

49. Almost half of the these privately run prisons are under contract with the Corrections Corporation of America, which is now the fourth-largest corrections system in the United States. For a discussion of this development, see David Masci, "Prison-Building Boom," in *Issues in Social Policy* (Washington, D.C.: Congressional Quarterly Press, 2000), pp. 146–148.

50. This opening to the private sector is discussed in Neil Gilbert, *Capitalism and the Welfare State: Dilemmas of Social Benevolence* (New Haven, Conn.: Yale University Press, 1983).

51. Neil Gilbert and Kwong Leung Tang, "The United States," in Norman Johnson, ed., *Private Markets in Health and Welfare* (Oxford: Berg, 1995).

52. Burchardt, *Boundaries Between Public and Private Welfare*.

53. Norman Johnson, "The United Kindgom," in Norman Johnson, ed., *Private Markets in Health and Welfare* (Oxford, Berg, 1995), p. 29.

54. Anna-Lena Almqvist and Thomas Boje, "Who Cares, Who Pays, and How Is Care for Children Provided? Comparing Family Life and Work in Different European Welfare Systems," in *Comparing Social Welfare Systems in Nordic Europe and France*. Text collected by Denis Bouget and Bruno Palier (Paris: DREES/MiRe, 1999), pp. 265–92.

55. Juhani Lehto, "Universal Right to Public Social and Health Care Services?" in *Comparing Social Welfare Systems in Nordic Eu-*

rope and France. Text collected by Denis Bouget and Bruno Palier (Paris: DREES/MiRe, 1999), p. 650.

56. Richard Titmuss, *Social Policy*, Brian Abel-Smith and Kay Titmuss, eds. (London: Allen & Unwin, 1974), p. 151.

57. Seven Olsson Hort and Daniel Cohn, "Sweden," in Norman Johnson, ed., *Private Markets in Health and Welfare* (Oxford: Berg, 1995), p. 183.

58. Tommy Lundstrom, "Non-governmental Actors, Local Administration, and Private Enterprise: New Models in Delivery of Child and Youth Welfare?" paper presented at the International Conference on Playing the Market Game? University of Bielefeld, Germany, March 9–11, 2000.

59. Ake Bergmark, Mats Thorslund, and Elisabet Lindberg, "Beyond Benevolence—Solidarity and Welfare State Transition in Sweden," *International Journal of Social Welfare*, 9:4 (October 2000), 238–49.

60. Tor Slettebo, "The Consequences of Marketization on Professional Practice and Identity—A Case Study of Outcontracting in the Residential Child and Youth Protection Servies in Norway," paper presented at the International Conference on Playing the Market Game? University of Bielefeld, Germany, March 9 to 11, 2000.

61. Jens Alber, "Recent Developments in the German Welfare State."

62. Dik Hermans, "Privatisation: From Panacea to Poison Pill, the Dutch Paradigm Shift," in Dalmer Hoskins, Donate Dobbernack, and Christiane Kuptsch, eds., *Social Security at the Dawn of the 21st Century* (New Brunswick, N.J.: Transaction Publishers, 2001).

63. For an analysis of governments' expanding use of voluntary, nonprofit organizations to provide services to physically, mentally, and sensorially handicapped persons in Italy, the Netherlands, the United Kingdom, and Norway, see Ralph Kramer, Hakon Lorentzen, Willem Melief, and Sergio Pasquinelli, *Privatization in Four European Countries: Comparative Studies in Government–Third Sector Relationships* (New York: M. E. Sharpe, 1993).

64. Émile Durkheim, *De La Division du Travail Social (The Division of Labor in Society)*, George Simpson, trans. (New York: Free Press, [1893] 1933), Alexis de Tocqueville, *Democracy in America*, Henry Reeve, trans. (New York: Knopf, 1963).

65. De Tocqueville, *Democracy in America*, pp. 181, 185.

66. Dan Coats, "Can Congress Revive Civil Society?" *Policy Review*, no.75 (January–February, 1996), 25.

67. "The Responsive Communitarian Platform: Rights and Responsibilities," *Responsive Community*, 2:1 (Winter 1991–92), 4.

68. Charles Krauthammer, "A Social Conservative Credo," *Public Interest*, 121 (Fall 1995), 17.

69. On this point, Zijderveld argues that when the organizations of civil society are financially dependent on the state, the central government sets the agenda and civil society loses "its stamina, its vitality and its much needed flexibility." Anton Zijderveld, *The Waning of the Welfare State* (New Brunswick, N.J.: Transaction Publishers, 1999), p. 53.

70. For a discussion of the lineage of this concept, see Ian Winter, "Major Themes and Debates in the Social Capital Literature: The Aus-

tralian Connection," in Ian Winter, ed., *Social Capital and Public Policy in Australia* (Melbourne: Australian Institute of Family Studies, 2000). pp. 17–42.

71. Jane Jacobs, *Death and Life of Great American Cities* (New York: Vintage Books, 1963), p. 138.

72. James Coleman, "Social Capital in the Creation of Human Capital," *American Journal of Sociology*, 94, Supplement (1988), S 95–120.

73. Robert Putnam, "Bowling Alone: America's Declining Social Capital," *Journal of Democracy*, 6:1 (1995), 65–78. Putnam's work caused quite a stir and, as one might expect, incited much criticism. For example, Everett Ladd, *The Ladd Report* (New York: Free Press, 1999), found that civic life was not so much diminishing as "churning," as new organizations come into existence; thus, the rise of soccer clubs offsets the fall in bowling leagues. Other critics question empirical measurements of social capital, which civic engagement is supposed to enhance, and the role of government, family, and firms, along with participation in voluntary associations, in the creation of social capital. See Ian Winter, ed., *Social Capital and Public Policy in Australia* (Melbourne: Australian Institute of Family Studies, 2000).

74. For the essential flavor of this debate, see Ladd, *Ladd Report*; and Robert Putnam, *Bowling Alone: The Collapse and Revival of American Community* (New York: Simon & Schuster, 2000).

75. See, for example, Krauthammer, "Social Conservative Credo," pp. 15–22; Peter Berger and Richard Neuhaus, *To Empower People: From State to Civil Society*, Michael Novak, ed. (Washington, D.C.: AEI Press, 1996); Stephen Osborne and Aniko Kaposavri, "Towards a Civil Society? Exploring Its Meaning in the Context of Post-Communist Hungary," *Journal of European Social Policy*, 7:3 (August 1997), 209–22; Zijderveld, *Waning of the Welfare State*.

76. For an excellent analysis of the blurring of lines in conceptualizations of the third sector, see Ralph Kramer, "A Third Sector in the Third Millennium?" *Journal of Voluntary and Nonprofit Organizations*, 11:1 (2000), 1–23.

77. This perspective is developed in Eva Cox and Peter Caldwell, "Making Policy Social," in Winter, *Social Capital and Public Policy in Australia*. pp. 43–73.

78. Alan Wolfe, "Developing Civil Society: Can the Workplace Replace Bowling?" *Responsive Community*, 8:2 (Spring 1998), 43.

79. U.S. Census Bureau, *Statistical Abstract of the United States: 1999* (Washington D.C., U.S. Government Printing office, 1999), p. 453.

80. Douglas Besharov, "Bottom-Up Funding," in Peter Berger and Richard John Neuhaus, *To Empower People: From State to Civil Society*, 20th Anniversary Edition, Michael Novak, ed. (Washington, D.C.: AEI Press, 1996), pp. 124–31.

81. Bear in mind that an average unit cost computed in this way is different from the marginal costs of adding one more unit of service. There are certain fixed overhead costs that do not expand proportionately with an increase in units of service.

82. These figures represent the hospital rates and ADFC and mental-health rates for residential care of severely emotionally disturbed children in northern California.

83. For a detailed analysis of 47 managed-care initiatives in child welfare, see Charolette McCullough and Barbara Schmitt, "Managed Care and Privatization: Results of a National Survey," *Children and Youth Services Review*, 22:2, (February 2000), 117–30.

84. Michelle Derr, Jacquelyn Anderson, Carole Trippe, and Sidnee Paschal, *The Role of Intermediaries in Linking TANF Recipients with Jobs* (Washington, D.C.: Mathematica Policy Research, February 2000). In examining what might have accounted for these differences the study found a high degree of variance in sites where the TANF program administrators just accepted the purchase price set by the private providers and in contrast, a high degree of comparability in prices in sites where the program administrators negotiated with providers on the price of services.

85. In North Carolina, for example, there is a paucity of providers for substance-abuse services. See Steven R. Smith and Judith Smyth, "Contracting for Services in a Decentralized System," *Journal of Public Administartion Research and Theory*, 6:2 (April 1996), 277–96.

86. See, for example, E. Kisker, S.L. Hofferth, D. Phillips, and E. Farquhar, *A Profile of Child Care Settings: Early Education and Care in 1990—Executive Summary* (Washington, D.C.: U.S. Department of Education, 1991).

87. Burton Weisbrod and Mark Schlesinger, "Nonprofit Ownership and the Response to Asymmetric Information: The Case of Nursing Homes," in Susan Rose-Ackerman, ed., *The Economics of Nonprofit Institutions* (New York: Oxford University Press, 1986).

88. Douglas Besharov and Nazanin Samari, "Child Care Vouchers and Cash Payments," in C. Eugene Steurele, Van Doorn Ooms, George Peterson and Robert Reischauer, eds., *Vouchers and the Provision of Public Services* (Washington, D.C.: Brookings Institution, 2000), pp. 195–223.

89. For an overview of this development, see Barbara Needell and Neil Gilbert, "Child Welfare and the Extended Family," in Jill Duerr Berrick, Richard Barth, and Neil Gilbert, eds., *Child Welfare Research Review* (New York: Columbia University Press, 1997), vol. II, pp. 85–99.

90. Data from 29 states that could identify kinship-care placements in 1991 showed that 31 percent of the children in legal custody of the states were placed with members of their extended family. See R. Kusserow, *State Practices in Using Relatives for Foster Care* (Dallas: Dallas Regional Office: Office of the Inspector General, 1992). In 1996 there were 5.3 million children in out-of-home placements as reported in U.S. Census Bureau, *Statistical Abstract of the United States: 1999*, p. 403.

91. For a more detailed discussion of this strategy for privatization, see Dennis Snower, "Challenges to Social Cohesion and Approaches to Policy Reform," in *Societal Cohesion and the Globalizing Economy: What Does the Future Hold?* (Paris: OECD, 1997), pp. 39–60.

92. Ibid.

93. See Robert Kuttner, "Rampant Bull: Social Security and the Market," *American Prospect*, July–August 1998, pp. 30–36.

94. However, this attraction must contend with paternalistic im-

ages of the not-always-benign company town, which the caring workplace evokes. In fairness to their capitalist architects, it should be said that company towns were not all as unpleasant as one tends to imagine. For an objective account, see Stuart Brandes, *American Welfare Capitalism: 1880–1940* (Chicago: University of Chicago Press, 1970).

5

Universal to Selective

Targeting Benefits

Social welfare policies are instruments to dispense cash, goods, and services outside of the regular channels of distribution in the market economy of industrialized nations. A basic principle of the welfare state is that the individual's right to welfare does not depend on valuations of the market. The central function of welfare, as T. H. Marshall put it, "is to supersede the market by taking goods and services out of it, or in some way to control and modify its operations so as to produce a result which it would not have produced itself."[1] In the market, people get the goods and services they can afford to purchase: ability to pay dictates the process of market exchange. In contrast, it is the collective will (or some might say a collection of special group interests) expressed by democratically elected officials that determines who receives benefits transferred through the social channels of the welfare state. Grappling with the fiscal and demographic necessities that confront the industrialized nations, policymakers are under intense pressure to concentrate public expenditures on those most in need. Among the fundamental questions that must be addressed by the architects of welfare reform, perhaps, none is more contentious than this: who shall be eligible?

Since the birth of the welfare state, policymakers have debated the defining principles that guide the allocation of social benefits. The classic line of this debate draws the distinction between universalism and selectivity.[2] Simply stated, universalism embodies the idea that welfare benefits should be made available to everyone as a social right. Selectivity is associated with the premise that benefits should be distributed on the basis of individual need, as determined by a test of income. Those who advocate selectivity claim that means testing, which dispenses benefits according to financial need, reduces overall spending and ensures that the limited resources in public coffers are directed to citizens in the most dire circumstances. Allocating benefits to the poor facilitates the redistribution of resources at the same time that it avoids asking taxpayers to subsidize people who can otherwise afford to meet their own needs. Champions of selectivity ask, Why should the state be involved in the churning of private incomes by collecting more taxes than necessary in order to distribute public benefits to people who really do not need them?

Those who favor universal policies maintain that allocating benefits as a right to all citizens avoids the division of society into separate groups of givers and receivers, which promotes solidarity and inhibits the attachment of social stigma to welfare consumption. They contend that programs designed for poverty-stricken people end up like their clients—in shabby quarters and poorly funded. Moreover targeting based on income-tested criteria always leads to the withdrawal of benefits as income rises, which creates disincentive effects that can discourage people from going to work or can spur their labor into the informal economy. As for the larger fiscal implications, although universal programs are more expensive than selective allocations, some argue that this expense is partially offset by the higher administrative tab associated with the transaction costs of conducting means tests and the continuous monitoring of eligibility.[3]

Universalism is widely acclaimed as one of the defining principles of the welfare state ideal as reflected in the Scandinavian–social democratic model, whereas selectivity represents the liberal regime of Anglo-American policies.[4] As we shall see, these principles are more complicated than are conveyed by this rudimentary account since selectivity can take many forms. But for the moment, this distinction serves to sharpen one line of analysis: that is, if there is convergence toward a new framework for social welfare governed by the enabling state, we would anticipate an increasing degree of means-tested selectivity in the social expenditures of the industrialized nations.

When targeting is based on means-tested need, eligibility for social benefits is determined by an individual's financial circumstances, evidence of which can be limited to income (sometimes referred to as an "income test") or may include both income and assets. After nearly two decades of meandering efforts to secure administrative reliability in the allocation of means-tested benefits in Italy, for example, a new instrument, the Indicator of Socio-Economic Conditions, was introduced by governmental decree in 1998. Popularly referred to as the "wealth meter," this instrument enumerates a comprehensive list of sources of income and assets that must be counted in determining eligibility for means-tested social benefits. Total household income adjusted for family size is the financial unit of reference. Surveying the Italian experience, Maurizio Ferrera concludes that over the last two decades the Italian welfare state has made increasing use of targeting and that in recent years "the overall coherence and 'rationality' of targeting rules and the efficacy of their actual administration have significantly improved."[5] He sees the Indicator of Socio-Economic Conditions as an administrative device for achieving greater social justice in the distribution of scarce resources, which sets the Italian welfare state on a promising course. The initial application of this instrument, however, has excluded many of the major means-tested benefits. Although these exemptions are explained by policymakers as an effort to experiment with new criteria at the margins before launching a full-scale application, Ferrera suggests that the underlying justification is the fear of imposing losses on many people who are currently receiving benefits but would no longer qualify under the new rules.[6]

The Drift toward Income-Tested Benefits

One set of findings from a major comparative study by Tony Eardley and his colleagues illustrates the change in income-tested expenditures as a proportion of all social security expenditures between 1980 and 1992 in a sample of OECD countries for which comparable data were available. As shown in table 5.1, these data lend themselves to several interpretations. If we were interested in ranking the countries, clearly some of them started out and ended up with a much higher proportion of income-tested social expenditures than others. But the focus of concern is on the overall direction and consistency of change. Over the 12-year period, income-tested social expenditures increased as a proportion of all social security expenditures among the vast majority (80 percent) of OECD countries in this sample. Averaging about 5 percent, the increase is not large, and with several of the countries registering climbs of 10 percent to 20 percent, the growth in most of the countries was below the average. But the direction and overall rates of change are clear and high enough that they cannot be attributed simply to random fluctuations over time. Also, to the extent that the spread among these countries changed, it was in the direction of convergence, toward the mean, though only to a slight degree. Although Denmark and Finland were not included in this table because the available data were not entirely comparable, income-tested benefits increased in Denmark from 6.1 percent to 7.8 percent between 1985 to 1992 and in Finland from .09 percent to 2.1 percent between

Table 5.1 Means-Tested and Income-Tested
Expenditures as a Proportion of Total Social Security
Expenditure: 1980 and 1992

Country	1980	1992
Australia	67.6	90.3
Austria	5.7	6.7
Belgium	2.3	3.0
Canada	19.6	18.9
France	3.5	6.4
Italy	9.1	9.1
Japan	7.3	3.7
Netherlands	8.3	10.9
New Zealand	82.8	100
Norway	2.5	4.8
Portugal	2.3	3.8
Spain	2.1	8.4
Sweden	4.6	6.7
United Kingdom	21.9	33.0
United States	29.3	39.8
Mean (C.V.)	17.92 (133.5)	23.03 (132.6)

$t = 2.79$; $p = .016$.

Source: Data adapted from figures in table 2.5 in Tony Eardley, Jonathan Bradshaw, John Ditch, Ian Gough, and Peter Whitford, *Social Assistance in OECD Countries: Synthesis Report* (London: HMSO, 1996).

1982 and 1991. Thus, the share of income-tested benefits rose in all of the Scandinavian countries. In Germany, the proportion of income-tested benefits also increased, from 7.1 percent to 11.9 percent, between 1980 and 1990. Over that decade, the proportion of the population that was receiving income-tested benefits climbed in almost every country.[7]

Data from Eurostat, the Statistical Office of the European Communities, confirm this trend. Examining the shift in eligibility for 14 European nations on which data were available from 1990 to 1997, figure 5.1 shows that the highest rate of change was in the area of benefits to children and families. Here means-tested allocations increased in 12 of the 14 countries for an overall average gain of 4.6 percent over the eight-year period. (In absolute terms the 4.6 percent gain is not large, although as a proportional gain it amounts to almost 25 percent in less than a decade.) This modest increase over a relatively brief period of time is statistically significant; that is, it is unlikely that the differences can be attributed to changes that would be expected to occur merely by chance.

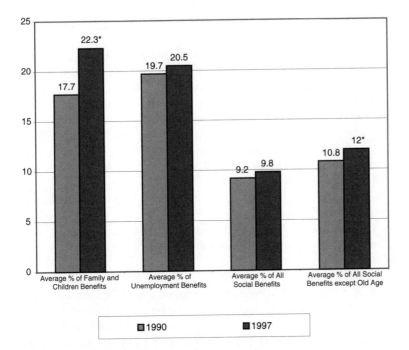

Figure 5.1 Means-Tested Benefits in 14 European Countries: 1990 and 1997. The countries included are Belgium, Denmark, Germany, Greece, Spain, France, Ireland, Italy, Netherlands, Austria, Portugal, Finland, United Kingdom, and Norway. *Note:* *p < .05 *Source:* Eurostat, Social Protection Expenditure and Receipts (Luxembourg: Office for Official Publication of European Communities, 2000), tables B3.1–19, C2 1.1–17.7.

To a lesser extent, the proportion of means-tested benefits in unemployment programs also increased in most of the countries, although in this area of provision the average change came to about 1 percent (or a proportional increase of 5 percent). Overall, means-tested benefits as a percentage of all social expenditures in these 14 countries, which include family and children, housing, old-age, unemployment, health, disability, and social exclusion benefits, increased very slightly—9.2 percent to 9.8 percent. When expenditures on old-age programs are excluded from the total social expenditure, the absolute increase overall is 1.2 percent (a proportional increase of 10 percent). Among the Nordic countries, although Finland and Denmark showed small net gains in the overall proportion of means-tested expenditures for the 1900–1997 period, Norway registered a small decline, as did Sweden from 1993 to 1997 (the period for which data were available).

The developments in Sweden during this period are interesting in that they reveal how a strategy to sustain universalism by flat across-the-board benefit reductions in one area can lead to an increase in means-tested benefits in other areas. To lower the budget deficit in the mid-1990s, children's allowances were substantially reduced for the first time. This was seen as a defensive strategy that allowed policy-makers to maintain the universal model rather than reducing the expenditure on child benefits through means testing.[8] At the same time, additional measures were instituted, such as imposing stricter income limits on eligibility for housing. Between 1995 and 1997, for example, spending on means-tested housing benefits declined from 19.8 billion to 15.9 billion Swedish krona.[9] As a result of these cuts, there was a substantial hike in expenditure on means-tested social assistance benefits.[10]

The slowly rising proportion of income-tested expenditures since 1980 is a change more aptly characterized as a drift than as a tidal wave. Taken as a whole, income-tested benefits still account for a relatively small proportion of social expenditures—an average of 23 percent according to the data on 15 countries from the study by Eardley and his colleagues and 10 percent according to the data on 14 countries from Eurostat. The discrepancy between these estimates reflects, in part, the inclusion of several countries with very high levels of income tested-benefits, such as the United States (39.8 percent), New Zealand (100 percent), and Australia (90.3 percent) in the former study.[11] In interpreting these figures, one should bear in mind that the proportion of income-tested benefits in both samples is ultimately constrained by the fact that the bulk of social expenditures is devoted to old-age pensions, which are fairly resistant to explicit income testing in most countries.

However, there is more than immediately meets the eye in the rise of income-tested benefits. Beneath the surface of explicit policies and program reforms that can be measured against income-tested criteria of eligibility, there are other currents of change that surreptitiously target benefits according to income. One form of covert targeting occurs when the state doles out cash benefits to everyone with the hand of public beneficence while quietly guiding the tax collectors' hand to take back a large portion of these benefits from those in the upper-income levels—a policy that begets means-tested allocations while maintaining the appearance of universalism. In the United States, for example, old-age pensions for retirees are taxed when a married couple's adjusted gross income plus half of their Social Security benefits amount to a middle-class income of $44,000. As noted in chapter 2, many countries claw back a substantial share of social welfare benefits by counting them as taxable income. Since these taxes tend to be progressive, the amount of benefits left in hand is ultimately a function of the recipient's level of income.

There are large differences among countries in the extent to which their tax systems are used to target the consumption of benefits on the basis of income. As illustrated in figure 5.2, the Scandinavian countries and the Netherlands have the highest proportions of social spending reclaimed by the treasurer after benefits are allocated, whereas the lowest taxes are levied on social benefits in the four Anglo-American countries, which rely more heavily on means-tested eligibility at the front end.

As Mike Reddin put it in 1969, the tax system can be employed to make public benefits universal at the point of distribution but selective at the point of consumption.[12] More recently, Theda Skocpol dubbed this approach "selectivity within universalism."[13] However one describes it, what we have is a sleight of hand through which the state distributes more in the way of social expenditures than citizens are eventually allowed to consume. All this churning of money maintains the illusion of universalism by diminishing the transparency of

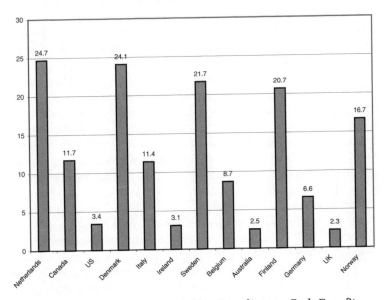

Figure 5.2 Percentage of Gross Public Spending on Cash Benefits Reclaimed Through Taxes: 1995. *Source:* Wilem Adema, *Net Social Expenditure,* Labour Market and Social Policy Occasional Paper No. 39 (Paris: OECD, 1999), table 3.

social allocations. But why go through these motions to manufacture the appearance of universality?

Avoiding Stigma or Advancing Equity

One answer traditionally given to preferences for universalism (or efforts to maintain the appearance of universalism) is to avoid the stigma attached to means testing. "The means test stigmatizes beneficiaries" is a mantra that has gained almost factual status from repetition. Yet this historical premise of social welfare policy rests on not a scintilla of evidence. If anything, some evidence shows that the means test per se is not an eventful source of indignation to public assistance recipients.[14] One can trace assertions made well over 30 years ago about the stigmatizing effects of the means test to the influential writings of Richard Titmuss, who characterized this approach to allocating social benefits as an "assault on human dignity."[15] Of course, the virulent exercise of bureaucratic authority and discretion can make almost any administrative procedure, from applying for a driver's license to registering for college classes, a demeaning experience. In the United States there were the humiliating "midnight raids" on public assistance clients to determine if they were living with a man or had made purchases that showed access to resources beyond their AFDC grants—an offensive method of means testing that was declared an invasion of privacy by the California Supreme Court in 1967.[16] But these disagreeable practices do not make a convincing case against the principle of means-tested policies; one must distinguish between the principle of mean testing and its bureaucratic administration. Administrative procedures are abusive and demeaning when the disclosure of income involves a stern and probing interview, conducted during an unscheduled home visit.[17] But if the determination of eligibility involves a simple dignified procedure, such as the self-disclosure of income and assets on a standard form, the process is relatively innocuous.

One must also take into account the level of income used to establish eligibility for social benefits. When the income threshold is set relatively high, a means test may be perceived as a method of allocation that denies eligibility to the very wealthy. When the threshold is set very low, the means test is seen as a device to benefit those in poverty. The premise that such tests create a stigma may reflect more the characteristics of the groups to whom this criterion of eligibility is often applied than the consequences of its application. That is, many poor people may feel stigmatized even *before* they make an application for benefits if, as some sociologists suggest, being poor is itself considered disreputable or embarrassing.[18] To the extent that people judge their self-worth according to their position on the scale of personal income, means tests that concentrate on the poor are serving a group that arrives from the start with some feelings of mortification.

All this is to say that despite the long-standing claims, there is nothing inherently demeaning in the means test as a procedure for allocating resources. College students in the United States, for example, appear unfazed by the means test when applying for financial aid. When asked about this approach, students in my department at the University of California, Berkeley, expressed a strong preference for means-tested selection over other criteria for scholarships. When average citizens fill out an annual income tax form, they must provide all sorts of information about their financial situation to calculate what they owe or what they will receive from the government—an exercise conducted without apparent damage to their sense of self-worth. In New Zealand, where almost all the basic social welfare benefits (with the exception of public pensions) are income-tested, Ross Mackay reports that this approach does not have pejorative associations. On the contrary, he notes that income testing is widely supported and even "carries a positive association of fairness" as a way to ensure that assistance is available to those who really need it.[19]

Although New Zealand is an extreme case, Mackay's comment on fairness resonates with a new discourse on means-tested policy that is beginning to surface. Under increasing fiscal pressures for reform, the traditional attractions of universalism to welfare state advocates on the Left are on the wane. As analysts and policymakers look for reasons to embrace income-tested allocations, they have rediscovered its merits, particularly as a method to promote equity. The need to reduce social benefits in response to budgetary limitations is clearly expressed by the ministers responsible for social policy in OECD countries in their 1992 endorsement of new orientations to social policy. They identify several ways to accomplish the reduction of social benefits, which include targeting by income, either directly or through taxes, and restricting eligibility criteria. In reviewing the alternatives, they suggest that subjecting benefits to a progressive income tax is the simplest and most equitable approach. Without putting too fine a point on it, in selecting among the targeting options, they conclude that "an emphasis on equity and a measure of altruism are necessary components."[20] This appeal to equity is exemplified in the reform of income-tested benefits under the French system of family allowances in the late 1990s. What began as a universal policy of family allowances has become increasingly means-tested over the last several decades. According to one estimate, means-tested allocations rose from

13.5 percent of all family benefits in 1970 to 45 percent at the end of the 1980s and climbed to 60 percent in the 1990s, if the *revenu minimum d'insertion* program is included.[21] Taking the means test to new heights, the Jospin government introduced in 1998 a measure to exclude rich households from receiving any family allowance payments. In a sleight-of-hand tax tradeoff, this reform was rescinded the following year at no cost to the government because at the same time the maximum child income tax credit was reduced so that wealthy families ended up paying in additional taxes what they then received in child-allowance benefits.[22]

Analyzing the French approach to family allowances as a Left-progressive strategy that converts "vice to virtue," Jonah Levy explains that by targeting these benefits, the government can reduce expenditures without compromising commitments to the poor and disadvantaged. "Efficiency and equity," he advises, "can be advanced together—or, at least, the gains of one need not be purchased at the expense of the other."[23] Bruno Palier, on the other hand, suggests that the new orientation toward means-tested benefits identifies the "transformation of social protection in France as a 'liberal' rather than 'universal' dynamic."[24] (In this context, "liberal" refers to the Anglo-American approach.) Whether the increased means testing reflects a strategy of the New Left or a move to the neoliberal Right, the emerging emphasis on equity is a case of doing the same thing but highlighting more noble motives than those previously associated with this approach. By definition, vertical redistribution—delivering benefits to those most in need, with little seepage to people with sufficient resources—has always been a feature of the means test, although the extent to which income-tested policy alleviates poverty varies among countries.[25]

Indeed, the attributes of equity and efficiency have traditionally stood in contrast to the presumed vices, such as stigmatizing the poor and dividing society into distinct groups of givers and receivers. Since the mid-1990s, as Denis Bouget points out, the new proponents of means-tested reforms in French governments of both the Left and the Right have lost sight of the presumed virtues of universalism—avoiding stigma; inhibiting the creation of poor programs for poor people; and perhaps most of all, promoting social cohesion.[26] But they have not vanished entirely. With the increasing prevalence of means testing, new distinctions are introduced into the traditional discourse that pay homage to the universal orientation by enlisting the terminology of universalism in the service of selectivity. One such effort contrasts "liberal universalism," which "implies flat rate benefits for all," with "socio-democratic universalism," which "allows for modulating benefits for vertical redistribution purposes and it incorporates targeting in the perspective of equal outcomes."[27] The primary method of adjusting benefits for vertical redistribution is through means testing, either at the point of distribution or of consumption. In addition to taxation, another way to reduce the relative consumption of "universal" benefits is to allow them to erode over time while increasing the value of means-tested benefits in the same functional category. Thus, in Belgium, the phrase "targeting within universalism," has been crafted to cover the shift toward more means-tested family allowance benefits between 1980 and 1995 in the cloak of universal ideals. In 1980, the means-tested allowance for a first child amounted to less than half the benefit of non-means-tested child allowances for employed people. By 1995, the value of means-tested allowances increased fivefold, rising substantially above non-means-tested allowances for employed people, which had actually declined by about 3 percent.[28]

Shrinking the Categories

The increasing drift toward means-tested social welfare policies, both directly at the point of distribution or indirectly at the point of consumption, is symptomatic of a broader retreat from the ideal of universalism in the advanced industrialized world. Among the proliferation of policies designed to target social welfare benefits, the universal versus means-test alternatives represent something akin to the outer rim and the bulls-eye—most of the targeting policy is going on in between. The bona fide universal schemes at the outer rim have always constituted a very thin band of policies. "Truly universal programmes," as Stein Ringen tells it, "are in fact very rare. Even large welfare states commonly have a large number of income-tested benefits, such as social assistance, housing support and family support for child care."[29] There are a few exceptions, such as the British National Health Service, which covers everybody and allows even people who may be healthy, but think they are sick, to visit doctors. However, programs that are frequently described as "universal" measures usually employ eligibility criteria under which benefits are available as a right to sizable groups—social security for the elderly and children's allowances—within the populations, regardless of individual income. But these measures almost always involve elements of selectivity. Both children's allowances and social security for the elderly, for example, are selective on the basis of age. In this sense the employment of selective policies goes back more than 100 years to the first designs for old-age pensions under Bismarck. If most of what have been categorized as "universal" schemes have involved some form of targeting, what is so different about the current trends?

The ideal of universal welfare provisions, which held sway from the 1960s to the 1980s, signified a broad and generous approach to the allocation of social benefits that added new categories and extended the borders of the welfare state. If the added benefits had eligibility criteria that did not fit entirely within the outer rim of bona fide universal coverage, they pushed in that direction. What distinguishes the approach to targeting since the mid-1980s is that it involves policy measures designed not so much to identify new groups that are broadly eligible for additional or supplementary benefits as to reform existing programs by narrowing the scope of current selection criteria. When the OECD advised in 1991 that "the welfare system should be refocused and made less generous in terms of eligibility and benefits," it was recommending a shift from policies that authorized criteria for social benefits that were additive and expansive to those that were reductive and constrictive—and describing a process that was already underway.[30] This is not to say that all polices during this period reduced the scope of social benefits to the broader population. There are cases of new social benefits and expanded eligibility, for example, the abolition of the income test in the form of a tax on public pensions in New Zealand and a new entitlement to publicly financed long-term care insurance for the elderly in Germany.[31] Such exceptions qualify but do not reverse the general trend.

Between the means test that strictly doles out aid on a measure of financial need and the universal provision to which an entire population is eligible, there are numerous criteria for allocating social benefits. The reductive approach to targeting is exemplified by the ways in which three basic criteria—age, behavior, and impairment—have been used to shrink the categories of people eligible for social benefits in recent times. In the 1990s, to ease the burgeoning costs of public pensions, eight western European countries and nine in central and eastern Europe have raised the statutory age of retirement at which workers become eligible for social security benefits, most often for women. Other countries, such as France, have increased the contribution period required to qualify for a full pension, another approach to raising the normal age of retirement.[32] In the United States, the 1983 Social Security Amendments authorized the gradual increase of the normal pensionable age from 65 to 67 between the years 2002 and 2026. Some Social Security analysts recommend raising the retirement bar even further, to 69 years of age for those who turn 65 in 2026.[33]

Shrinking the pool of recipients through targeting by age has several implications. One could interpret this reform as an adjustment for the increase in life expectancy since the advent of social security. However, this may come as cold comfort to recipients because most people are currently taking retirement earlier than the standard age, even before that age is raised. From the early 1900s to 1970, the labor force participation rates for men over the age of 65 decreased markedly, from about 50 percent to 20 percent, whereas the participation rates for those aged 60 to 64 remained relatively stable and high. Since 1970, however, not only has the labor force participation rate of men over the age of 65 continued to decrease, but also the rates for those aged 60 to 64 have declined substantially. By 1995, for example, the participation rate for men aged 60 to 64 was less than 20 percent in France and about 30 percent in Italy; at the same time, the rates for men aged 55 to 59 were 60 percent in Italy and about 65 percent in France.[34] All of these data suggest that although work may be a source of satisfaction—which lends meaning to life, an opportunity for congenial association, and a sense of personal achievement for many writers, thinkers, policy analysts, academicians, and legislators who promote raising the age of retirement, it represents a daily activity that coal miners, bus drivers, salespeople, postal workers, plumbers, and employees in a host of other occupations apparently wish to discontinue as soon as possible.

Raising the age of retirement affects recipients differently according to their gender, minority status, and income. The life expectancy for black males at age 21 in the United States, for example, is 46 years, whereas it is 53 years for white males and 59 years for white females. Hence, the average black male who begins working at 21 and lives to age 66 can expect no retirement benefits on a lifetime of contributions to social security (not that an individual who lives to age 66 receives much of a return by retiring at the standard age of 65, but when the retirement age rises to 67, that return declines by 100 percent). There is also persuasive evidence that mortality rates vary according to income, independent of race, with low-wage earners having a shorter life expectancy than high-wage earners.[35]

Although raising the age of retirement may lower the total amount of benefits that are paid out by the system, the savings would appear to affect most heavily the proportional return on social security to workers in low-income and minority groups—that is, if we ignore the "bubble effect" of targeting measures designed to shrink the existing categories. As these measures are applied, it has become evident that old-age pensions, unemployment payments, sickness and disability benefits, and social assistance form an interconnected package that resembles a balloon of welfare expenditures, one that bubbles up on one side when squeezed down on the other. Thus, targeting policies that constrict eligibility in one of these programs often shifts beneficiaries and public expense to other areas.

In the Netherlands, for example, there are strong indications that employers have been using disability insurance as an early retirement scheme for superfluous labor.[36] Similarly, in Britain, growth in the duration of invalidity benefits is attributed to the use of long-term incapacity as a bridge between early exit from the labor market and retirement, as well as to the tightening of administrative controls on unemployment benefits.[37] In the United States, elimination of Supplemental Security Income (SSI) benefits for people judged disabled because of drug addiction and alcoholism was accompanied by a shift among this group to general assistance, where costs increased.[38] In New Zealand, the number of people on unemployment benefits declined after eligibility requirements were tightened, but the savings to society were offset by an increase in the growth of those receiving sickness and invalidity benefits.[39] In light of these experiences, it is conceivable that much of the savings on pensions achieved by lifting the age of retirement in the United States and elsewhere will show up as additional costs in other programs, particularly disability and social assistance.

Targeting that links eligibility for social welfare benefits to behavioral criteria is sometimes referred to as social engineering. Behavioral requirements articulated through the contractual obligations for public assistance and unemployment benefits are an essential feature of contemporary reforms designed to activate recipients. These contracts stipulate a wide range of behaviors—searching for work, participating in training, and performing voluntary services—that recipients must perform to remain eligible for unemployment benefits and public assistance. Reforms of public assistance programs in the United States embody the most extensive use of measures devised to couple benefits with socially approved behaviors. Many eligibility criteria under the Temporary Assistance for Needy Families (TANF) program are designed, as Jill Berrick notes, "to encourage women to engage in more traditional behaviors, which include heterosexual marriage, and more important, childrearing under the umbrella of marriage."[40] To influence women to refrain from having additional children while on TANF, for example, 20 states had initiated a family cap policy by 1999, which denied or limited increases in financial aid for children born to mothers already on the welfare roll. More than half of the states also initiated behavioral requirements that impose parental responsibility to ensure that their children attend school and receive the standard immunizations.[41]

Targeting on the basis of impairment maintains the appearance of constancy while diminishing the scope of coverage. A program continues to serve the original category of social need, but the threshold of eligibility is jacked up several notches for people within that category to qualify for benefits. The program seems to remain the same, until one looks beneath the surface. Analyzing the "flight from universalism" in Sweden, for example, Sune Sunesson and his colleagues note in 1998 that needs tests for elderly care have tightened to the degree that benefits are shifting from "services like help with household chores to personal and medical care for the weakest and frailest." However, some research suggests that middle-class recipients are better able to negotiate the needs test than the working-class elderly, for whom home help has decreased much more than for others.[42] This trend toward providing aid to fewer elderly people while concentrating on those with the most functional impairment is reconfirmed by some of the same Swedish researchers a few years later.[43] A similar trend is documented in the allocation of home help and home-care services for older people in England. Between 1992 and 1997, the number of contact hours among households receiving home care had increased at the same time that there was a decrease in the number of households being served. This trend is clearly seen as an effort to lower costs by targeting comprehensive home-care services on fewer households that contain recipients with high levels of impairment who would otherwise require more expensive care in residential or nursing-home placements.[44]

New, more rigorous definitions of functional impairment have been imposed on disability programs, perhaps more than in any area. Reforms of eligibility criteria in the Dutch program (described in chapter 3) resulted in three out of five cases being diagnosed with a lower degree of disability than previously assessed.[45] In Germany, the 1999 pension reform law (passed in 1997), introduced slightly more stringent degrees of incapacity under which a claimant would be eligible for a disability pension.[46] Certification for invalidity benefits in Britain has been made more demanding by shifting the responsibility for evaluating incapacity from family doctors to state-appointed assessors and by introducing a new "work test" that evaluates the claimants' incapacity to perform not just their current job but any job on the market.[47] In the United States, measures to reform the SSI program in the mid-1990s not only eliminated drug addiction and alcoholism as functional impairments that qualified for disability benefits but also narrowed the criteria employed to assess children's disabilities. The Individual Functional Assessment, a diagnostic tool used to capture a wide range of behavioral disorders in children related to learning, anxiety, and attention deficit problems, was replaced by new criteria that limited disability benefits to those who suffer from "medically determined physical or mental impairments, which results in marked and severe limitations."[48] Since the 1980s, the increased targeting by age, behavior, and functional impairment has reformulated the categories of people who are expected to care for themselves and those who qualify for public support.

Transparency and Solidarity

Restrictive targeting is politically delicate since it involves taking benefits away from people, a deed that politicians loathe to perform and prefer not to admit. Among the approaches noted above, targeting by age is possibly the least politically damaging. Age limits can be introduced in measured increments that begin far enough down the road so that current beneficiaries and those poised for takeup experience no benefit reductions, and the decision makers may not even be around when the new requirements go into effect. This approach is also reasonably transparent—everyone knows one's age and can anticipate exactly when it will change.

In contrast, targeting that is concentrated on behavioral requirements and measures of impairment involve criteria that are often opaque. In many instances, for example, measures of impairment embody complex indices of psychological functioning and physical competence, as well as statistical allocation formulas, which lend a veneer of scientific objectivity to decisions that are based ultimately on social values and political considerations such as cost containment or preferences for certain groups. At the same time, the adoption of claw-back taxes to introduce income testing for social benefits at the point of consumption makes it very difficult for citizens to calculate the real value of these benefits or to perceive the differential benefits awarded to people at various levels of income. The increasing use of the income tax system as conduit for distributing indirect transfers through a range of tax exemptions and refundable credits, as well as discounting the consumption value of direct transfers by subjecting these benefits to progressive taxes, creates an allotment of social subsidies that is virtually unfathomable to the average citizen. Few people, for example, have the faintest idea of the tax and credit subsidies received by farmers, homeowners, students, and other groups.[49] In fact, a large proportion of people who might qualify for the largest cash transfer program for low-income parents in the United States—the Earned Income Tax Credit—are unaware that this program exists.[50]

As the trend toward more restrictive targeting of social benefits unfolds, the lack of transparency in the design of eligibility criteria is likely to gain increasing saliency, if for no other reason than that it presents a copious opportunity for policy analysts to ply their craft. It will also pluck the curiosity of social activists on the Right and the Left, who are always occupied by the question of "who gets what" in matters of public spending. Voltaire once said that the art of government consists of taking as much money as possible from one class of citizens to give to the other—and, he might have added, without being too obvious about it. As long as universal benefits are being reduced and expenditures are concentrated more narrowly on groups with the greatest need, legislators have an abiding interest in blurring the line between winners and losers, givers and receivers, so as not to estrange potential constituencies. There is much bending of the concept to design selective policies within a "universal" mold. Thus, for example, Juhani Lehto explains that the "universal" provisions of child day care and care for the elderly in the Nordic countries is more restricted than the "universal" right to education. The first type of restriction involves the imposition of income-related user fees, which can only be determined by eligibility criteria that include an income test. Here, as with the use of claw-back taxes, the universal allocation of benefits translates to different levels of benefit consumption, based on income. The second type of restriction consists of needs testing, such as favoring single working mothers in the allocation of day-care placements and targeting care for the elderly to those with the highest levels of disability.[51]

The characterizations of targeting by taxing and using income-related user fees and needs tests as selectivity within universalism or sociodemocratic liberalism reflect traditional social and political objectives of the welfare state. The political objective is to maintain as broad a constituency as possible. As long as the middle class benefits from social welfare programs, it is assumed they will defend the adequacy of social provisions, although this assumption about the political advantage of universalism is not universally held. Evidence from Australia, at least, suggests that a system marked by extensive income testing can marshal a high degree of public support and deliver an adequate level of benefits.[52] But even if the link between middle-class support and benefits received were firmly established, the middle-class stake is being whittled down under the grinding restrictions of selectivity within universalism. At some point, policymakers may have to own up to Lehto's conclusion that "all in all, it may be that the concept of universalism is not quite well adapted to describing the concept of social rights."[53] Whether the middle classes will balk at increasingly selective social welfare benefits that are designed to offer public support for private responsibility remains to be seen.

The social objective of maintaining at least the appearance of universal benefits involves the presumed impact of this arrangement on social solidarity. At the same time that the promotion of equity is invoked to justify measures that increase selectivity and income testing, the banner of social solidarity unfurls to cloak the precise results of these measures in the garb of "universal" benefits. Indeed, the idea that universal policies reinforce social solidarity is widely taken for granted. According to this view, means-tested policies are divisive, fracturing society along income lines that separate donors from welfare beneficiaries, whereas universal schemes foster social cohesion by emphasizing common needs and entitlements to benefits. As with the charge that means testing creates stigma, the assertion that universalism breeds solidarity rests on doctrine firmly held, rarely challenged, and faintly demonstrated.

NOTES

1. T. H. Marshall, "Value Problems of Welfare Capitalism," *Journal of Social Policy*, 1:1 (January 1972), 19–20.

2. For a sample of this discussion, see Irwin Garfinkel, "Economic Security for Children: From Means Testing and Bifurcation to Universality," in Irwin Garfinkel, Jennifer Hochschild, and Sara Melanahan, eds., *Social Policies for Children* (Washington, D.C.: Brookings Institution, 1996), pp. 33–82; Sheila B. Kamerman and Alfred J. Kahn, "Universalism and Income Testing in Family Policy," *Social Work*, July–August 1987, pp. 277–80; Mike Reddin, "Universality Versus Selectivity," *Political Quarterly*, January–March 1969, pp. 13–20; Neil Gilbert and Paul Terrell, *Dimensions of Social Welfare Policy*, 4th ed. (Boston: Allyn & Bacon, 1998).

3. OECD, *New Orientations for Social Policy* (Paris: OECD, 1994), p. 14. The debate does not end here. Titmuss, for example, suggests that if access to medical care entails a time-consuming, demeaning means test, clients may hesitate in seeking service until the problem has reached an advanced stage that is more expensive to treat than if they had come in at the first signs of illness. Viewed over the long term, he infers a cost savings to the community from the relative ease of access to this type of universal provision. Richard Titmuss, *Commitment to Welfare* (London: George Allen & Unwin, 1968), pp. 69–71.

4. Gosta Esping-Andersen, *Three Worlds of Welfare Capitalism* (Princeton, N.J.: Princeton University Press, 1990).

5. Maurizio Ferrera, "Targeting Welfare in a 'Soft' State: Italy's Winding Road to Selectivity," in Neil Gilbert, ed., *Targeting Social Benefits: International Perspectives and Trends* (New Brunswick, N.J.: Transaction Publishers, 2001), pp. 184.

6. Ibid., pp. 182–83.

7. Tony Eardley, Jonathan Bradshaw, John Ditch, Ian Gough, and

Peter Whitford, *Social Assistance in OECD Countries: Synthesis Report* (London: HMSO, 1996).

8. Joakim Palme and Irene Wennemo, "Swedish Social Security in the 1990s: Reform and Retrenchment," Centre for Welfare State Research, Working Paper 9, Copenhagen, 1997.

9. Eurostat, *Social Protection and Expenditure Receipts: 1980–1997* (Luxembourg: Eurostat, 2000), p. 170.

10. Sune Sunesson, Staffan Blomberg, Per Gunnar Edebalk, Lars Harrysson, Jan Magnusson, Anna Meeuwisse, Jan Peterson, and Tapio Salonen, "The Flight from Universalism," *European Journal of Social Work*, 1:1 (March 1998), 19–29.

11. The data are also reported for different years and drawn from different sources. Eurostat analyzes data collected by its member countries; the total social security expenditure data in the study by Eardely et al., *Social Assistance in OECD Countries*, were drawn from the OECD Household Transfer Database.

12. Reddin, "Universality Versus Selectivity," pp. 12–14.

13. Theda Skocpol, "Sustainable Social Policy: Fighting Poverty Without Poverty Programs," *American Prospect*, 2 (Summer 1990), 59–67.

14. See, for example, Joe Handler and Ellen Hollingsworth, "How Obnoxious Is the 'Obnoxious Means Test'? The View of AFDC Recipients," Institute for Research on Poverty Discussion Paper, University of Wisconsin, Madison, January 1969; Richard Pomeroy and Harold Yahr, in collaboration with Lawrence Podell, *Studies in Public Welfare: Effects of Eligibility Investigation on Welfare Clients* (New York: Center for the Study of Urban Problems, City University of New York, 1968); and Martha Ozawa, "Impact of SSI on the Aged and Disabled Poor," *Social Work Research and Abstracts*, 14 (Fall 1978), 3–10.

15. Titmuss, *Commitment to Welfare*, p. 122.

16. Walter Trattner, *From Poor Law to Welfare State* (New York: Free Press, 1999).

17. For a more detailed description of such practices, see Frances Fox Piven and Richard Cloward, *Regulating the Poor: The Functions of Public Welfare* (New York: Pantheon Books, 1971), pp. 147–82; and Betty Mandell, "Welfare and Totalitarianism: Part I. Theoretical Issues," *Social Work*, 16: 1 (January 1971), 17–25.

18. David Matza, "Poverty and Disrepute," in Robert Merton and Robert Nisbet, eds., *Contemporary Social Problems*, 2nd ed. (New York: Harcourt Brace & World, 1966), pp. 619–69, views the disreputable poor as a small segment of all people in poverty—the hard core—but allows that poverty itself "is slightly disreputable" (p. 620). See also Chaim Waxman, *The Stigma of Poverty* (New York: Pergamon, 1977).

19. Ross Mackay, "The New Zealand Model: Targeting in an Income-Tested System," in Neil Gilbert, ed., *Targeting Social Benefits: International Perspectives and Trends* (New Brunswick, N.J.: Transaction Publishers, 2001), p. 33.

20. OECD, *New Orientations*, p. 14.

21. Claude Martin, "Reframing Social Policies in France Towards Selectivity and Commodification: The Case of Family and Frail Elderly Policies," presented at the European Forum, Centre for Advanced Studies Conference on Reforming Social Assistance and Social

Services: International Experiences and Perspectives, Florence, December 11–12, 1998.

22. Jonah Levy, "Vice Into Virtue? Progressive Politics and Welfare Reform in Continental Europe," *Politics & Society*, 27:2 (June 1999), 239–73. For a description of the family allowance reform, see ISSA, *Trends in Social Security* (Geneva: ISSA, 1998), no. 3.

23. Ibid. p. 245.

24. Bruno Palier, "A Liberal Dynamic in the Transformation of the French Social Welfare System," in Jochen Clasen, ed., *Social Insurance in Europe* (Bristol: Policy Press, 1997), p. 104.

25. See, for example, Christina Behrendt, "Do Means-Tested Benefits Alleviate Poverty? Evidence on Germany, Sweden, and the United Kingdom from the Luxembourg Income Study," *Journal of European Social Policy*, 10:1 (February 2000), 23–42.

26. Denis Bouget, "The Juppé Plan and French Social Welfare," *Journal of European Social Policy*, 8:2 (May 1998), 152–72. Interpreting the French experience, Bouget splits the difference between Palier's view of a shift to a "liberal" welfare regime and Levy's perception of the workings of a New Left strategy, suggesting instead that reforms of social protection in France over the last decade represent "a doctrinal split of the French unitarian model, the creation of the juxtaposition of several models, rather than a shift from one model towards another" (p. 165).

27. Jean-Claude Barbier and Bruno Theret, "The French System of Social Protection: Path Dependencies and Social Coherence," paper prepared for the Conference on Continuities and Change in the Welfare State, Bellagio Study and Conference Center, Italy, August 7–11, 2000.

28. Mark Andries, "The Politics of Targeting: The Belgian Case," *Journal of European Social Policy*, 6:3 (1996), 209–23.

29. Stein Ringen, *The Possibility of Politics* (Oxford: Clarendon, 1987), p. 12.

30. OECD, *Economic Surveys: Netherlands.* (Paris: OECD, 1991), p. 89.

31. For discussion of these cases, see Ross Mackay, "Remaking the Welfare State in New Zealand," and Jens Alber, "Recent Developments in the German Welfare State: Basic Continuity or Shift of a Paradigm," paper prepared for the Conference on Continuities and Change in the Welfare State, Bellagio Study and Conference Center, Italy, August 7–11, 2000.

32. Susan Devereux, "Pension Systems Reform in Response to the Growth in Retired Populations," in Dalmer Hoskins, Donate Dobbernack, and Christiane Kuptsch, eds., *Social Security at the Dawn of the 21st Century* (New Brunswick, N.J.: Transaction Publishers, 2001).

33. C. Eugene Steuerle and Jon Bakija, *Retooling Social Security for the 21st Century: Right and Wrong Approaches to Reform* (Washington, D.C.: Urban Institute, 1994).

34. Ole Sorensen, "Variability of Retirement Age Practices: An Appropriate Response to Labour Market Developments?" in *Harmonizing Economic Developments and Social Needs: ISSA Technical Conferences 1997, 1998* (Geneva: ISSA, 1998).

35. See, for example, Eugene Rogot, Paul Sorlie, and Norman Johnson, "Life Expectancy by Employment Status, Income, and Education

in the National Longitudinal Mortality Study," *Public Health Reports*, 107 (1992), 457–61 and Jack Hadley and Anthony Osei, "Does Income Affect Mortality? An Analysis of the Effects of Different Types of Income on Age/Sex/Race-Specific Mortality Rates in the United States," *Medical Care*, 20 (1982), 901–14.

36. OECD, *Economic Surveys*.

37. Ken Judge, "Targeting Social Provisions in Britain: Who Benefits from Allocation Formulae?" in Neil Gilbert, ed., *Targeting Social Benefits: International Perspectives and Trends* (New Brunswick N.J.: Transaction Publishers, 2001), pp. 65–97.

38. Deborah Podus, Katherine Watkins, and Emilia Lombardi, "Drug Use and Disability Payments in Los Angeles County After SSI Reform," *California Policy Research Center Brief*, 12:8 (2000).

39. Mackay, "Remaking the Welfare State." He also notes that the cut in unemployment benefit rates was accompanied by a sharp rise in demand for assistance from voluntary food banks; the number of food parcels distributed climbed from 1,226 to 10,261 during the first quarter of 1990 to 1992.

40. Jill Duerr Berrick, "Targeting Social Welfare in the United States: Personal Responsibility, Private Behavior, and Public Benefits," in Neil Gilbert ed. *Targeting Social Benefits: International Perspectives and Trends* (New Brunswick, N.J.: Transaction Publisher, 2001), p. 135.

41. Gretchen Rowe, *Welfare Rules Databook: State TANF Policies as of July 1999* (Washington, D.C.: Urban Institute, 2000).

42. Sunesson et al., "Flight from Universalism," p. 25.

43. Staffan Blomberg, Per Gunnar Edebalk, and Jan Petersson, "The Withdrawal of the Welfare State: Elderly Care in Sweden in the 1990s," *European Journal of Social Work*, 3:2 (July 2000), 151–63.

44. Linda Bauld, Ken Judge, and Iain Paterson, "Cross-National Study of Continuities and Change in the Welfare State," paper prepared for the Conference on Continuities and Change in the Welfare State, Bellagio Study Center, Italy, August 7–11, 2000.

45. Piet Keizer, "Targeting Strategies in the Netherlands: Demand Management and Cost Constraint," in Neil Gilbert, ed., *Targeting Social Benefits: International Perspectives and Trends* (New Brunswick, N.J.: Transaction Publishers, 2000).

46. Alber, "Recent Development in the German Welfare State."

47. Judge, "Targeting Social Provisions."

48. Berrick, "Targeting Social Welfare," p. 143.

49. For an analysis of tax expenditures in the United States, see Neil Gilbert and Barbara Gilbert, *The Enabling State: Modern Welfare Capitalism in America* (New York: Oxford University Press, 1989).

50. About 55 percent of low-income parents with less than a high school education have never heard of the Earned Income Tax Credit Program. For a more detailed analysis, see Katherin Phillips, "Who Knows About the Earned Income Tax Credit," Urban Institute Project on Assessing the New Federalism, Series B, No. B-27, Washington, D.C., January 2001.

51. Juhani Lehto, "Universal Right to Public Social and Health Care Services?" in *Comparing Social Welfare Systems in Nordic Europe and France*, text collected by Denise Bouget and Bruno Palier (Paris: DREES/MiRe, 1999), pp. 641–59.

52. See, for example, E. Papadakis, "Class Interest, Class Politics, and Welfare State Regime,"*British Journal of Sociology*, 44:2 (1993), 249–70; and Peter Whiteford, "Income Distribution and Social Policy Under a Reformist Government: The Australian Experience," *Policy and Politics*, 22:4 (1994), 239–55.

53. Lehto, "Universal Right?" p. 657.

6
Citizenship to Membership

Restoring Solidarity?

Social solidarity is a term of art that has been bandied about for decades in connection with the welfare state, particularly among scholars and politicians in western Europe. The term refers to an integrative bond—a sense of belonging—that connects individuals by creating group loyalty, trust, and mutual obligation, which lubricate collective action. This may have a familiar ring since solidarity gives rise to what has been described elsewhere in this book as social capital. But if solidarity is the bond that produces social capital, how is this bond forged in an advanced industrial society?

One answer is that solidarity is fused through the social rights of citizenship. This line of thought posits that the transition from preindustrial to modern society created a need for new structures to regenerate the social cohesion that was depleted by the unraveling of traditional group bonds. In preindustrial societies, traditional human relationships were based mainly on ascribed status, which was determined at birth—people knew where and to whom they belonged.[1] With the advent of industrial society, geographic and social mobility undermined traditional relations and new forms of attachment were required to integrate individuals within the larger polity of emerging nation-states.[2] According to T. H. Marshall, the status of citizenship endowed residents of a nation with civil, political, and social rights, which reinforced a sense of belonging to the larger polity. Marshall sees the rights of citizenship as an evolutionary process, with the eighteenth century as the formative period of civil rights, the nineteenth century as the era of political rights, and the twentieth century as the period in which social rights became a major component in the status

of citizenship.[3] Although there is no dispute about the advent of citizenship rights in the modern nation-states, the exact order in which
they evolved is open to question. Germany is a case in point: here
social insurance entitlements were granted in 1880, well before political rights were fully bestowed.[4]

The social rights of citizenship range "from the right to a modicum
of economic welfare and security to the right to share to the full in
the social heritage and to live the life of a civilized being according
to the standards prevailing in the society."[5] In formulating this definition of social rights, Marshall recognized the state's function to promote social inclusion, long before the term became fashionable. As he
envisioned it, the life of a "civilized being," according to prevailing
standards, embodied the education, employment, housing, social provisions, and community involvement of mainstream society. The glue
of social cohesion dissolves for those excluded from participation in
the customary life of mainstream society.[6]

Marshall was fully cognizant that social rights of citizenship had
to be balanced by obligations. As he put it, these rights required citizens to behave with "a lively sense of responsibility toward the welfare of the community."[7] And among these responsibilities, the duty
to work was of paramount importance. Joined to the reciprocal duties
of citizenship, social rights to a degree of economic security and social
inclusion offer not only a floor of protection against the risks of modern life but also a bridge of mutual expectations that connects the
individual to the nation-state. In the latter capacity, the rights of citizenship foster social cohesion on a macro level, within the borders
of the nation-state. In addition, Marshall thought that although social
rights would not create complete equality, they would at least mitigate
the degree of economic inequality among citizens. This outcome
raises the question of the extent to which economic equality might
also contribute to solidarity. Although there are no well-established
measures of solidarity, some empirical evidence suggests that levels
of economic equality are directly related to the degree of citizens' trust
in one another, which is assumed to be a reflection of solidarity.[8] However, correlation is not causality; the causal relationship here might
run in either direction.

Although Marshall recognized that rights were accompanied by obligations, his emphasis on the social rights of citizenship is widely
perceived, in Gosta Esping-Andersen's words, "as the core idea of a
welfare state."[9] Less widely acknowledged is Marshall's observation
that the right to social benefits does not necessarily imply the right to
receive them free of charge. The cost of benefits may be recovered, he
suggests, "by levying *ad hoc* charges in proportion to the ability to
pay, ranging from the full cost of the service received down to noth-

ing."[10] His view of universal allocations includes income-tested user charges, which are seen not as an impairment of the right to welfare but as a fulfillment of it. Overall, Marshall's analysis of the social rights of citizens to universal provisions (even if income-tested) endorses the familiar idea that a generous welfare state, strong on universal entitlements, heightens social solidarity. Let us call this idea the *conventional solidarity hypothesis*.

Alternative views on solidarity support competing hypotheses, among which the perceptive work of French sociologist Émile Durkheim has stood the test of time. Observing the changing fabric of social life at the turn of the twentieth century, Durkheim analyzed how the bases of social cohesion seemed to be evolving—from what he labeled "mechanical" to "organic" solidarity—in the shift from preindustrial to industrial society.[11] Mechanical solidarity is the sense of belonging that stems from commonality with others. This form of solidarity develops under conditions in which social and moral homogeneity are reinforced by strong ties to kinship, localism, and religion. Durkheim explains that "the term does not signify that it is produced by mechanical and artificial means. We call it that only by analogy to the cohesion that unites the elements of an inanimate body, as opposed to that which makes a unity out of the elements of a living body."[12] Organic solidarity derives not from social uniformity but from the interdependence of complementary roles under the division of labor in society, which became fully articulated in modern times. This solidarity is analogous to the interdependent molecules that form the unity of an organism—hence, the designation "organic."

However, as Robert Nisbet points out, on further reflection Durkheim was doubtful that organic solidarity could replace the fundamental elements of mechanical solidarity at the core of social cohesion.[13] In the preface to the second edition of *The Division of Labor in Society*, Durkheim stressed the continuing need for social and moral homogeneity as the foundation of a solidarity that contributes harmony and order to modern society. Anticipating the contemporary discourse on how voluntary associations contribute to the accumulation of social capital, Durkheim thought that occupational associations might substitute for the erosion of older structural ties—kinship, localism, and religion—which formed the communal strands of mechanical solidarity in preindustrial society. Even with the interdependence that accompanies the division of labor, feelings of solidarity require "a certain intellectual and moral homogeneity, such as the same occupation produces."[14] These occupational associations had an important function to play as mediating bodies between the state and the individual, which constitute the building blocks of communal life and the springboard of collective activity. The state, in his view, was not well positioned to animate collective activity because it "is too remote from individuals; its relations with them too external and intermittent to penetrate deeply into individual consciences and socialize them."[15] Voiced almost 100 years ago, Durkheim's ideas about the functions of secondary groups, aligned between the individual and the state, resonate with the modern debate on the need to strengthen mediating structures for the revitalization of civil society.[16]

According to Durkheim, the cultivation of social solidarity within secondary groups not only served as an integrating mechanism for establishing unity and order in the larger sociopolitical structure but also had beneficiary effects on the level of individual well-being. The relation between collective forces and individual behavior is illustrated in his classic study of suicide, which found that suicide rates are lower among individuals who benefit from the mutual support of belonging to socially cohesive groups. "They cling to life more resolutely," Durkheim writes, "when belonging to a group they love, so as not to betray interests they put before their own. The bond that unites them with the common cause attaches them to life and the lofty goal they envisage prevents their feeling personal troubles so deeply."[17] This nineteenth-century proposition is buttressed by more recent evidence from a nine-year study of 6928 residents in California, which found that people with extensive social ties were less likely to die of all causes than those with few social contacts.[18]

The Roots of Solidarity

The works of Durkheim and Marshall submit two competing views on the source of social solidarity, which have profound implications for the relation between solidarity and the welfare state. For Durkheim, solidarity stems from the soil of intellectual and moral homogeneity. It is nurtured by a commonality of values, norms, and beliefs that are braced by ties of kinship, localism, and religion. He saw this soil eroding in modern society and believed that it might be restored through the creation of secondary groups that are bound by the moral and intellectual affinities of occupational association. The common risks, economic interests, involvement in a field of activity, and patterns of daily interaction of occupational groups give rise to a level of social homogeneity that promotes identification and mutual trust. Since in this analysis social uniformity is a condition of solidarity, let us call the Durkheimian view the *conditional hypothesis of solidarity*. Although social uniformities were stronger within the communities of preindustrial society than in modern times, one still finds varying degrees of homogeneity among the populations of modern nation-states.

The conditional hypothesis certainly qualifies, perhaps inverts, the proposition that a generous welfare state, in which an array of benefits are guaranteed as rights of citizenship, breeds social solidarity—the cause-effect relationship posited by the conventional hypothesis. That is, small, comparatively homogeneous societies, such as Denmark, Finland, Sweden, and Norway, start with more fertile soil for a relatively high degree of social solidarity than large, heterogeneous countries. Finland, for example, is a country of about 5 million Caucasian people, living for many generations close to the arctic circle in the shadow of the Russian empire, whose language bears no resemblance to those of its Scandinavian neighbors. In contrast, we might consider, not the United States, but just the city of Los Angeles, with a population of more than 9 million people—a blend of Hispanics, non-Hispanic Caucasians, Asians, Native Americans, and African Americans, many of whom are first-generation citizens—against which the Finnish society looks almost tribal in its social uniformity. At some level, the relationship between Finns and their government is virtually familial: almost everyone has at least a third cousin in some public office and numerous relatives working for the state. It stands to reason that all other things being equal, Finns would be more predisposed than the residents of Los Angeles to trust their government, to cooperate, and to share their society's resources with one another. I insert the ceteris paribus proviso in recognition of the fact that intellectual and moral homogeneity may be predisposing factors underlying social solidarity but are not entirely sufficient for its realization. Although people may behave according to the same moral code, traditions, and norms, if the moral code dictates that above all else individuals should maximize the advantage of the nuclear family, with social bonds based on kinship displacing other forms of association, the result is what Edward Banfield labeled "amoral familism."[19] This type of kindred solidarity gives rise to communities that are marked by social atomization and low levels of trust beyond the family circle.[20]

Is the formation of solidarity an outcome of the universal welfare state, or is the universal welfare state an attribute of societies initially distinguished by a high degree of solidarity? If the conditional hypothesis ceteris paribus is correct, it is not so much that a generous system of social rights creates solidarity as that small, homogeneous societies (unhampered by amoral familism) have a high propensity for social solidarity, which, in part is expressed through the creation of a generous welfare state. "A sense of unity and solidarity," Alain Noel maintains, "cannot be constructed solely from the centre."[21] This argument, of course, turns the conventional hypothesis upside down. It is more likely, however, that cause and effect interact, and both hypotheses explain the formation of solidarity as a dynamic process. That is, solidarity, germinating in the seedbed of social and cultural homogeneity, fosters the mutual trust and collective action that gives rise to universal welfare benefits, the availability of which in turn amplifies public trust and a sense of belonging. Trust in the state cannot be cultivated in a vacuum: it is established in the course of the state's meeting citizens' expectations of fairness, justice and social protection. The social rights of citizenship have come to form an important set of expectations, the satisfaction of which augments trust in government and justifies its existence. The communal provision of security and welfare is important because, as Michael Walzer explains, "if we did not provide for one another, if we recognized no distinctions between members and strangers, we would have no reason to form and maintain political communities."[22]

Assuming that Durkheim and Marshall offer complimentary perspectives, one might still ask, How deeply must the roots of solidarity be embedded in the soil of social and cultural homogeneity to support the rise of citizenship rights? Speaking in 1990 on the subject of immigration, Norman Tebbit, a former chair of the British Conservative Party, asked: When Asian and Afro-Caribbean citizens of the United Kingdom watch a cricket match between teams that represent the United Kingdom and their former homelands, "which side do they cheer for?"[23] The "cricket test," as it came to be called, suggestively inquires whether the rights of citizenship can prevail over cultural, historic, racial, and religious differences to inspire a sense of loyalty to the right team. The degree to which the solidarity that emanates from the social rights of citizenship is conditioned on a preexisting level of social cohesion that derives from homogeneity remains an open question—one that will be acutely tested as the rising waves of immigration carry strangers who aspire to become citizens across the borders of the advanced industrialized nations.

In the meantime, however, the rights of citizenship to an array of universal social benefits are changing in terms of substance, scope, and delivery. These developments have already been examined and documented in much detail. Substantively, the balance between rights and responsibilities embedded in social policies has been fundamentally altered. Social benefits for unemployed workers and people with disabilities, which were initially formulated around the right to income maintenance, are increasingly contingent on the duty to work and behave responsibly. Analyzing what he calls "the path-breaking change in Danish welfare policy" in these areas after 1992, for example, Jorgen Andersen suggests that this change represents a shift from policies that emphasized the rights of citizenship to those that lend weight to the duties of citizenship to work and to be engaged in community life.[24]

The scope of welfare benefits has narrowed under increasing pressure to incorporate measures of eligibility, such as income-related user charges, claw-back taxes, and stringent tests of need, which maintain an outer shell of universalism while shrinking the inner kernel of social provision that is available for consumption. And in almost every area of social provision, the delivery of social benefits is inexorably shifting to the private sector. At the same time that public support for private responsibility thickens the private ingredient in the public-private mix of social welfare, it delimits trust in the state, not because the state has become untrustworthy, but because there is simply less activity for it to be trusted with.

On the whole, these changes constitute a contraction of the social rights of citizenship and a reformulation of the state's role in delivering benefits based on these rights. Thus, to the extent that solidarity is indeed reinforced by social rights, the abatement of these rights has abraded a unifying strand of universal entitlement, which connected citizens and joined them in a trusting relationship to the state. At the same time, other forces are at play. As Marshallian solidarity which is fostered by the social rights of citizenship, is on the wane, Durkhemian solidarity, which is advanced through voluntary association, is waxing with new energy. With the balance between public and private responsibility for the provision of social services shifting toward the private sector, the use of community-based, voluntary organizations has drawn increasing political support. This approach to service delivery responds to the antistatist, market-oriented ideology of the Right; to the citizens' empowerment objectives of the Left; and most of all, to the modern infatuation with civil society on both sides of the political spectrum.[25] In the United States, Bill Clinton and Al Gore frequently expressed support for the communitarian ideals of civic involvement during the 1992 presidential campaign.[26] And in his 2001 inaugural speech, President George W. Bush repeatedly referred to the ideals of civil society and civic duty. Invoking the spirit of voluntarism, he asked the American public to be "responsible citizens building communities of service and a nation of character."[27] In western Europe, Anton Zijderveld writes, "the revitalization of the market after 1980 was soon accompanied by the call for civil society's revitalization"—a movement referred to in the Netherlands as *social renewal*.[28]

The Penalties of Belonging

The enabling state contributes to the revival of civil society through the devolution of responsibility for social protection and care from the state to the private sector, in which community-based, voluntary enterprises are well represented. The resurrection of civil society promotes solidarity that is based on common interests and experiences bred by association in intermediary groups that reside between the restricted circle of kinship and the national borders of citizenship. Solidarity incubates a spirit of belonging and a sense of trust, which encourage social cooperation, build social capital, and correlate with economic prosperity. Since social processes rarely work completely to the well and good, however, one is compelled to ask: What is missing from this picture? To this point, solidarity has been viewed largely from a functional perspective and marked by overwhelmingly positive implications for social cooperation and economic productivity. To complete the analysis, we must examine solidarity from an alternative perspective, one that considers some of the potentially negative implications of the much applauded functions of intermediary groups.

On animating productivity, there is evidence that membership in a tightly linked religious or community group can have a mixed influence on entrepreneurial activity. Mutual aid and trust facilitates the startup of a business, but the obligation to assist members of the community hinders the expansion of the entrepreneur's firm once it is established.[29] Indigenous entrepreneurs who own shops in villages near the town of Otavalo in Ecuador, for example, often become Protestants to escape the numerous claims on their profits that are associated with the duties and social charges of membership in the Catholic Church. Thus, the trust and normative obligations found in solidaristic communities have given rise to "a gigantic free-riding problem."[30] Then there is the question of distinguishing cause and effect: "Do trust-building social networks lead to efficacious communities," asks Steven Durlauf, "or do sucessful communities generate these types of social ties?"[31]

On the matter of trust and cooperation, at the same time that participation in religious, occupational, and other service-oriented, community-based groups imbues members with a positive sense of belonging and common purpose, it can also form an enormous wellspring of conflict with other groups. Thus, drawing on Georg Simmel's classic analysis of conflict and group life, Lewis Coser extrapolates several propositions about the divisive effects of group solidarity.[32] First he suggests that a group's internal cohesiveness is increased by conflict, which sets boundaries between groups, strengthening group consciousness and awareness of separateness. Moreover, he finds that such groups, as industrial unions and farmers' organizations tend to seek out enemies in order to maintain and increase group cohesion. "Since continued conflict is a condition of survival for these groups," Coser explains, "they must perpetually provoke it."[33] These propositions raise some important questions about the extent to which the sum total of cooperation and trust is advanced by a solidarity that is based on the shared experiences, norms, and common interests of membership in intermediary groups. The Boy Scouts, for example, exclude homosexuals, infuriating gay rights organizations. Advocacy groups organized around the interests of children, rape victims, civil rights, gender rights, the elderly, the homeless, disabled people, and people suffering from various addictions increasingly compete for public funds to study and serve their members. Many of these groups do not hesitate to attack anyone who questions their measurement and interpretation of the problems they experience and the efficacy of programs they develop to address these problems.[34] Wistful analyses of the need to rejuvenate the lost sense of community tend to disregard the practical reality that communities are bounded by principles of exclusion, as well as inclusion.[35]

Indeed, in the United States, much of the so-called culture war is conducted around the turf of mediating groups. When it comes to specifics, the general discourse about revitalizing civil society through public support of intermediary groups often sticks on the issue of what norms and values these groups represent. When the Left and the Right extol the virtues of voluntary associations, do they have in mind the core values and norms of women's liberation as represented by the National Organization of Women or those of paternal authority as expressed by the Promise Keepers? Although they might disagree about the benevolence of these intermediary groups, both sides of the political spectrum would no doubt concur on the value of contributions to civil society made by that legendary voluntary association known as the Hell's Angels. But one need not invoke the Hell's Angels to appreciate the palpable moral undertone in discussions of civil society. The manifesto "A Call to Civil Society," published by the Council on Civil Society, is subtitled "Why Democracy Needs Moral Truths"—truths that are in large part biblical and religious.[36] The culturally liberal Left tends to disapprove of President Bush's plans to expand federal support for the provision of social services by faith-based organizations, fearing that the government will end up in the business of promoting religious interests that oppose the lifestyles and values of cultural liberalism. The culturally conservative Right tends to favor these plans because they increase consumer choice and bolster religious communities. However, although conservatives are positively inclined toward expanding the activities of faith-based groups,

they, too, have reservations. Which religious communities will benefit? There are a plethora of faith-based organizations in the United
States, and conservatives worry that this plan might increase the
power of certain religious cults that are "fundamentally at odds with
the ethos of American institutions and antipathetic to integration
within the nation state."[37]

However, the divisive repercussions of intermediary groups are not
entirely dysfunctional for the social order. On the contrary, Coser suggests that in the larger scheme of things, conflict serves unifying functions. First, he submits that conflict binds antagonists since the act of
entering into conflict not only establishes relations where none may
have previously existed but also compels the establishment of norms
and rules to govern the conduct of hostilities. Second, conflict
prompts the search for allies and the formation of coalitions among
previously unrelated groups. And third, conflict helps to establish a
balance of power since the struggle reveals the relative strength of the
parties; once their relative strengths are "ascertained in and through
conflict, a new equilibrium can be established and the relationship
can proceed on this new basis."[38] Thus, we arrive at the paradoxical
conclusion that even if solidarity based on membership in intermediary groups promotes conflict, it may still serve an integrative function because, as Coser puts it, "conflict rather than being disruptive
and dissociating, may indeed be a means of balancing and hence
maintaining society as a going concern."[39]

The proposition that it may generate conflict, even that which
somehow binds adversaries, is much at odds with the argument put
forth for the social merits of solidarity—trust and cooperation—fostered by either entitlement to citizenship rights or participation in
voluntary groups. These views, pro and con, remain largely untested
because empirical measures of solidarity and its consequences are difficult to formulate, comparative data are rarely available, and measures that might be employed yield baffling results. One might expect
to find, for example, relatively low rates of crime in societies marked
by high levels of solidarity, which induce trust and cooperation. Following this vein of thought, Francis Fukuyama posits that the decline
of voluntary participation in community life has led to the deterioration of social trust in the United States, as evident in relatively high
and rising rates of crime.[40] Writing in the early 1990s, Fukuyama recognized that crime rates in the United States were beginning to decline, but he noted that "these trends do little to affect the overall
magnitude of the level of crime in the United States when compared
to other developed countries."[41]

However, if crime rates are taken as an operational definition of
levels of solidarity, findings from the 2000 International Crime Victim-

ization Survey paint a mystifying picture. Organized and published by the Dutch Ministry of Justice, these findings draw on the most highly standardized and rigorous analysis of victimization rates in the industrialized countries conducted over the last decade. Among the 17 industrialized nations surveyed, the United States is tied in fourth place with Belgium and France on the overall prevalence rates, a measure that reports the percentage of people victimized once or more in 1999 by any of the 11 crimes covered by the study. Some of the historically most generous, universally oriented welfare states, such as Denmark, Sweden, and the Netherlands, are among the 8 countries with higher prevalence rates than the United States, as shown in figure 6.1. Of course, it is well known that in the Netherlands, Sweden, and Denmark, the theft of bicycles is relatively higher than in other countries; they are also among the countries in which people own the most bicycles. But in Denmark and Sweden, a higher percentage of people are victimized by car theft than in the United States, where the prevalence of automobile theft is about equal to that of the Netherlands. In the United States, proportionately more people reported having something stolen from their car, such as luggage and radios, than in Denmark, Sweden, and the Netherlands. On the summary

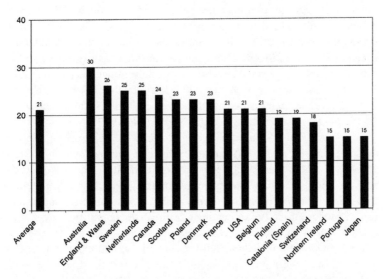

Figure 6.1 Criminal Victimization: Percentage Victimized Once or More in 1999. *Source:* John van Kesteren, Pay Mayhew, and Paul Nieuwbeerta, *Criminal Victimisation in Seventeen Countries: Key Findings from the 2000 International Crime Victims Survey* (The Hague: Ministry of Justice, 2001), p. 38.

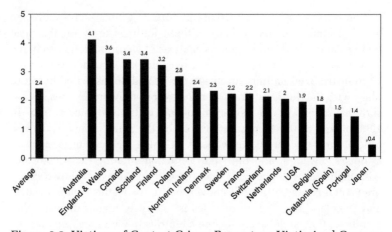

Figure 6.2 Victims of Contact Crime: Percentage Victimized Once or
More in 1999; Selected Contact Crime (Robbery, Sexual Assault, and
Assault with Force). *Source:* John van Kesteren, Pay Mayhew, and
Paul Nieuwbeerta, *Criminal Victimisation in Seventeen Countries:
Key Findings from the 2000 International Crime Victims Survey*
(The Hague: Ministry of Justice, 2001), p. 33.

measure of aggressive contact crime—robbery, assaults with force, and
sexual assaults—in which perpetrators come face to face with those
on whom they prey, the United States's prevalence rate ranked below
those of Denmark, Sweden, and the Netherlands, as illustrated in figure 6.2. When measures that reflect the total number of victimizations
per 100 inhabitants in 1999 are taken into consideration, the United
States reports a higher rate than Denmark but still remains below the
incidence rates of Sweden and the Netherlands.[42]

In general, the victimization survey concludes that crime rates in
most of the industrialized countries have fallen between 1995 and
1999, with the largest decline in the United States. There is no consensus about exactly what accounts for this trend; though explanations usually refer to several demographic, economic, and social factors. Demographically, since most crimes are committed by males
aged 15 to 24, the falling crime rates to some extent reflect the decreasing proportion of this high-risk group, which accompanies the
aging of the populations in western Europe and the United States.
Improved police techniques and, in the United States, a general hardening of political responses toward crime—the "Guiliani factor"—
may also bring down the rates. Although a sizable portion of the decline in the United States is often attributed to the substantial increase
in imprisonment of criminals, this efect is not replicated by European

experiences, where marked variations in the rates of imprisonment fail to explain the reduction in property crime.[43] Improved security measures, particularly the increasing use of household security systems and antitheft devices, may inhibit burglaries. And one cannot discount the impact of the favorable economic climate in the United States and western Europe on crime rates since the mid-1990s. "Finally, and most speculatively of all," the authors of the Dutch report on criminal victimization venture, "it is conceivable that intricate cultural and social change is at work. It is a tall order to document this, but not preposterous to wonder whether change is operating in some way to 'civilise' at least at the margins those who in the past would have offended, or whether crime is simply becoming a less fashionable pursuit for high-risk age groups."[44]

Mention of social solidarity and the welfare state is noticeably absent in these various explanations, as it should be since no pattern emerges among the countries to suggest that those with the historically most comprehensive and universal social rights have relatively low rates of criminal activity. Indeed, the report's final speculation about the "civilizing" influences of social change hints at the possibility that the shift toward welfare policies that emphasize civic duties and responsibilities may reinforce law-abiding behavior more than policies previously designed to extend rights and entitlements. In any case, with the overall decline in victimization rates in western Europe and the United States coming at a time when universal social rights are on the wane, one is hard pressed to argue that social rights of citizenship heighten solidarity, fostering an environment of trust and cooperation, which restrains criminal activity. Curiously, in fact, Denmark, Norway, and Sweden had a sharp climb in crime rates during the 1970s, right in the midst of the golden era of welfare state expansion, when social rights were on the rise.[45] These comparisons are not to imply that the Scandinavian countries, which continue to maintain some of the most comprehensive systems of social protection and are arguably the most egalitarian nations in the advanced industrial world, suffer a paucity of social solidarity.[46] It is just that over time the effects of solidarity on crime rates do not appear to vary directly with welfare state activity.

Citizen or Shareholder: Solidarity with Whom?

To say that its effects are potentially divisive, as well as integrative, and in either case difficult to detect empirically is not to deny the importance of social solidarity. Since the rise of capitalism and the dissolution of traditional bonds, philosophers, social scientists, and politicians have been preoccupied with the question of what integrative mechanisms might evolve to bind individuals in stable, productive social relations. Durkheim and Marshall see the possibility for solidarity to be forged at different levels of society, with private, voluntary associations providing the institutional glue for cohesive relations in community life and publicly conferred social rights of citizenship serving this function in the larger societal context of the nation-state.

The rights of citizenship, as already noted, are contracting. At the same time, one might predict that their connection to social solidarity will become increasingly ambiguous as the psychological boundaries of the nation-state start to fade under the pressures of globalization. According to Christopher Lasch, the psychological process is already underway in the United States and other industrial nations with the rise of a new class of elites. They are "symbolic analysts," manipulators of information whose "fortunes are tied to enterprises that operate across national boundaries. They are more concerned with the functioning of the system as a whole than with any of its parts. Their loyalties—if the term is not itself anachronistic in this context—are international rather than regional, national, or local."[47] Agreeing that globalization is undermining the established model of citizenship, Jean Cohen argues that citizenship of the future should incorporate multiple levels of belonging to local, national, regional, and global institutions of governance.[48] This view, of course, begs the question of the "cricket test"—to which group they owe first loyalty, when there is an inevitable clash of interests.

Whatever the future holds, national boundaries, within Europe, at least, have currently come to be seen more as impediments to the flow of labor than as political preserves for the cultivation of citizenship rights. Thus, the European Commission identifies the difficulty in transferring accrued pension rights to another member state of the European Union as an obstacle to free movement of workers, one that needs to be removed.[49] But how will social benefits based on the rights of citizenship within the context of fuzzy national boundaries serve as instruments of solidarity on the national level? The extension of social entitlements across national boundaries raises an intriguing question about the viability of social rights as an instrument for solidarity on an international scale. As the psychological and practical implications of national boundaries diminish, those who argue that the social rights of citizenship promote solidarity must confront this issue: solidarity at what level and with whom? Responses to this question may stretch all the way from members of a local parent-teachers' association to citizens of a supranational governing unit.

But what about the market? By emphasizing the responsibility of local private units for the delivery of social services, the enabling state encourages a solidarity that is linked to membership in law-abiding, community-based, voluntary associations, which fosters the accumulation of social capital. At the same time, however, the push for privatization also includes support for tax expenditures that subsidize private retirement schemes through work-related pensions, as well as individual retirement accounts, which promote the accumulation of economic capital. These measures have enabled citizens to become shareholders in the national and international financial marketplace and to partake in the benefits of global capitalism on an unprecedented scale. In the United States, for example, the number of people who owned stock or mutual funds climbed by 126 percent over the 15 years from 1984 to 1999, by which time there were an estimated 76 million shareholders in 43 percent of the nation's households—history's first mass class of worker-capitalists. In 1995, over 40 percent of the shareholders had stock portfolios valued at $25,000 or more.[50] The proportion of shareholders in Australia is even higher. In the United Kingdom, about 25 percent of the population owns shares in the equity market. The proportion is somewhat smaller, but growing, in Germany, where there are more equity shareholders than trade union members.[51] As the movement toward partial privatization of old-age pensions gains momentum, a large proportion of the workers in Germany, Sweden, and many other advanced industrialized countries will join the growing ranks of worker-capitalists over the next several decades.

Might this trend establish an alternative foundation for social solidarity, which is partly subsidized by the enabling state through tax expenditures? Shareholders experience a proprietary sense of belonging to the private sector; they are joined by common relations to the means of production and mutual interest in the international market's productive capacity, which transcend national borders; they also share in the returns from this market; finally, they still have their governments to thank for promoting their stake in corporate ownership through indirect expenditures on retirement accounts. Those who favor strengthening civil society will say that solidarity stems from the active daily experiences of people who form personal ties and moral commitments through participation in local associations. Owning stock is a passive experience that requires a very limited range of personal interactions; in many cases acquisitions can be made on the Internet. Yet, at the societal level, social solidarity that stems from the rights of citizenship does not entail active participation in local networks. Social rights confer a psychological sense of belonging that is positively reinforced by access to benefits and accompanied by the obligation to work and be independent. Shareholders are obliged to work since it is mainly through this activity that they gain access to private retirement accounts, and their sense of affiliation to the world of corporate business is positively reinforced over the long run by access to financial rewards—though in the short run they may have to absorb the shock of stock market declines.

In the passage from the welfare state to the enabling state, Durkheim trumps Marshall as the emphasis shifts from the solidarity of social rights on the societal level to that of civic responsibilities in local communities. At this stage it is premature, and perhaps will always remain too far a stretch, to suggest that the conventional mechanisms of social solidarity will extend to encompass a common stake in the private sector, which transcends local and national boundaries. Whether the basis of solidarity on the societal plane will evolve from state-guaranteed citizenship rights to public benefits to state-subsidized shareholder claims on the private market remains to be seen. But such a development would not be inconsistent with the market-oriented ethos of the enabling state.

NOTES

1. For the classic analyses of status and contract relationships, see Ferdinand Tonnies, *Community and Society*, Charles Loomis, trans. and ed. (New York: Harper Torchbooks, [1887] 1963), pp. 181–97; and Henry Sumner Maine, *Ancient Law* (London: John Murray, 1906).

2. Rimlinger agrees that "the development of social rights inevitably plays a crucial role in the handling of civic reintegration. The establishment of socially guaranteed rights to protection from want is one of the major means by which a new status can be secured for the industrial masses." See Gaston Rimlinger, *Welfare Policy and Industrialization in Europe, America, and Russia* (New York: Wiley, 1971), pp. 335–36.

3. T. H. Marshall, *Class, Citizenship, and Social Development* (New York: Anchor Books, 1964).

4. For a discussion of this case, see M. Mann, *The Sources of Social Power, Vol. II, The Rise of Classes and Nation-States, 1760–1914* (Cambridge: Cambridge University Press, 1993).

5. Marshall, *Class, Citizenship and Social Development*, p. 78.

6. Contributing to the modern discourse on social exclusion, more than 30 years after Marshall's analysis, the Organization for Economic Cooperation and Development notes how "isolation from the mainstream of society can lead to a total loss of economic and social adhesion for those affected." OECD, *Beyond 2000: The New Social Policy Agenda* (Paris: OECD, 1996), p. 11.

7. Marshall, *Class, Citizenship and Social Development*, p. 123.

8. Bruce Kennedy, Ichiro Kawachi, and Deborah Prothrow-Smith, "Income Distribution and Mortality: Cross Sectional Ecological Study

of the Robin Hood Index in the United States," *British Medical Journal*, 7037:312 (1996).

9. Gosta Esping-Andersen, *The Three Worlds of Welfare Capitalism* (Princeton, N.J.: Princeton University Press, 1990), p. 21.

10. T. H. Marshall, *The Right to Welfare and Other Essays* (London: Heineman Educational Books, 1981), p. 92.

11. Émile Durkheim, *De la Division du Travail Social* (*The Division of Labor in Society*), George Simpson, trans. (New York: Free Press, [1893] 1933).

12. Ibid., p. 130.

13. Robert Nisbet, *Emile Durkheim* (Upper Saddle River, N.J.: Prentice Hall, 1965).

14. Durkheim, *Division of Labor*, p. 26.

15. Ibid., p. 28.

16. See, for example, Peter Berger and John Neuhaus, *To Empower People: From State to Civil Society*, Michael Novak ed. (Washington, D.C: AEI Press, 1996); Charles Krauthammer, "A Social Conservative Credo," *Public Interest*, Fall 1995; Stephen Osborne and Aniko Kaposari, "Towards a Civil Society? Exploring Its Meaning in the Context of Post-Communist Hungary," *European Journal of Social Policy*, 7:3 (1997).

17. Émile Durkheim, *Suicide*, John Spaulding and George Simpson, trans. (New York: Free Press, 1951), p. 209.

18. These findings are supported by other epidemiological studies in different communities. See Ichiro Kawachi, Bruce Kennedy, and Kimberly Lochner, "Long Live Community: Social Capital as Public Health," *American Prospect*, 35 (November–December 1997). A study of Scandinavians shows that people who commit suicide are "likely to be, in classic Durkheimian fashion, unmarried, residents of large cities, and without siblings or friends." Alan Wolfe, *Whose Keeper? Social Science and Moral Obligation* (Berkeley: University of California Press, 1989), p. 148.

19. Edward Banfield, *The Moral Basis of a Backward Society* (Glencoe, Ill.: Free Press, 1958), p. 85.

20. Confirming Banfield's observations, Putman's study of southern Italy 40 years later found community life marked by low levels of civic association and a high degree of distrust. Robert Putnam, *Making Democracy Work: Civic Traditions in Modern Italy* (Princeton, N.J.: Princeton University Press, 1993). However, other data suggest that although institutional trust in Italy is lower than in other member states of the European Union, interpersonal trust and contact with friends is well within the middle range. For an analysis of familism that raises some interesting questions about the conventional view, see Antonio Mutti, "Particularism and the Modernization Process in Southern Italy," *International Sociology*, 15:4 (December 2000), 579–90.

21. Alain Noel, "Is Decentralization Conservative? Federalism and the Contemporary Debate on the Canadian Welfare State," paper prepared for the Conference on Decentralization: Dimensions and Prospects in Canada, p. 26, Political Economy Research Group, University of Western Ontario, London, October 23, 1997. See also Will Kymlicka, *Multicultural Citizenship* (Oxford: Oxford University Press, 1995).

22. Michael Walzer, *Spheres of Justice: A Defense of Pluralism and Equality* (New York: Basic Books, 1983), p. 64.

23. Cited in John Lanchester, "The Land of Accidents," *New York Review of Books*, February 8, 2001, p. 29.

24. Jorgen Andersen, "Work and Citizenship," paper prepared for the Resesarch Symposium on Social Democracy in a Post-Industrial World, p. 31, Vedbaek, Denmark, September 23–24, 1999.

25. As Noel, "Is Decentralization Conservative?" p. 10, explains, new perspectives from the Left emphasize decentralization "in the name of local development, community association, and empowerment." In Britain, the New Right also believed that in breaking the monopoly of public services, a shift to the market would empower citizens. See Howard Glennerster and James Midgley, *The Radical Right and the Welfare State* (Hemel Hempstead: Harvester Wheatsheaf, 1991), p. 173.

26. William Galston, "Clinton and the Promise of Communitarianism," *Chronicle of Higher Education*, 39:15 (1992), 52.

27. George W. Bush, text of the president's inaugural speech, reprinted in *San Francisco Chronicle*, January 21, 2001, p. A10.

28. Anton Zijderveld, *The Waning of the Welfare State: The End of Comprehensive State Succor* (New Brunswick, N.J.: Transaction Publishers, 1999), p. 140.

29. The mixed effects of solidarity are also found among extended families in traditional societies. See E. Wayne Nafizger, "The Effect of the Nigerian Extended Family on Entrepreneurial Activity," *Economic Development and Cultural Change*, 18:1 (October 1969), 25–33.

30. Alejandro Portes and Julia Sensenbrenner, "Embeddedness and Immigration: Notes on the Social Determination of Economic Action," in Mary Brinton and Victor Nee, eds., *The New Institutionalism in Sociology* (New York: Russell Sage Foundation, 1998), p. 140.

31. Steven Durlauf, "The Case 'Against' Social Capital," *Focus*, 20: 3 (Fall 1999), 3.

32. Lewis Coser, *The Functions of Social Conflict* (New York: Free Press, 1956). Coser's propositions are extrapolated from Georg Simmel, *Conflict*, Kurt Wolff trans. (Glencoe, Ill.: Free Press, 1955).

33. Coser, *Functions of Social Conflict*, p. 104

34. See, for example, Neil Gilbert, *Welfare Justice: Restoring Social Equity* (New Haven, Conn.: Yale University Press, 1995), pp. 84–128; Joel Best, "Promoting Bad Statistics," *Society*, 38:3 (March–April 2001), 10–15.

35. For a critical perspective on the attributes of voluntary association see Wilfred McClay, "Community and the Social Scientist," *Public Interest*, 143 (Spring 2001), 105–10.

36. John Fonte, "Why There Is a Culture War: Gramsci and Tocqueville in America," *Policy Review*, 104 (December 2000–January 2001), 15–31.

37. Jerry Muller, "Dilemmas of Conservatism,"*Public Interest*, 139 (Spring 2000), 64.

38. Coser, *Functions of Social Conflict*, p. 137

39. Ibid.

40. Francis Fukuyama, *Trust: The Social Virtues and the Creation of Prosperity* (New York: Free Press, 1995), pp. 309–10.

41. Ibid., note 8, p. 415. If voluntary association creates trust, it is

not clear why the United States would have higher crime rates than other industrialized countries since even with the decline of participation, the rates of voluntary association are still higher than in many other countries.

42. John van Kesteren, Pay Mayhew, and Paul Nieuwbeerta, *Criminal Victimisation in Seventeen Countries: Key Findings from the 2000 International Crime Victims Survey* (The Hague: Ministry of Justice, 2001).

43. M. Aebi, G. Barclay, J. Jorg-Martin, and M. Killias, *European Sourcebook of Crime and Crminal Justice Statistics: Key Findings* (Strasbourg: Council of Europe, 1999).

44. Ibid., p. 99.

45. Wolfe, *Whose Keeper?* pp. 148–49.

46. There is a question, however, of whether the degree of solidarity in these countries has declined over the last decade. An analysis of the situation in Sweden suggests that although there is no clearcut answer, there are signs of greater segmentation in the population and a decline in the level of social protection. The authors conclude that "it is too soon to say whether what we have witnessed is merely a temporary decline or the beginning of a more permanent change of course." See A. Bergmark, M. Thorslund, and E. Lindberg, "Beyond Benevolence—Solidarity and Welfare State Transition in Sweden," *International Journal of Social Welfare*, 9:4 (October 2000), 248.

47. Christopher Lasch, *The Revolt of the Elites and the Betrayal of Democracy* (New York: Norton, 1995), p. 35.

48. Jean Cohen, "Changing Paradigms of Citizenship and the Exclusiveness of the Demos," *International Sociology*, 14:3 (September 1999), 245–268.

49. Philippe Pochet, Cecile Barbier, Enrique Moro Lavado, Michel Paternotre, and Claude Vernay, "Digest," *Journal of European Social Policy*, 7:4 (1997), 340–48.

50. Richard Nadler, "The Rise of Worker Capitalism," *Policy Analysis*, 359 (November 1, 1999), 1–27.

51. "Global Equity Markets: The Rise and Fall," *Economist*, May 5–11, 2001, Survey section, p. 7.

PART III

SOCIAL IMPLICATIONS

7

The Triumph of Capitalism—
and Its Discontents

Do the changes analyzed in the previous chapters amount to a paradigm shift? If so, why isn't it readily apparent to and widely debated by policymakers currently responsible for reformulating the basic principles of social protection? The answer, in part, is given by scholars who are studying welfare reforms in Denmark and France. Examining recent initiatives in the Danish welfare state, Jorn Loftager agrees that "a closer look at the new social and labour market policies which have been introduced in the 1990s reveals dramatic changes of principles. Correspondingly, a new discourse has clearly manifested itself and so it seems wholly sensible to talk about a paradigm shift." The fundamental changes to which Loftager refers involve the dominant emphasis on activation and selectivity (among the lines of convergence discussed in part II). "Compared to the old paradigm," he writes, "these changes constitute dramatic reductions and tightenings. However, in the discourse of the policy elite responsible for the reforms, these new measures are presented as an important social improvement. More than anything else this documents that a new paradigm of welfare-state thinking has been established." Why do the policy elites present these changes simply as beneficial adjustments rather than as a basic reorientation? "Right wing demands to roll back the welfare state and reduce the number of public employees have to a large extent disappeared," Loftager explains, "while *the Social Democratic/Radical Liberal coalition government has carried through policies which used to be associated with right-wing principles*"[1] (emphasis added).

Analyzing the social policy initiatives of the French Socialist-Green-Communist coalition that came into power under the leadership of Lionel Jospin in 1997, Jonah Levy identifies three guiding principles of the Left: targeting the affluent; favoring the constituents of the Left in policies that entail structural welfare reform; and "even when pursuing policies associated with the right and neo-liberalism, these policies should be redirected to the maximum extent along left-progressive lines." Levy concludes that *"while operating on the ideological terrain of the right, however, Jospin has gone to great lengths to show that his actions are consistent with the ideals of the left"*[2] (emphasis added).

If Loftager and Levy have it right, as I believe they do, the traditional supporters of the welfare state in both Denmark and France now find themselves trying to carve out a new agenda for the Left on, as Levy so aptly put it, the ideological terrain of the Right—a paradigm shift for the welfare state if there ever was one.[3] Naturally, these conditions would induce a certain amount of political denial about the exact direction toward which recent social welfare policies are headed—as welfare state backers on the Left struggle to distinguish their proposals from those advanced by the Neo-Liberal Right. Bringing the metaphorical "tides of change" to closure, one might say that even though the ships of state have turned in a new direction, their political leaders assure the citizen-passengers that there is no cause for concern: "We are staying the course—just tacking at the moment to make progress against the headwinds of capitalism."

Veering to the Right: On Many Headings

But the course has changed as new market-oriented principles transform the conventional ideal of the welfare state. However, convergence toward the enabling state paradigm does not mean that national systems of social protection will all follow the same heading and come to operate in exactly the same way. Although social welfare policies are increasingly being framed by new principles that emphasize work, privatization, individual responsibility, and targeted benefits, there certainly will be differences—rhetorical as well as substantive—in the way in which countries interpret and apply these principles. Some will justify targeting on the basis of equity; others will accentuate efficiency. Different methods of targeting will be employed with varying grades of transparency.[4] The range of activities that qualify as "work" will differ, as will the extent to which employment policies will invest in human capital, job creation, and wage subsidies and the degree to which part-time, paid employment is normalized. There will be alternative approaches to privatization, from top-down contracting for services to bottom-up vouchers and earmarked tax credits. Contracting for services will be organized through varied arrangements that involve nonprofit organizations in the voluntary sector, which are committed to delivering services in the context of broader social goals and community participation, as well as profit-making organizations dedicated mainly to the immediate business of providing services.[5] Examining the way in which some private arrangements are taking shape in France, for example, Levy identifies the creation of private pension funds along Left-Progressive lines as arrangements managed collectively by employer and union organizations, rather than by private companies.[6]

Finally, diverse expectations will unfold concerning the nature of individual and family rights and responsibilities. In Germany, for instance, the Constitutional Court ruled that at the end of 2004, childless workers will have to pay a higher premium into the country's compulsory nursing insurance scheme than will workers with children. The reasoning behind this decision is that childless workers have an unfair financial advantage in that they do not bear the main costs of raising the next generation of contributors to the pay-as-you-go insurance, and they reap the benefits from the insurance premiums paid by the younger generation.[7]

Although all of these are significant shifts in how money is being spent, we would expect only a slight decline in the overall rate of social expenditures in the coming years if there is no sharp downturn in the economies of the advanced industrial nations. But even a modest decline in social expenditures will be experienced as an appreciable tightening of welfare provisions as the increasing demands of aging populations encounter constrained resources. In 2001, the gloomy economic forecast for the industrial nations, exacerbated by the terrorist atrocities in the United States, raises the possibility of economic stagnation, if not recession, which would perforce increase social spending on unemployment, early retirement, and public assistance. (In mid-2001, *The Economist's* reading of industrial production estimates puts the world economy on the verge of the first global recession of the twenty-first century.[8]) In either case, the point is that if one looks only to spending, the institutional arrangements for social welfare are not being dismantled—this was never a serious option. But the fundamental principles that now guide social expenditures no longer conform to those that served as the polestar for the advancement of the modern welfare state.

The new principles, it is worth repeating, will be applied in different ways, which is to say that there will be assorted renditions of the enabling state. Freud's axiom concerning the "narcissism of minor differences" suggests that the closer nations come to resemble each other, the more they magnify minute dissimilarities as a means to reinforce social cohesion.[9] If this proposition is correct—with English rapidly becoming the lingua franca of the European Union and the enabling state identified most closely as an Anglo-American construct—policymakers from other countries are likely to go to great lengths to differentiate their social welfare initiatives from those of the United States and the United Kingdom. The Nordic countries will have their version of the enabling state, as will France, Germany, and others, including, perhaps, the eastern European countries. But when one peels back the outer layers of rhetoric and sorts through the different measures to advance privatization, targeting, employment, and individual responsibility, we arrive at a common core of market-oriented social policies that in essence represent the triumph of capitalism.

Serving the Market

Adopting Margaret Thatcher's outlook, the protective blanket of the welfare state has become widely perceived as smothering the vigorous virtues—initiative, diligence, commitment, fair play, and enthusiasm—in the name of charity, patience, kindness, and sympathy.[10] From increasing the age of retirement to narrowing the criteria of disability, from tax credits for the working poor to competitive bidding on social service contracts, the norms and values that frame the design of social welfare policies for the enabling state, in all its renditions, tend to celebrate economic productivity and private responsibility over social protection and public aid. This framework corresponds to what Richard Titmuss once called the "industrial achievement-performance" model of social policy, in which social welfare institutions serve as handmaidens to the market economy, rather than as a counterforce that supports alternative values and objectives. This model of social policy, Titmuss explained, "holds that social needs should be met on the basis of merit, work performance and productivity. It is derived from various economic and psychological theories concerned with incentives, effort, and reward."[11] One might take issue with the idea of needs met strictly on the basis of merit and productivity and policies that draw on incentives, effort, and reward, but disagreement surely would not be carried so far as to advocate the opposite position—needs met on the basis of malfeasance and sloth and polices that generate disincentives. At one level, there is much to commend the advent of the enabling state as a beneficial corrective to the welfare state, which over time came to pay too little attention to the implications of social policy for productivity, merit, and responsibility.

At another level, however, the declining role of the state and the primacy of the free-market ethos in shaping the future course of social welfare poses some troubling implications for the moral character and benevolence of modern society in the global world. In the long-standing deliberations about morality and the free market, the severe version of the economic marketplace as morally negative—red in tooth and claw—and the more moderate claims that it is morally neutral must give some ground to those who argue that markets have positive moral implications and effects. David Marsland, for example, suggests that markets require the practice of honesty "to ensure fair dealing, and the virtues of thrift, diligence, and curiosity as guarantors of the self-reliant enterprise." More than in the sheltered confines of domestic life and the narrow band of voluntary association, the competitive marketplace is the main arena in which people are put to the test, and "real reputations are made on the basis of genuine images of authentically virtuous action."[12] Marsland shares James Q. Wilson's view that trust and honesty facilitate commercial practices of buying, selling, lending, and borrowing, which in turn inculcate habits of fair dealing.[13]

From a historical perspective, as Albert Hirschman points out, the creation of markets allowed "passions" for honor and glory, usually expressed on battlefields and dueling grounds, to be redirected into "interests" in material gain pursued through commercial interactions and governed by reason, which commenced in a handshake rather than in the waving of battleaxes.[14] By channeling competitive energies or providing an opportunity for, as Freud might say, the sublimation of instinctual aggression, the introduction of markets exercised a civilizing influence. Freud thought that although the sublimation of instincts through the practice of artistic and intellectual activity yielded what he deemed finer and higher satisfactions, "their intensity is mild compared with that derived from the sating of crude and primary instinctual impulses."[15] From this one might extrapolate that the sublimated pleasures of success on the market were not quite as intense as putting one's enemies to rest on the battlefield.

Markets reward patterns of behavior marked by diligence, initiative, postponement of gratification, straight dealing, and other vigorous virtues—but not entirely. The staunchest supporters of the market as a seedbed of morality recognize the need for some degree of regulation. Even before the advent of modern capitalism, one finds in the ruins of Pompeii an ancient equivalent of the bureau of weights and measures, where the locals went to be sure the tradesmen weren't putting too much thumb on the scales.[16]

Those who argue for the moral benefits of markets, particularly in a historical context, have a point, but in pressing this point deeply into the realm of modern-day capitalism they are asking for too much ground. In response, Barry Schwartz's claim "that the market contributes more to the erosion of our moral sense than any other modern social force" cedes not an inch.[17] Citing numerous industrial horror cases, in which the drive for profit has brought about death, destruction, and abuse, Schwatrz suggests that rather than a breeding ground for probity and diligence, competitive markets are places where "dishonest and inhumane practices will drive out the honest and humane ones."[18] He argues that self-control is undermined by the constant expansion of demand needed to keep the market prosperous—demand fueled by the enticements of modern advertising for unrestrained consumption. Others have made this case for the devious effect of the forces of advertising. John K. Galbraith called it the "dependence" effect, which posits that advertising incites consumers' desires for new, often trivial merchandise, the continual production of which satisfies what is essentially a manufactured demand.[19] The classic rebuttal to that argument distinguishes between needs and wants. Beyond the biological necessities of life, wants are by their very nature psychological and boundless; advertising simply provides information about the worth and value of a product—the pleasures that await those who drive a BMW—so that people can exercise knowledgeable choices in deciding how to maximize their satisfactions.[20] President John Kennedy relaxed by reading James Bond novels. Who is to judge what merchandise is trivial? Still, there is a nagging suspicion that advertising seeks to influence behavior by creating wants more than informing choice—to render consumption and the pleasures it affords as a way of life.

Capitalism was not always so closely associated with hedonism and cupidity. According to Max Weber's time-honored account, the rational and systematic attitude that marked the founding spirit of capitalism was incompatible with impulsive gratification. During the early stages of capitalism, Weber observes, human appetites were tempered by the Protestant ethic and Puritan restraint, under which work assumed the character of a religious calling and the accumulation of wealth was evidence of virtue.[21] In time, however, those qualities changed. Daniel Bell suggests that the Protestant ethic was undermined by the capitalist invention of instant credit. Whereas previously one had to save before buying, credit cards permitted the immediate gratification of consumptive urges. With the erosion of the Protestant ethic, Bell observes, "only hedonism remained, and the capitalist system lost its transcendental ethic."[22]

Is the capitalistic marketplace an academy for hedonistic practices to which honesty and probity are denied entry or a school of virtuous activity? Judging from the arguments and evidence of its strongest supporters and detractors, the market incorporates the potential to serve both functions. How this potential is realized depends, in large measure, on the prior habits, traditions, and moral values that human actors bring to the domain of commerce. These human dispositions are initially shaped and nurtured in the bosom of family life. And since family life is not immune to the pervasive influences of capitalism, the extent to which virtue or vice prevails hinges on a dynamic interaction between market forces and family relations. On this matter Schwartz argues that in modern times market forces have undermined family relations, which in turn have diminished the moral expectations that animate people's lives and how they approach commercial activity. He cites the works of Fred Hirsch and Gary Becker, which suggest "that in the last few decades there has been an upsurge in what might be called the 'commercialization of social relations'—that choice has replaced duty and utility maximization replaced fairness in relations among family members."[23] These observations echo Joseph Schumpeter's prescient analysis of the deterioration of family values more than half a century ago.[24] Claiming no animus against capitalism, Schumpeter nevertheless believed that this system was headed for self-destruction as its commercial success diluted the vital forces of family life that shaped entrepreneurial habits and values. As he saw it, the traditional bond of family life was a mainspring of the entrepreneurial spirit. Parents postponed gratification, in order to plan and invest, in anticipation of future gains that might be fully reaped only by their children. According to this view, the entrepreneurial drive was deprived of a basic motivating force when high rates of divorce, infertility, and single parenthood joined with low birthrates to sap the vitality and continuity of family life. But what accounts for the depletion of stable family life and parenthood?

Schumpeter was among the first economists to link the material success and widespread adoption of capitalist ideas—cost-benefit analysis, rational self-interest, choice, and maximization of utility— to the deterioration of family values. He attributed the thinning of family bonds to "the rationalization of everything in life, which we have seen is one of the effects of capitalist evolution." Thus, as soon as people "acquire the habit of weighing the individual advantages and disadvantages of any prospective action—or as we might also put it, as soon as they introduce into their private lives a sort of inarticulate system of cost accounting—they cannot fail to become aware of the heavy personal sacrifices that family ties and especially parenthood entail under modern conditions."[25] On the bottom line, the un-fathomable, transcendental joys of parenthood elude the cost account-ing of rational self-interest in search of wealth, leisure, and the pleasures of alternative lifestyles. It could all be summed up, as Schumpeter explained, by the question in many potential parents' minds: "Why should we stunt our ambitions and impoverish our lives in order to be insulted and looked down upon in our old age?"[26]

In an address on the pending demise of capitalism delivered in 1949, Schumpeter noted, "The best method of satisfying ourselves as to how far this process of disintegration of capitalist society has gone is to observe the extent to which its implications are being taken for granted both by the business class itself and by the large number of economists who feel themselves to be opposed to (one hundred per-cent) socialism and are in the habit of denying the existence of any tendency toward it."[27] This statement about the decline of capitalism bears an uncomfortable resemblance to my previous discussion of the present-day denial of the triumph of capitalism by welfare advocates on the Left—I say "uncomfortable" since time has disproved his di-agnosis of how the tendencies observed during that period would log-ically evolve.

Today we know that Schumpeter was wrong, at least in one re-spect, to assume that as the capitalist orientation toward rational cost-benefit analysis spread into the realm of personal affairs it would un-dermine family life and that in turn the erosion of family life would stall the entrepreneurial engine of capitalism. The decline of family values and the traditional stability of family life has not slowed the rise of capitalism. Indeed, one could turn the assumption upside down and make as much sense by arguing that once capitalism takes root, strong, stable, future-oriented families are not a prerequisite for its growth. The decline of stable family life promotes market expan-sion by accelerating both consumer demand and the supply of labor. A thriving market economy requires not only entrepreneurs—people with daring ideas who will plan, save, and invest to fuel greater pro-ductivity in the future—but also a large, flexible work force and a mass of people who fuel demand by seeking immediate gratifications and consuming without the restraint of future-oriented concerns, which children impose. Low marriage rates and high divorce rates result in isolated individuals who consume proportionately more—televisions, cars, phones, stereos, refrigerators—than family units. Di-vorce is a painful matter to those involved but a thriving source of business for lawyers, therapists, and real estate agents. Among those who are married, there is very little about traditional family life, which included considerable household production, that is inherently advantageous to the market economy. Indeed, the market economy expands when a woman's traditional work has a shift in venue, for instance, from chef in the family kitchen to chef in the local restaurant, from caring for her own children to watching other people's children in a day-care facility, and from managing household affairs to managing a business office. Although the shift of labor from hearth to market increases family income, once the "hidden" production of traditional household work is taken into account, along with the cost of work-related expenses and increased income taxes, the value of what families consume is considerably less than the amount of additional earned income would suggest. And as Stein Ringen notes, when the heightened stress of two-earner families is also thrown into the equation, the shift of labor does not necessarily translate into a better standard of living.[28]

If Schumpeter did not have it entirely right about how the decline of family values impairs the vitality of capitalism, his ideas concerning the effects of the capitalist ethos on the breakdown of stable family life seem to have stood the test of time, judging, at least, from the writings over the last three decades of Schwartz, Becker, Hirsch, and others.[29] Everyone would not necessarily agree with this diagnosis or at least would not place the entire onus on capitalism. Some see the deterioration of family norms and values as a casualty of the culture wars waged by radical feminists, atheists, gay rights activists, and advocates of the conventional welfare state. Although the diverse forces of secularization, sexual liberation, technological advancement, and the unanticipated consequences of some public interventions weigh into the equation, it would be insensible to discount the powerful implications of capitalism for the breakdown of traditional family bonds.

Under the triumph of capitalism, the dispositions and affairs of both family and state are increasingly shaped by the ethos of competition, individual choice, the weighing of measurable costs and benefits, and the maximization of gain. With the enabling state serving as a handmaiden to the market and the expanding commercialization of the family roles, the balance among state, family, and market in shaping the quality of life in modern society is shifting considerably toward market-oriented determinants. Why is this a matter of concern?

Reviving the Public Sphere

In response to the issue raised above, we must begin by recognizing that the market is a marvelous mechanism. Who in full possession of their senses would choose to live in the pork-barrel aesthetics of public housing over privately designed architecture, tailored to individual tastes, or to dine at the buffet of a state-run restaurant over a private table at Chez Panisse? Whose children would rather be taken to the state-run fair than to Disneyland? There is much to appreciate about the free market for material consumption within the domain of commercial life. Those who rail against the free market should try celebrating their anniversary at a restaurant in Moscow.

However, the domain of commercial life is just one arena of human interaction—an arena in which people engage in exchange and the satisfaction of material wants. Is it a virtuous domain? On this question the evidence, as I read it, suggests that we remain agnostic. The free market is a place where vigorous virtues vie with villainous vices, and morality and immorality are practiced without prejudice. Although others may disagree, whether one prefers the argument that virtue trumps vice in the market or vice versa, no one suggests that the free market is an incubator of the gentle virtues—charity, sympathy, kindness, public service, sacrifice, tolerance, mutual aid, and the like. The vigorous virtues—initiative, diligence, enthusiasm, and productivity—are immensely functional within the domain of the market, but that is not the only plane of human activity and interaction. The value system of competition, choice, and profit yields vast material benefits but little in the way of communal security.

When the habits and attributes of commercial life permeate the other spheres of human activity, the economic order engulfs society. A vague sense of apprehension about this development emanates from religious, academic, and political quarters. Addressing the moral implications of market activity, Christian social thinkers are forging a theory of what is termed *economic personalism*, inspired by the writings of Pope John Paul II.[30] In seeking a synthesis of theology and economics, "the idea is to promote a humane economic order that benefits from market activity but does not reduce the human person to just another element in economic phenomena."[31] This humane order requires restraints on the market that are exercised not so much by political structures as by individual behavior that is influenced by moral instruction and socialization primarily through family and church and by a moral code promoted through voluntary associations. In academic circles, the goals of communitarian economics go beyond increasing the productivity of the economy to incorporate social and political ends that serve the common interests and shared values of all citizens. Government is seen as having a distinct role in furthering these objectives, which include a safety net to protect the neediest members of society from the ruin of poverty and disease.[32] In the political arena, George W. Bush's 2000 presidential campaign ran on a platform of "compassionate conservatism," which relayed an evocative, though ill-defined expression of the need to somehow incorpo-

rate the gentle virtue of compassion into his party's free-market ideology.

In this context, the cause for concern about the emergence of the
enabling state is not so much that it promotes work-oriented policies,
limits entitlements, and heightens public support for private responsibility as that in so doing it bows too deeply as a handmaiden to the
market. As it has evolved since the early 1990s, the enabling state
generates no counterforce to the capitalist ethos, no larger sense of
public purpose that might be served beyond increasing productivity,
no clear ideal of public service, and dwindling support for the goals
of social protection and security. In many respects, the course of the
enabling state endorses antistatist attitudes, which lends weight to the
movement toward a market-dominated society.

What can be done to create a healthier balance between the enabling state and market forces, one that incorporates the self-serving
vitality of private enterprise and the humanity of shared public purpose. "The greatest asset of public action," Albert Hirschman muses,
"is its ability to satisfy vaguely felt needs for higher purpose and
meaning in the lives of men and women, specially of course in an age
in which religious fervor is at a low ebb in many countries."[33] One
need not return to expansive entitlements of the conventional welfare
state to revive the legitimacy of public purpose, the ideals of public
service, and appreciation for the state's special ability to ensure social
protection against the vicissitudes of the market and to organize communal security in the face of illness, disability, and the inevitabilities
of old age.

In efforts to revive the public sphere, the words used to frame social policy choices are important in clarifying the public purposes to
be served. If policy choices are posed, for example, between active
and passive social benefits, there is little doubt that all would prefer
an active benefit. The word *active* speaks of life's energy, whereas
passive suggests a state of mild depression. But if the choice is between *activation*, which presses disabled people, women with young
children, and unemployed workers into the labor force, and *social
protection* against the risks of modern capitalism, the tendency to embrace activation would be less compelling. Policies devoted entirely
to cultivating independence and private responsibility leave little
ground for a life of honorable dependence for those who may be unable to work. And although work-oriented policies designed to increase productivity are insulated with amorphous claims of empowerment and social inclusion, they are rarely confirmed as measures
that ensure people more freedom to live fuller lives.

Ultimately, if the enabling state is to emerge as more than a handmaiden to the market, public officials must articulate the policy

choices, such as those that are masked by the rhetoric of passive and active measures. They also need to clarify the core functions and appropriate role of the state in serving both private enterprise and the common good. Generally, such efforts should include a practical design to consolidate the profusion of social welfare measures generated by the welfare state, which address, often piecemeal, the need for work, income maintenance, and social care; an honest and transparent accounting of social transfers and to whom they are targeted; a creative response to fiscal restraints that is perceived as fair by beneficiaries and contributors; and a compassionate plan for addressing the needs of people who for whatever reasons are not able to work in the market economy—a group that has been ignored in the rush to embrace market reforms.

Finally, beyond a broad summons for programmatic streamlining, transparency, fairness and compassion, several specific measures would revitalize the enabling state as an independent force that is devoted to social purposes that transcend the well-being of the market. A comprehensive package of family-friendly policies, for example, that address the life-cycle needs of modern families could do much to counterbalance the emphasis on work-oriented reforms that advance economic productivity and competitiveness. Currently, the main thrust of "family policy" tends to be synonymous with publicly supported day care. Compensating for the absence of parental child care in families with two wage earners or a single-parent wage earner, this approach subsidizes the performance of caring functions outside of the home. Since day-care provisions assist parents to engage in paid employment at the same time that they transfer domestic activities rendered for devotion into market services driven by pecuniary motives, one might ask: Should these benefits be considered threads of family-friendly supports or the ligaments of employment policy that brace the shift of informal labor, mainly the unpaid family work of mothers, to the formal economy? For those cases in which parents of young children, particularly mothers, want to work, publicly subsidized day-care provisions in the form of vouchers, tax credits, and free (or sliding-scale fees for) services are practical conveniences that help families to achieve their objective. At the same time that many mothers welcome the opportunity to enter the paid labor force, evidence from a number of surveys in Europe and the United States suggest that a large proportion, somewhere around 50 percent, of mothers with young children would prefer either not to work outside of the home or to engage in paid employment on only a part-time basis.[34] The problem for this half of the population is they can only benefit from subsidized day care if they go to work. This arrangement creates a financial incentive to shift responsibility for the care of children from the hearth to the market.

The financial incentive is not trivial. Child care is an immensely labor-intensive operation. In Sweden, for example, with trained staff, a supervisory ratio of two adults for every five children under the age of 3, and well-equipped facilities, day-care services are subsidized by as much as $11,900 per child.[35] But Swedish parents who might want to care for their children at home cannot choose between consuming this "free" day-care service and receiving a tax rebate equal to its cost. Parents who invest their labor in domestic child-care activities miss out on a huge public subsidy, while continuing to pay the taxes that support it. Although state-supported child-care services are popular in Sweden, there is some indication that many mothers would prefer more opportunity for other arrangements, particularly during the early years of childhood. A widely reported survey showed that rather than increasing public investment in state-run day-care centers, 60 percent of the Swedish women polled favored putting the resources toward a child-care allowance that would help parents who wanted to stay home with their children or to purchase care privately.[36]

An authentically family-friendly policy would start if the enabling state helped to socialize the costs of child care through a refundable tax credit available to all families with young children on a sliding scale that is calibrated according to family income, the number of children, and their ages. This arrangement allows families to decide how they wish to invest their time and effort between domestic life and paid employment during the early years of child rearing, without being penalized by the loss of subsidies that now help only those who participate in the labor force. The benefit could be used to pay for outside child care when parents are employed full time and to compensate for the reduction in income when one parent withdraws from the labor market to care for a child at home. Along with refundable child-care tax credits, parents who stay home to provide care during the early years of child rearing might receive pension credits toward retirement—a benefit already provided in varying amounts by Austria, Sweden, Britain, France, and Hungary.[37]

The early child-rearing years are a distinct stage of the family life cycle. As these years draw to a close, the value of a parent's personalized care and home-centered activities to their families and to society declines. The duties of housewife and mother constituted a lifelong occupation when families were much larger than today and life expectancy much shorter. Nowadays, the start of elementary school marks the end of the period during which child rearing demands a parent's full time and energy. From a life-cycle perspective, a comprehensive package of family-friendly policies would include measures to facilitate the transition of labor from the household to the market at the point of diminishing returns in the full-time homemaker's social and economic contribution to family life. One such measure could involve the establishment of family social credits, awarded by the government for up to the first five years of full-time child care. (Variations on this scheme might provide social credits to those who care for disabled relatives and give additional weight to home care for children with special problems.) These credits would be transferable for tuition for undergraduate and graduate school education and technical training courses or for preference points on federal civil service examinations. In spirit, this scheme is akin to veterans' benefits, which are granted, in part, to compensate for career opportunities sacrificed while serving the nation. Homemakers contribute to the national well-being in shaping the moral, physical, and intellectual stock of future citizens. Refundable tax credits for child care and family social credits lend practical support for this contribution and publicly affirm the values of duty and care in family life.

Another initiative that would temper the market-oriented emphasis of the enabling state involves the promotion of national service. To strengthen the value of public service, society must provide outlets for its expression. In the United States, more than 162,000 volunteers have served in the Peace Corps since it was launched in 1961, and more than 200,000 volunteers have served in AmeriCorps, the program of national service initiated by the Clinton administration in 1994. AmeriCorps volunteers provide such services as organizing after-school activities, aiding the elderly in assisted-living facilities, tutoring children in low-income neighborhoods, combating floods and forest fires, working in national parks, and building homes for low-income families. Senator John McCain recommends the substantial expansion of programs such as these so that every young person who wants to serve has the opportunity to do so. McCain sees national service as a crucible for forging a sense of national unity and an appreciation for how sacrifice for a cause that transcends self-interest invests one's "life with the eminence of that cause."[38] National service might rapidly become a normative rite of passage for young people if colleges and universities encouraged (or even required) applicants to take a year after their graduation from high school to experience the obligations and rewards of active citizenship.

In fleshing out these sketchy proposals for family-friendly measures and national service programs, the devil, as they say, resides in the details. My purpose in this book, however, is not to provide blueprints for policies that would temper the enabling state's zeal for market-oriented reforms but to cast light on the challenge ahead. Before leaders can chart a constructive course that joins social purpose and economic productivity, they must find a way to steer through the dense fog of political denial about the transformation of the welfare state—and the silent surrender of public responsibility.

NOTES

1. Jorn Loftager, "Solidarity and Universality in the Danish Welfare State: Empirical Remarks and Theoretical Interpretations," pp. 5, 8, draft of a paper prepared for the 7th BIEN International Congress, Amsterdam, September 10–12, 1998.

2. Jonah Levy, "France: Directing Adjustment?" in Fritz Scharpf and Vivien Schmidt, eds., *From Vulnerability to Competitiveness: Welfare and Work in the Open Economy* (Oxford: Oxford University Press, forthcoming), pp. 39–41.

3. Examining only the shift toward privatization of service delivery in the advanced industrialized countries, Evers suggests that "whatever the level of public financing may be, it is a commonality of all these operations that, by handing over the provision of welfare services to private organizations, they insert a component of economic liberalism in the traditional architecture of social welfare." Adalbert Evers, "Welfare Dynamics, the Third Sector and Social Quality," in Wolfgang Beck, Laurent van der Maesen, Fleur Thomese, and Alan Walker, eds., *Social Quality: A Vision for Europe* (The Hague: Kluwer Law International, 2001), p. 219.

4. Within the European Union, Ferrera sees a "process of gradual institutional transformation" that could lead to a "qualitative convergence among the various systems." However, he suggests that in relation to targeting for instance, such convergence would still be characterized by different countries that employ different methods. See Maurizio Ferrera, *A New Social Contract? Four Social Europes: Between Universalism and Selectivity* (Badia Fiesolana, Italy: European University Institute, 1996), p. 13.

5. Evers, "Welfare Dynamics," distinguishes between the neoliberal approach to privatization, which emphasizes the business of service delivery, and an approach that lends primacy to social goals, community involvement, and the strengthening of civil society by voluntary, nonprofit providers.

6. Levy, "France."

7. "No German Children? Then Pay Up," *Economist*, April 7–13, 2001, p. 54.

8. "A Global Game of Dominoes," *Economist*, August 25–31, 2001, pp. 22–24.

9. Sigmund Freud, *Civilization and Its Discontents*, James Strachey, trans. and ed. (New York: Norton, 1961), p. 61. Freud linked the narcissism of minor differences as a way to express hostility to outsiders, and thereby satisfy the human inclination to aggression, while binding together the insiders.

10. Shirley Letwin, *The Anatomy of Thatcherism* (London: Fontana, 1992).

11. Richard Titmuss, *Social Policy*, Brian Abel-Smith and Kay Titmuss, eds. (London: George Allen & Unwin, 1974), p. 31.

12. David Marsland, "Markets and the Social Structure of Morality," *Society*, 38:2 (January–February 2001), 34–35.

13. James Q. Wilson, *The Moral Sense* (New York: Free Press, 1993).

14. Albert Hirschman, *The Passions and the Interests* (Princeton, N.J.: Princeton University Press, 1977).

15. See Freud, *Civilization*, pp. 26–27.

16. This point about the practice of larceny in the market was expressed in a publication that typically devotes little space to advocacy for public intervention. Vermont Royster, " 'Regulation' Isn't a Dirty Word," *Wall Street Journal*, September 9, 1987, p. 36.

17. Barry Schwartz, "Capitalism, the Market, 'the Underclass,' and the Future," *Society* 37:1 (November–December 1999), 37.

18. Ibid., p. 41

19. John K. Galbraith, *The Affluent Society* (New York: Mentor Books, 1958), p. 205.

20. Friedrick Hayek, "The Non Sequitur of the 'Dependence Effect,' " in Edmund Phelps, ed., *Private Wants and Public Needs* (New York: Norton, 1962), pp. 37–42.

21. Max Weber, *The Protestant Ethic and the Spirit of Capitalism*, Talcott Parsons, trans. (New York: Scribner, 1958).

22. Daniel Bell, *The Cultural Contradictions of Capitalism* (New York: Basic Books, 1976), p. 21.

23. Schwartz, "Capitalism," p. 40; and Fred Hirsch, *Social Limits to Growth* (Cambridge, Mass.: Harvard University Press, 1976). For a formal microeconomic analysis of marriage as a form of utility maximization, see Gary Becker, *A Treatise on the Family* (Cambridge, Mass.: Harvard University Press, 1981).

24. Joseph Schumpeter, *Capitalism, Socialism, and Democracy* (New York: Harper & Row, Publishers, [1942] 1950). Although his book was published in 1942, an initial draft of the chapter analyzing the deterioration of family life was presented in 1936 and referred to the rising number of childless marriages after World War I, which led many analysts of that time to envision the decline of the nuclear family. This decline was interrupted by the rising marriage rates, baby boom, and resurgence of familism after World War II. Since the mid-1960s, however, the deterioration of family life and the sinking birthrates lend a prophetic aura to Schumpeter's observations.

25. Ibid., p. 157.

26. Ibid., p. 158.

27. Ibid., p. 418.

28. Stein Ringen, *The Family in Question* (London: Demos, 1998). Ringen calculates that when the loss of family production is accounted for, the income measure of economic growth in Britain declines by between one-third and one-quarter (p. 24). In the United States, Vickery estimates that 34 percent of the wife's income in a two-earner family is consumed by work-related expenses and increased taxes due to the higher bracket into which the second salary ratchets family income. See Clair Vickery, "Women's Economic Contribution to the Family," in Ralph Smith, ed., *The Subtle Revolution/ Women at Work* (Washington, D.C.: Urban Institute, 1979).

29. Schwartz, "Capitalism"; Becker, *Treatise on the family*; Hirsch, *Social Limits to Growth*; and Robert Bellah, "The Invasion of the

Money World," in David Blankenhorn, Steven Bayme, and Jean Bethke Elshtain, eds. *Rebuilding the Nest* (Milwaukee, Wisc.: Family Service of America, 1990), pp. 227–36.

30. For a review of the historical, philosophical, and practical aspects of economic personalism, see Gregory Gronbacher, "The Need for Economic Personalism," *Journal of Markets and Morality*, 1:1 (March 1998), 1–34.

31. Ibid., p. 29.

32. For a statement of the goals of communitarian economics and how this perspective differs from the traditional ways of thinking about economic issues, see Norton Garfinkle, "Communitarian Economics," paper delivered at the 1996 Communitarian Summit, Geneva, July 12–14, 1996.

33. Albert Hirschman, *Shifting Involvements: Private Interests and Public Action* (Princeton, N.J.: Princeton University Press, 1992), p. 126.

34. Data from a 1997 survey of families in the United States show that 49 percent of women agree with this statement: "When children are young, mothers should not work outside the home." See Richard Wertheimer, Melissa Long, and Sharon Vandivere, "Welfare Recipient's Attitudes Toward Welfare, Nonmarital Childbearing, and Work: Implications for Reform?" Series B, No. B-37, Urban Institute, Washington D.C., June 2001. A similar reluctance for full-time employment when children are young is expressed by Danish mothers, despite the fact that in Denmark public day care is provided from the age of 6 months, and 90 percent of mothers of young children are employed for an average of 34 hours per week. When asked to describe the ideal arrangement for a nuclear family with children of nursery-school age, only 3 percent of the mothers preferred to have both parents working full time, 15 percent chose to have the mother home full time as a housewife, 42 percent favored part-time employment for the mother, and 40 percent preferred to have both parents working part time; see Ministry of Social Affairs, *Danish Strategies: Families and Children at Work and at Home* (Copenhagen: Ministry of Social Affairs, 1992). In response to a nationwide Gallup poll in America in 1980; 55 percent of the women who wanted to be married and have children did not wish to have a full-time job or career outside the home; see Gallop Organization, "American Families—1980," report submitted to the White House Conference on Families, Princeton, N.J., June 5, 1980. In the annual Virginia Slims survey of 3000 women in the United States, the proportion of women who said that if free to choose they would prefer to have a job (rather than stay home to take care of the family) rose from 36 percent in 1974 to 52 percent in 1985 but then declined to 42 percent in 1989. See Norval Glenn, "What the Numbers Say," *Family Affairs*, 5:1/2 (Summer 1992), 5–7. These findings are supported by other surveys. Whitehead and Blankenhorn cite the *Washington Post* poll and a survey by Mark Baldassare and Associates, which reveal that a majority of working mothers sampled in Washington, D.C., and Los Angeles would prefer to stay home with young children if finances permitted. Barbara Defoe Whitehead and David Blankenhorn, "Man, Woman, and Public Policy: Difference and Dependency in the American Conversation," Working paper, Institute for American Values, New York, 1991.

35. Swedish Institute, *Child Care in Sweden* (Stockholm: Swedish Institute, 1992).

36. Sven Svensson, "Vardnadsbidrag fore dagis," *Dagens Nyheter*, April 12, 1987.

37. In Austria, for example, women receive one year of credit for each child, and Sweden awards a credit to either spouse for each year he or she cares for a child under the age of 3. In Britain, people who interrupt work careers to assume care-giving duties are compensated through the Home Responsibility Protection policy, which credits both men and women with a minimum level of contribution during the years they spend caring for children or the disabled. Pension benefits are increased by 10 percent for insured persons in France who have raised at least three children, and Hungary grants an increased benefit for three years of infant care. See Nicholas Barr and Fiona Coulter, "Social Security: Solution or Problem?" in John Hills, ed., *The State of Welfare: The Welfare State in Britain Since 1974* (Oxford: Clarendon, 1990); and Martin Tracy and Patsy Tracy, "The Treatment of Women as Dependents Under Social Security: After 50 Years How Does the United States Compare to Other Countries?" *Journal of Applied Social Sciences,* 111 (1987), 5–16.

38. John McCain, "Putting the 'National' in National Service," *Washington Monthly*, October 2001.

Index